THE GESTAPO

THE GESTAPO

A HISTORY OF HITLER'S SECRET POLICE
1933–45

RUPERT BUTLER

CASEMATE
HAVERTOWN, PA

This edition first published in 2004 by

CASEMATE
2114 Darby Road
Havertown, PA 19083

Library of Congress Cataloging-in-Publication Data available.

ISBN: 1-932033-24-6

Editorial and design by
Amber Books Ltd
Bradley's Close
74-77 White Lion Street
London N1 9PF
www.amberbooks.co.uk

Project Editor: Michael Spilling
Design: Jerry Williams
Picture Research: Natasha Jones

Printed in Italy by Eurolitho

ACKNOWLEDGEMENTS
The author would like to thank Peter Padfield for letting him use an extract from his book, *Himmler Reichsführer-SS*
(Macmillan Ltd, 1990). The author would also like to thank the Evangelischen Akademie in Berlin for allowing him to
use the material they hold on Prinz-Albrecht-Strasse 8, as well as acknowledge the valuable help from the London
Library, the Institute of Contemporary History and the Wiener Library, The Imperial War Museum and the German
Historical Institute. John Coughlin was especially valuable with research and assistance.

PICTURE CREDITS
AKG-Images: 44, 63, 69, 70, 99, 102, 128, 173;
Corbis: 64, 79, 165, 167, 172;
Photos12.com – KEYSTONE Pressedienst: 18, 23, 82, 140, 145, 156, 177; **Oasis:** 41, 61, 148;
Hachedé: 86; **Bertelsmann Lexikon Verlag:** 131, 146;
POPPERFOTO.COM: 29, 36, 55, 60, 66, 67, 89, 125, 151, 164, 180, 183;
Süddeutscher Verlag: 16, 17, 21, 24, 26, 30, 34, 43, 46, 49, 56, 73, 77, 81, 85, 109, 114, 126, 132,
135, 137, 143, 147, 155, 158;
Topham Picturepoint: 10, 33, 39, 40, 52, 108, 139, 160, 168, 182, 185;
TRH Pictures: 6, 8, 13, 15, 17, 20, 27, 31, 38, 42, 50, 59, 74, 76, 80, 90, 92, 95, 96, 97, 100, 104, 105, 107,
110, 111, 113, 117, 118, 121, 123, 129, 134, 153, 157, 162, 171, 175, 179;
Ukrainian State Archive: 122.

Contents

CHAPTER 1

FOUNDATIONS

German defeat in World War I heralded the Weimar Republic, a regime soured with cynicism and breeding violence in the streets. But with the advent of Hitler came the hope of a new dawn.

E ven though the Gestapo, as the Secret State Police dedicated to maintaining the National Socialist regime, perished along with Nazism in 1945, much of its influence and power survived until the collapse of Communism. Five years after the end of World War II, the infamous *Ministerium für Staatssicherheit* (Stasi) was established in East Germany, using methods that were only too familiar to many Germans: controlled media, a vast network of informants to repress subversives, the encouragement of family members to spy on one another through physical threats and the fear of blackmail. By the late 1980s, the Stasi, which maintained a force of more than 90,000 uniformed and plain-clothed agents, had around 175,000 official informants on its books – roughly one for every hundred people. Many of its most experienced early operatives were former Gestapo members.

The existence of the Stasi was a reminder, although an extreme one, that all governments, of whatever complexion, rely on some form of covert law enforcement, using various measures to uncover possible conspiracies against the state and perceived threats to civil order. The more authoritarian the government concerned, the harsher are likely to be its methods.

Members of the Ochrana, for example, as the servants of Imperial Russian autocracy, carried out mass arrests and torture against political opponents between 1881 and 1917. Following the 1917 October Revolution,

Left: Two years into power, Adolf Hitler, with some of his closest associates, including Joseph Göbbels, Rudolf Hess and Hermann Göring, attending a ceremony in the State Opera House, Berlin. Representatives of the military are present and have been given an honoured place with their own box, but it is clear where real authority lies.

Above: Adolf Hitler is seen here with President von Hindenburg on 30 January 1933, the day he became Chancellor. The near senile Hindenburg, with less than a year to live, had previously declared: 'I have little time for that Bohemian corporal.'

they were succeeded by the Cheka (the Extraordinary Committee Against Sabotage and Counter Revolution), which took over many of the characteristics of its tsarist predecessor, using penetration agents and agents provocateurs. The organizations later introduced by the Communists, the Soviet Military Intelligence (OGPU) and the Committee of State Security (KGB), had a broad network of special departments to probe the armed forces, industry and all major government institutions. As in all dictatorships, their agents recruited a large number of informers whose task was to ensure the observance of security regulations and to monitor the activities of employees. All relied to different degrees on terror and intimidation. No one knows precisely how many people were sent to camps during the era of Stalin's purges, but it has been estimated that between four and five million people were detained before and after World War II.

The first sophisticated methods of covert law enforcement by Germany were modelled on the achievements of Napoleon Bonaparte, who had organized espionage as an integral part of his military system of operations. Karl Stieber from Saxony, a former barrister and Socialist turncoat, worked undercover at the behest of the King of Prussia. He gained the post of

Polizeirath, which rendered him independent of normal police control and equipped with the tools to create a comprehensive intelligence system the agents of which rooted out enemies of the state. The basis of the system Steiber evolved remained more or less intact until Germany's defeat in 1918.

THE OLD ORDER

The Weimar Republic between the two world wars was characterized by shifting political loyalties underpinned by a surge in street violence. Although there was an official ban on an all-German secret police apparatus, one had been established in Berlin nevertheless, with steadily creeping powers 'to prevent and prosecute … all penal offences that have a political character'. Thus there were already a power base and personnel to run the Gestapo when it was founded in Prussia. Until then it had been subject to the rule of civil law, but this state of affairs was soon to change.

The death throes of Weimar had long been obvious to alarmed observers outside Germany, but it was not until 30 January 1933, when President and *Generalfeldmarschall* Paul von Beneckendorf und von Hindenburg, the aged icon of the old order, met with Adolf Hitler, the Austrian rabble-rousing populist of the National Socialist Workers' Party (NSDAP), that the fate of the world for the succeeding 15 years was finally decided. Hitler assumed the title of Reich Chancellor despite von Hindenburg's earlier contemptuous declaration that the 'Austrian corporal' was barely fit to be minister of post.

THE WEIMAR REPUBLIC

The Weimar Republic, which emerged from the ashes of German defeat in 1919 and lasted until the birth of the Third Reich in 1933, was named after the town, 240 km (150 miles) southwest of Berlin, where the signatories of a national assembly had accepted the Versailles Treaty. This required Germany to reduce its territory and to disarm, even though the army and civil service were retained.

It had been intended that the Constitution of the new Republic should take as its model the achievements of long-established democracies – the form of cabinet government existing in Britain and France, the election of a president along American lines and, where appropriate, the employment of referenda, as in Switzerland. This was to be expressed in fine phrases that seemed irreproachable: 'Political power emanates from the people … All Germans are equal before the law … All inhabitants of the Reich enjoy complete liberty of belief and conscience.'

But these high aspirations were overshadowed by the Versailles Treaty, which was anathema to both the army and to conservative politicians, who refused to accept it as a treaty of peace or the Republic that ratified it. Opposition to Weimar hardened further when the Mark plunged, heralding disastrous inflation and making German currency worthless. A plea by Germany to suspend moratorium payments was rejected and French troops occupied the Ruhr, effectively tearing the heart out of the country's economy. The masses of the people, saddled with a useless currency, turned their wrath on the architects of the Weimar Republic, much of it manifest in street violence.

Above: Two policemen stand amid the rubble of the German Reichstag on 27 February 1933. Who torched the building remains a mystery. What is indisputable is that, following the fire, civil liberties perished along with the flames, paving the way for unrelenting Nazi oppression.

TAKING CONTROL

The Nazis' exploitation of propaganda through brilliantly staged street theatre was demonstrated spectacularly in Berlin on the evening of Hitler's appointment. A triumphant march wound through the city's Brandenburg Gate, its progress lit by a million torches. Past German history was recalled in song: the triumphs of Bavarian kings, of Frederick the Great of Prussia and of Bismarck. The voice of the new Germany could also be heard, however, in the songs of the black and silver-garbed *Schutzstaffel* (SS, 'Protection Squad').

On 24 February, with the Nazis in office for barely one month and following the announcement of new elections, Prussian police contingents made a lightning raid on Karl-Liebknecht-Haus, the Communist headquarters in Berlin. Hermann Göring, the police supremo, announced the discovery of incriminating files, 'proving' that the Communists were on the brink of a long-planned revolution. He backed his claims with an official Prussian government statement alleging that 'Government buildings, museums, mansions and essential plants were to be burnt down. Women and children were to be sent in front of the terrorist groups …'. It scarcely mattered that no proof of such allegations was produced. Suspects were rounded up in military-style trucks, while in the early dawn cars screeched through the streets to decant agents in front of private houses and apartment blocks. It was not only the main protagonists of the left who were singled out. The families of suspects were also rounded up and herded into the cellars of the Columbia-Haus in Columbiadamm, which was known among the Gestapo by the grisly nickname of the 'Columbia Bar'.

However satisfied Göring may have been with the Karl-Liebknecht-Haus raid, a spectacular event three days later aided his cause still further. Just before nine o'clock that evening, a man crossing the square in front of the imposing Reichstag parliamentary building suddenly heard the sound of breaking glass. He froze for a moment at the sight of a figure on the first-floor balcony brandishing a burning torch, then sped to seek help. Before the fire brigade arrived, however, the cavernous building's restaurant and vast Sessions Chamber were an inferno. Three policemen moved in with guns drawn on a figure, bare to the waist, who emerged from the rear of the chamber and surrendered meekly. One of them yelled, 'Why did you do it?' and received the muttered reply, 'As a protest.' Precisely 24 minutes after the fire had been discovered, 24-year-old Marinus van der Lubbe from Leiden in the Netherlands was marched from the building.

'FOR THE PROTECTION OF THE PEOPLE'

Göring was on the spot at once, publicly denouncing the Communists for committing arson and accusing the weak-minded van der Lubbe, a muddled Communist idealist, of being their agent. Beside himself, Göring yelled, 'This is the beginning of the Communist revolution! We must not wait a minute. We will show no mercy. Every Communist official must be shot.' On his arrival, Hitler was led through the corridors that were still accessible, taking the opportunity to cry: 'This is a sign from God. No one can now prevent us from crushing the Communists with a mailed fist.'

The reign of terror in Berlin began on the night of the fire. Even the mildest anti-Nazis were arrested and flung into gaol. At Hitler's behest, President von Hindenburg was prevailed upon to sign a decree 'For the Protection of the People and the State', intended as a 'defensive measure against Communist acts of violence endangering the State'. The decree stated: 'Restrictions on personal liberty, on the right of free expression of opinion, including freedom of the press, on the rights of assembly and association; and violations of the privacy of postal, telegraphic and telephonic communications; and warrants for house searches, orders for confiscation as well as restrictions on property, are also permissible beyond the legal limits otherwise prescribed.' A number of leading Communists stood in the dock as well as van der Lubbe, but in the end only the Dutchman was convicted and shambled to the guillotine early the following January.

The whole truth about the Reichstag fire, and whether the pathetic van der Lubbe was solely responsible, will never be known; recent historians incline towards this view, pointing out that he had attempted to torch other buildings without success. What is certain is that the fire marked the beginning of Göring's war on the Communists, providing a useful pretext.

It was only the start. In early May the *Deutsche Allgemeine Zeitung* newspaper was running headlines proclaiming 'The National Socialists take over the Trade Unions / The Leaders Arrested / Action throughout the Reich'. Massed contingents of Prussian police swooped on trade union headquarters, brandishing official decrees signed by Hermann Göring. Significantly, by then the police were operating under the new name of Gestapo (*Geheime Staats Polizei*, 'Secret State Police'). Accompanying them were the street bully boys of the Third Reich, members of the *Sturmabteilung* (SA, 'Storm Detachment'), who were generally known as the Brown Shirts and mostly drawn from the post-war nationalistic paramilitaries and freebooters, the *Freikorps* ('Free Corps'). The SA leader was the scar-faced Ernst Röhm, whose membership of the Nazi party dated back to the earliest days. But the fact that the Gestapo and SA were working together on this occasion was not an indication of a harmonious alliance, as was soon to be shown.

> The Nazi rise to power provided opportunities for ambitious power seekers, many of whom had served in the Great War and had found it difficult to adjust to civilian life.

THE RISE OF GÖRING

Hermann Göring was a colonial official's son from Rosenheim, Upper Bavaria. He had gained a dashing reputation in the air force as a combat pilot, becoming commander in 1918 of the celebrated 'Flying Circus' fighter group made famous by Baron Manfred von Richthofen. Göring had emerged from World War I with the *Pour le Mérite* medal and the Iron Cross (First Class). After a stint with the Fokker aircraft company, he became an adviser to the Danish government, a stunt flyer and then a commercial pilot for Svenska Lufttraffik in Sweden. Even at this time his high ambitions had brought him to the attention of the German legation in Stockholm, who reported to Berlin that Göring was describing himself as 'a candidate for the post of Reich president'.

But Göring had little money and meagre qualifications for earning a living outside flying and soldiering. His fortunes changed with his marriage to the Swedish divorcée Carin von Kantzow, whose first husband had given her a generous settlement. The couple set up home in a hunting lodge at Hochkreuth in the Bavarian Alps, some 80 km (50 miles) from Munich. At this time Göring made a half-hearted attempt to remedy a sparse education by enrolling at Munich University for a course in political science and history, but a restless temperament made him impatient with any form of academic discipline. Rather, he was drawn to Munich as a city that, like the rest of Bavaria, was embracing an extreme nationalism expressed in demonstrations against the burning injustices inflicted by victors who had reduced Germany to armed and economic impotence in 1918. The fault lay, declared the rabble-rousers, with those responsible for concluding the armistice of 11 November 1918, whom they dubbed the *Novemberverbrecher* ('November criminals').

Virulent political groups were mushrooming daily, but seemingly few were capable of coming up with any coherent political strategy. One exception was a militant force of malcontents who had banded together as the *Nationalsozialistische Deutsche Arbeiter Partie* (NSDAP, 'National Socialist German Workers' Party'). It had burning contempt for those advocating gradual change and its demands were stark: a violent revolution, a new state, a drastically modified society. Scarcely anyone living in Munich in 1922 could have been unaware of the NSDAP's most voluble exponent. It was late that same year that Göring first saw Adolf Hitler in the crowd at a demonstration against the Allied powers' call for the extradition of

Below: On a summer's day in 1929, *Sturmführer* Horst Wessel leads the *Sturmabteilung* (SA, 'Storm Detachment') through the Nuremberg streets. The son of a Protestant chaplain, Nazi street-fighter Wessel was later murdered in a brawl. Leaving behind lyrics for 'Horst Wessel Lied' (the Horst Wessel Song), he was elevated to the status of national hero.

Germany's military leaders; Hitler, who considered this particular protest mere bombast with no power to back it up, had declined to speak. Later the two men met face to face, an encounter reputedly engineered through Carin Göring's link with key figures in the NSDAP.

On this occasion, Göring later recounted, 'Hitler spoke about the demonstration, about Versailles … and the repudiation of the Treaty … The conviction was spoken word for word as if from my own soul. On one of the following days I went to the business office of the NSDAP … I just wanted to speak to him at first to see if I could assist him in any way. He received me at once and after I had introduced myself he said it was an extraordinary turn

FREIKORPS

In the feverish post-war climate of a defeated Germany, discontented bands of voluntary paramilitaries, known as the *Freikorps*, played a brief but significant role in the country's political life. Originally formed in Berlin, their influence can be traced from Kaiser Wilhelm II's abdication in 1918 until the abortive Beer Hall Putsch of 1923. The name *Freikorps* was adopted as a tribute to Ludwig Freiherr von Lützow, who in 1813 had organized a voluntary corps as the kernel of an army designed to win liberation from Napoleon.

Members of the new-style *Freikorps* were composed of former officers, demobilized soldiers, military adventurers, ardent nationalists and unemployed youths, all burning to crush those whom they believed had betrayed the Fatherland by acceptance of the harsh terms of the Treaty of Versailles. The *Freikorps*, which was illegal and politically right wing, also blamed Germany's demoralization on Social Democrats and Jews. One of its chief architects was Captain (later General) Kurt von Schleicher, the future German Chancellor, who worked with the political department of the *Reichswehr*, the army of 100,000 soldiers allowed to the German Republic by the Versailles Treaty. The *Reichswehr* was responsible for secretly equipping and paying for *Freikorps* units, initially to protect the country's eastern borders and then to quell revolution at

home. These units were sworn opponents of the rigid hierarchical structure of the old German army.

One of the key targets of the *Freikorps* in Germany was the left-wing government of Bavaria, which was crushed by some 3000 adherents in 1919 under the command of Franz Xaver Ritter von Epp. As the *Freikorps* consisted mostly of small, self-contained units rather than large army formations under a chain of command, its forces lacked a consistent discipline and were difficult to control. This was particularly true in Bavaria, where they dragged government supporters to the gaols and beat them with rifle butts preparatory to slaughter. During battle with a group of 350 Communists, 21 unarmed medical orderlies were captured and murdered.

But the days of the *Freikorps* were numbered. Adolf Hitler had established his powerbase in the politically volatile city of Munich. With the formation of his *Sturmabteilung* (SA, 'Storm Detachment') within the newly named *Nationalsozialistische Deutsch Arbeiterpartei* (NSDAP, 'National Socialist German Workers' Party'), the *Freikorps* units began to break up. Many were recruited into the SA.

The *Freikorps* were formally dissolved in 1921, and their last descendants were stood down at a ceremony in Munich in November 1933 to mark the tenth anniversary of the Beer Hall Putsch.

of fate that we should meet … He had long been on the lookout for a leader who had distinguished himself in some way in the last war … so that he would have the necessary authority. Now it seemed to him a stroke of luck that I, in particular, the last Commander of the Richthofen Squadron, should place myself at his disposal.'

The encounter may have dazzled Göring, but Hitler, forever the cynical opportunist, confided to colleagues: 'Excellent propaganda! Moreover he has money and doesn't cost me a cent.' Göring's considerable personal magnetism also lent a respectable face to the Nazi party. By the following January, after his first meeting with Hitler, Göring was appointed supreme commander of the storm troopers. His task, it was made clear, was to mould the ill-organized rabble of the SA into something approaching a disciplined private army.

By no means everyone within the SA was happy with Göring. The roughest elements, many of them unemployed former soldiers, saw him as rooted in the past, associated with the bourgeois trappings of privilege, plutocracy and the officer class. There was widespread conviction among its followers that the SA should be in the vanguard of genuine revolution – above all, sufficiently socialist to sweep away the old order. Under Göring, but by no means relishing the position, was the swashbuckling Ernst Röhm, obese, bullet-scarred, red-faced and with a weakness for young males. To Röhm, people were pigeonholed as soldiers or civilians, friends or enemies,

Above: In Berlin during March 1919, a disparate band of mainly youthful *Freikorps* assembles with a flame thrower before an Erhardt armoured car, preparatory to battling with the Spartacists, forerunners of the German Communist Party during the days of the Weimar Republic.

boasting, 'Since I am an immature and wicked man, war and unrest appeal to me more than good bourgeois order.' Attracted to Hitler's oratory, he had become one of the earliest members of the Nazi party as well as a close friend of the putative *Führer* ('leader'), in whose defence Röhm assembled a motley band, consisting at first of a stationery salesman, an amateur wrestler, a watchmaker and a beer-hall bouncer. The new bodyguard was designated *Stosstrupp* ('Storm Troopers') and became suborned to Röhm's 2000-strong SA, later to be replaced by the *Stabswache*, or Headquarters Guard, forming the basis of the *Schutzstaffel*, the SS.

THE BEER HALL PUTSCH

In the dying months of 1923, a major crisis threatened not only the state of Bavaria, but also the entire German Republic. Chancellor Gustav Stresemann, a conservative with monarchist sympathies, announced the end of the policy of passive resistance in the Ruhr, Germany's industrial heartland under French occupation. Further, he declared that there must be a resumption of reparation payments to the victors: he reasoned that, if Germany was to be saved and a drift to anarchy stemmed, some sort of agreement had to be negotiated with the Allies so as to give the Republic a breathing space before regaining its economic strength. To meet inevitable opposition, Stresemann persuaded President Friedrich Ebert to declare a state of emergency. Bavaria verged on hysteria, uniting both nationalists and communists in fierce

Right: Running brawls on the streets of German cities were part of the political and social landscape until the Nazis achieved power in January 1933. Workers, encouraged by the Communists to oppose the Republic, are seen here in the previous March facing the batons of the Munich police.

denunciation of the Republic. For Hitler it seemed an opportunity sent from heaven. His best chance of gaining political power, he reasoned, lay in allying his party with the Bavarian right and launching a march on Berlin. However, what Hitler and his fellow Nazis, for the most part street rowdies of the SA, conspicuously lacked was a respectable face. Hitler considered he had found it in General Erich Ludendorff, a military hero and advocate of the extreme right. Such an ally would be invaluable in the company of Bavaria's ruling triumvirate: Central State Commissioner Gustav Ritter von Kahr, Armed Forces Commander General Otto von Lossow and Bavarian State Police chief Colonel Hans von Seisser. Orders from Berlin were imperiously ignored by von Kahr, despite a warning that any uprising would be resisted by force.

In a classic case of counting unhatched chickens, Hitler distributed a poster that declared: 'Proclamation to the German people! The regime of the November criminals is today declared deposed. A provisional German national government is formed.' Appended was Hitler's name and that of the triumvirate. On 8 November 1923, Hitler struck, choosing as his base the Burgerbraukeller, a fashionable rendezvous on the outskirts of Munich where von Kahr was addressing a patriotic meeting. With the aid of Göring and Ernst Röhm's motley collection of SA, the cellar was surrounded and Hitler burst in on the meeting, dashing a stein of beer to the ground, firing a shot from his Browning into the ceiling and shouting, 'The national revolution has begun. The hall is surrounded by 600 heavily armed men and no one may leave. The Bavarian government and the Reich government have been deposed and a provisional Reich government will be formed.'

Von Kahr and the others were forced into a back room and their cooperation demanded. In a desperate bid to play for time, von Kahr agreed to continue his support; however, the courage of the triumvirate was rapidly running out. It was then that Hitler made the mistake of agreeing to allow the men leave the hall. All too soon they were reneging. Von Lossow lost no time in getting to a telephone and ordering troop reinforcements to be rushed to the beer hall. Worse, warrants were issued for the arrest of a fleeing Hitler, Ludendorff and others involved in the putsch, which was heading for failure.

Above: In this retouched portrait, Hermann Göring – the former *Luftwaffe* ace who in 1918 became Commander of the Flying Circus made famous by Baron Manfred von Richthofen – is seen sporting the *Pour le Mérite* decoration. By the end of World War I, he had won conspicuous popularity as a dashing knight of the skies.

Hitler, however, confident in his backing from Ludendorff, was not prepared to give up. On the next day, with a phalanx of SA and *Stosstroop*, rifles slung over their shoulders, the party made for the centre of Munich. As they reached the Odeonsplatz, near the Felden Halle, about a hundred state police opened fire on 3000 Nazis. Within seconds 16 Nazis and three police lay dead. Hitler promptly subsided to the pavement, while Göring, less lucky, received a bullet to the thigh. Unfazed, Ludendorff continued marching straight ahead, moving through the ranks of police who, in a gesture of respect for the old war hero, turned their guns aside.

In the confusion, Hitler was whisked away by car, while Göring was given first aid by the Jewish proprietor of a nearby bank and eventually smuggled out of the country. Ahead of him, in the company of Carin, stretched four years of exile in Austria, Italy and finally Sweden. Pain from his wound was considerable and he had recourse to ever-mounting doses of morphine. The effect was alarming. Not only did he become obese and swollen with excessive weight, but he also underwent a startling personality change that boded ill for anyone who stood in his way.

'HONOURABLE CONFINEMENT'

Hitler, along with Ludendorff and Röhm, whose SA had been to the forefront in the attempted putsch, was eventually arrested and brought to trial before a court that, according to observers, tolerated an atmosphere of goodwill between prosecution and defence. Hitler grasped the chance to dominate the court,

Below: SA supporters stand at barricades during the attempted Munich Beer Hall Putsch of November 1923. Second from the left in the picture stands a gaunt-faced Rudolf Hess, with SA chief Ernst Röhm third from the left. Next to him, carrying aloft the imperial standard, is pebble-spectacled Heinrich Himmler, the future SS supremo.

intoning, 'I alone bear the responsibility. But I am not a criminal because of that … There is no such thing as high treason against the traitors of 1918 … I believe that the hour will come when the masses, who today stand in the street with our swastika banner, will unite with those who fire upon them.' He made it clear that he alone had the necessary courage and will to lead the struggle against the 'Jewish republic'. He was sentenced to five years' 'honourable confinement', with the understanding that he would be released on probation after a year. Röhm was held in Stadelheim gaol and Ludendorff was acquitted of all charges. A ban was slapped on the NSDAP in Bavaria.

One of Ernst Röhm's industrious acolytes at the putsch attracted scant notice at this time. A photograph survives of an owlish, bespectacled nonentity gazing over flimsy barricades and barbed wire. Heinrich Himmler's sole involvement of any note in the proceedings had been to hold aloft the traditional imperial standard. His established place in the Nazi climb to power was still to come.

Before his trial and imprisonment, Hitler recognized his tactical error in attempting revolution by direct action instead of working at winning over the masses, attracting financial support and then easing his way to political supremacy through legal means. Nevertheless, the putsch was far from being a total failure because the trial had brought his hitherto obscure Nazi movement headlines in a number of countries. Even as morale within the Nazi party shrank to what was probably its lowest ever level, while attention shifted to groups on the left, Hitler was prepared to bide his time, for the moment at least. He insisted on maintaining public silence until the ban upon his party was lifted. At the end of February 1925, two months after his release from Landsberg castle, he made his first address. The choice of location was an act of calculated defiance: a rousing speech at the Burgerbraukeller calling for party unity. In pursuit of this aim he was quite prepared to horse-trade, forging backstairs deals with the right and centre while he waited for his opportunity.

Not only did Göring become obese and swollen, but he also underwent a startling personality change that boded ill for anyone who stood in his way.

POWER AT LAST

The final phase of the ongoing Nazi struggle for power came on 30 May 1932 with von Hindenburg's appointment of Franz von Papen as Chancellor. A patrician who had served as a member of the extreme right wing of the Catholic Centre Party, von Papen had sought his support from the army (the *Reichswehr*) and the industrial barons. He was, however, widely regarded as a lightweight, leading André-François Poncet, the French Ambassador in Berlin, to declare that the appointment 'was greeted at first with incredulous amazement. Everyone smiled. There is something about von Papen that

prevents either his friends or his enemies from taking him entirely seriously. He bears the stamp of frivolity.' But this was a frivolity that masked a streak of ruthlessness. Regarded by many as a Trojan horse for the Nazis, he had been in office scarcely two weeks when he raised a ban on the SA and Nazi uniforms that had been instituted by his predecessor, Heinrich Brüning. Von Papen went on to dismiss the governments of various provinces and, in the face of protests from the administration in Prussia, assumed control as Reich Commissioner. His support for Hitler was expressed in a promise to supply the financial muscle of the Rhineland industrialists.

All of which suited the Nazis, who were riding the crest of a wave. In the elections of July 1932, the National Socialists secured 230 seats and became Germany's most powerful party. As it turned out, von Papen's time as Chancellor was brief. His place was taken by Kurt von Schleicher, a previous Minister of Defence and master intriguer, who offered to support a National Socialist government on condition that Hitler appoint him to the cabinet and allow him to direct the *Reichswehr*. He was outmanoeuvred when Hindenburg appointed Hitler Chancellor and von Papen as Vice Chancellor.

As for Göring, he had returned from exile after treatment for morphine addiction and a spell in a psychiatric hospital, where he had been diagnosed as having schizophrenic tendencies expressed in bouts of lachrymose sentimentality and violent rages. Propelled by tireless energy, possibly fuelled by the effects of morphine, his devotion to politics became all consuming, serving to overcome the devastation he felt following Carin's death from tuberculosis. In 1928 he had been one of the first Nazis to be elected to the Reichstag and was re-elected two years later, serving as Hitler's political agent in Berlin and ultimately achieving the office of Reichstag President. Other offices were eagerly grabbed: Reich Minister without portfolio, Reich Commissioner for Air, Prussian Minister President and Prussian Minister of the Interior. In addition, he sought a cocoon of security that would match Röhm's SA. His prime attention, though, fastened on the Prussian police, and he lost little time in seeking an ally within, a figure who would be at the very centre of power in Berlin.

DIELS TO THE FORE

While a student of medicine and law at the universities of Giessen and Marburg, Rudolf Diels, the son of a prominent landowner, had spent much of his time avoiding academic work in favour of mammoth drinking bouts with members of a duelling corps. The legacy was a slash of livid scars across his cheeks. At the age of 30 he had entered the Prussian Ministry of the Interior as a specialist on Communist affairs. Designated 1A and concerned with the security of the state, it was in fact a puny office, under-staffed and under-financed, barely capable of dealing with a German Communist Party that in 1930 claimed 250,000 adherents and 4000 political cells.

For Göring, fuelled with visions of a revolt from the left within Germany that would mirror the one that had gripped Russia in 1917, the office was ripe for reform, and Diels was earmarked for a key role. For all its existing limitations, it soon became obvious to Göring that in Berlin police headquarters he had inherited a treasure trove, much of it comprising closely detailed dossiers on a variety of personalities. Drawing on information in these documents, no time was lost on the launch of a ruthless purge, beginning inside the Prussian police itself, where officers from the days of the old Republic were abruptly removed to be replaced by dyed-in-the-wool Nazis. The main campaign, however, of interrogation and terror was, predictably, aimed at the Communists.

On 26 April 1933, Göring established by decree the *Geheime Staats Poleizeamt* (Gestapa, 'Secret State Police Office'), to be renamed *Geheime Staats Polizei* (Gestapo). With the advent

Below: Rudolf Diels, the great survivor. Originally an official of the Prussian Ministry of the Interior, he progressed to heading the new branch of the secret political police, later the Gestapo. He was dismissed following the power struggle between Göring and Himmler. Accused of disloyalty, Diels was arrested following the July bomb plot in 1944, but survived the collapse of the Third Reich and after the war was employed again in local government.

THE ENABLING ACT

Within months of becoming Chancellor on 30 January 1933, Adolf Hitler had transformed the frail democracy that was Germany into a dictatorship imposed by a package of terror, intimidation and skilful propaganda. The election had brought the Nazis 288 seats and their Nationalist allies 52. Together the two parties had won more than half the votes and, with the Communists banned after being blamed for the Reichstag fire, the Nazis had a clear majority. A sign of the way Germany was shaping could be judged on 23 March when the newly elected deputies arrived at the Kroll Opera House, the Reichstag's meeting place after the fire, making their way through tight cordons of SS and armed SA Brown Shirts. The show of force worked. With the necessary two-thirds majority, the Nazi and Nationalist deputies passed an Enabling Act, which gave Hitler dictatorial powers to rule without reference to the Reichstag.

The Enabling Act (*Gesetz zur Erhebung der Not von Volk und Reich*, 'Law to remove the distress of people and state') laid the foundations of the dictatorship by making key alterations to the Weimar constitution. In five brief paragraphs, the power of legislation, approval of treaties with foreign states and the creation of amendments to the Constitution were divorced from Parliament and handed over to the Reich cabinet.

By 7 April, Hitler had appointed Reich Governors (*Reichstatthälter*) in all the states, empowering them to appoint and remove local governments, dissolve the diet and control the appointment or dismissal of state officials. The powers of these new governors were sternly controlled, however, because they were required to carry out 'the general policy laid down by the Reich Chancellor'.

Hitler celebrated the first anniversary of achieving power by promulgating a 'Law for the Reconstruction of the Reich'. Here 'reconstruction' meant the dissolution of the states' sovereign powers, which were transferred to the Reich, with all state governments answerable to the administration of the Reich Minister of the Interior. The Enabling Law was renewed in 1937, 1939 and 1942. Each time parliamentary power was further dissipated, as the Reichstag became a constitutional fiction that met only a dozen times up to 1939, its only voice that of Adolf Hitler and the Nazi leadership.

of the Gestapo as an official body, the words of British journalist Douglas Reed neatly encapsulated life in Hitler's Germany for countless citizens, many of whom had little or no interest in politics: 'When Germany awoke a man's home was no longer his castle. He could be seized by private individuals, could claim no protection from the police, could be indefinitely detained without preferment of charge; his property could be seized, his verbal and written communications overheard and perused; he no longer had the right to foregather with his fellow countrymen and his newspapers might no longer fully express their opinions.'

This underlined what had happened the previous March following elections in which, despite the atmosphere of terror and repression, the Nazis had only just secured an overall majority with the aid of the Nationalist party.

Even though the Communists had gained around five million votes, they were forbidden to take their seats. Before the members of the Reichstag assembled in the Kroll Opera House, Hitler opened the debate on the Enabling Act, which provided the constitutional foundation for the Nazi dictatorship and confined the Weimar Republic to the history books. Parliamentary approval was no longer required, and most of those who would have opposed it were already in gaol. The Nazis had taken a crucial step forward: from being masters of the street they had become masters of the state.

The Gestapo's power, which had previously been confined to Berlin, was extended to every police department in Prussia. Although it appeared that the Communists had, for a while at least, been neutralized, Göring itched with impatience to expand his empire. His position, though, was by no means unassailable, as Ernst Röhm's SA had expanded its strength considerably: three million men could now be mobilized. In addition, there were 300,000 members of *Stahlhelm* ('Steel Helmet'), the ex-servicemen's organization. The thuggish activities of these adherents of the SA had grown with the force of their numbers and showed clear signs of being beyond control. But, as it turned out, a powerful and sinister corrective was soon in sight.

Below: Hitler's first cabinet on taking office was a broad coalition. Besides Hitler himself, there were two other Nazis, Hermann Göring, future *Reichsmarschall*, and Wilhelm Frick, appointed Reich Minister of the Interior. The cabinet became a rubber stamp for Nazi policies, its final meeting taking place in February 1938.

CHAPTER 2

RIVALRY

With the Nazis firmly the masters of Germany, Göring and Himmler pursued their ultimate goal: control of a secret police whose tentacles would stretch throughout the Reich and beyond.

Heinrich Himmler, the prissily bespectacled nonentity from the edge of the semi-farcical Beer Hall Putsch, was now casting covetous eyes at the ever-growing strength in Berlin of the SS and Gestapo. The rank of 'Acting Police President' had been tossed to him, but he regarded it as scarcely good enough, even with the addition of the grandiose title of *Reichsführer-SS*. The son of a solidly respectable Bavarian schoolmaster, and once a fertilizer salesman, he had originally enrolled in the SS as Member No. 168. His undistinguished wartime army career had afforded him the rank of orderly room corporal, in which capacity he established the reputation as a sneak and tireless collector of the weaknesses and indiscretions of his colleagues. But this was only part of the man who believed wholeheartedly in the racial tenets and pseudo-mystic trappings of National Socialism, and who eagerly absorbed the misunderstood superman theories of Friedrich Nietzsche, along with ancient Teutonic legends of a Germany of forests and hunters living by sword and dagger.

As the late Hugh Trevor-Roper, the British historian, wrote: '… to Himmler they were, every iota of them, the pure Aryan truth, which if a man keep not pure and undefiled, he shall without doubt perish everlastingly. With such a narrow pedantry, with such black-letter antiquarianism, did Himmler study the details of this sad rubbish'. Those who worked with Himmler had similar assessments: Albert Krebs, for example, during his time as Gauleiter

Left: On 20 April 1934, Himmler – with a formal handshake – takes over from Göring the directorship of the Secret State Police Office, embracing the Gestapo. It led to a massive assumption of power by Himmler, whose sole responsibility was to Göring in the latter's offices of Minister-President of Prussia and Interior Minister.

Above: *SS-Gruppenführer* **Reinhard Heydrich, who rose to head the entire SS security apparatus. A ruthless careerist, Heydrich was feared by Nazis and opponents alike. Although a paragon of Aryan manhood, he had a secret fear – the insinuations of many enemies that he possessed 'impure blood', a partially Jewish ancestry.**

of Hamburg, once shared a long railway journey with Himmler and endured a tedious monologue, described in Krebs's post-war memoirs as 'political nonsense' and 'stupid and fundamentally empty claptrap'. These Nordic ravings and fantasies, however, were also fuelled by the all-consuming pursuit of power – above all, the determination to gain absolute control ultimately of the black-uniformed SS.

THE RISE OF REINHARD HEYDRICH

In the wake of von Schleicher's appointment as Reich Chancellor, a previous ban imposed on both the SA and the SS had been lifted, resulting in a surge of violence that caused great alarm among conservative business circles, whose support was vital to the Nazis. Himmler began to prepare for what amounted to Germany's civil war – and his ultimate enemy was the SA. The search was on for promising subordinates. Outstanding among these was Reinhard Eugen Tristan Heydrich, from Halle an der Salle in Saxony, whose appointment as deputy was due not least to the fact that he was tall, blond and athletic, seemingly the very model of the blond Nordic species so besotted of Himmler.

Heydrich, whose musician father had founded the First Halle Conservatory for Music, Theatre and Teaching, had served in the German navy. What should have been a promising career, however, had ended in court martial and dismissal in 1931 for dishonourable conduct. No solid record of the reason has survived: the most favoured of the many rumours involved an affair with the daughter of an officer in the Hamburg naval dockyards. Heydrich himself was not prepared to offer any enlightenment. He contributed a sentence to his SS dossier that read, 'At the end of April 1931, I was dismissed from the service on non-service grounds by a decision of the Reich President against the advice of my immediate superiors.'

At this time Heydrich was engaged to Lina von Olsen, the flaxen-haired daughter of a village schoolmaster from the Baltic island of Fehmarn. Whatever the cause of Heydrich's disgrace, it seemingly made no difference to the relationship. In any case, the bond went beyond mere family – the Olsens and the young Reinhard shared an ardent devotion to nationalism. Lina's brother, Jürgen, had fallen under Hitler's spell in 1928 after hearing him speak, and Lina herself had joined a National Socialist women's group. It seemed that an opening in the NSDAP could be established for Heydrich, but initially he was not attracted to the idea, judging the Nazis by the crude image of the SA. As it turned out, it was Heydrich's own family who forced the pace through knowing Baron Karl von Eberstein, at that time an *SS-Oberführer* who had the ear of Himmler and engineered a meeting.

There could scarcely have been a greater contrast between the colourless, narrow-minded Himmler, meek and bespectacled, and the infinitely brighter Heydrich, a linguist and talented violinist, tall and impressive with a wide sensual mouth and ice-pick eyes. Ironically the meeting, according to some later accounts, had arisen initially through a misconception: Heydrich had served in the navy as a *Nachrichtenoffizier* (wireless officer), a term confused by both von Eberstein and Himmler with *Nachrichtendienstoffizier* (intelligence officer). It was the latter position that Himmler was most anxious to fill. As he had secured the interview with some difficulty, Heydrich did not see fit to disabuse the *Reichsführer-SS*.

Himmler gave him just 20 minutes to describe in writing how he would organize an intelligence service for the SS. Heydrich drew on the sketchy knowledge he had gathered at navy intelligence seminars, spicing it with memories of the books, many of them fictional thrillers, read to while away long hours at sea. For verisimilitude, he included what he hoped were suitable and correct examples of service terminology. Himmler, after studying the result, pronounced himself satisfied. Heydrich was given the job

Below: This early photograph of the SS shows many key figures. Heinrich Himmler (front row, centre) became *Reichsführer-SS* and at first controlled just 280 men. To the left of Himmler is Kurt Daluege, who served originally with the SA, becoming a senior SS officer in 1928. A young Reinhard Heydrich (third row, second from right), the future SD chief, can also be seen, as well as Josef ('Sepp') Dietrich, future *Waffen-SS* and panzer corps commander.

and told to make ready for the journey to Munich from his home in Hamburg. On 14 July 1931, Reinhard Heydrich, with the lowly rank of *Rottenführer*, joined the Hamburg SS, which consisted largely of young social misfits who had to be prised away from the city's red-light district and beer cellars. This lowly apprenticeship did not last long. Party Headquarters Hamburg was alerted by a message from Munich on 5 October: 'Party Member Reinhard Heydrich, Membership No. 544916, will, with effect from October of this year, be carried on the strength of Party Headquarters as a member of the staff of the *Reichsführer-SS*.' The transfer to the Bavarian capital brought promotion to the rank of *Sturmbannführer*, or platoon leader,

HIMMLER'S WORLD

Behind the high walls of Wewelsburg Castle, in forests near the ancient Westphalian town of Paderborn, Heinrich Himmler fashioned his own special world. It was nursed not by a prim, pebble-spectacled bureaucrat, but by Himmler the romantic, creator of a shrine dedicated to the ritualistic trappings of Freemasonry with its uniforms and elaborate regalia.

Acquired by Himmler in the summer of 1934, Wewelsburg was his Camelot, reflecting deep readings of the legends of King Arthur and his 12 Round Table Knights – transformed now into 12 personally selected *Obergruppenführers*, proclaimed as 'an aristocracy of blood and soul'. The chosen *Obergruppenführers* were required to gather regularly at a large oak table in a dining room. Here, Himmler was able to draw on beliefs acquired in the mid-1920s when he had been a member of the Thule society, an organization that believed in the greatness of German history, reaching back to the ninth century AD. Then the Teutonic tribes had defeated the Roman army, thus proving the superiority of an Aryan race of ancient northern Europeans. The danger now, he declared, hailed from the east, from the detested Slavs who were part of a spawning Judeo-Bolshevik conspiracy.

In a corner of the castle was a room set aside to house the Holy Grail, a sacred symbol that Himmler believed Christians had stolen from a far older Aryan religion and which he felt should be found. The crypt housed 12 stone pedestals into which the ashes of dead latter-day 'knights' would be placed along with their SS daggers and personal weaponry.

Himmler's extensive collection of weapons and a large library were dedicated to King Heinrich I ('Henry the Fowler'), founder of the first German Reich and from whom Himmler firmly believed he was descended. At the stroke of midnight on the anniversary of his hero's death, Himmler would commune with the Fowler in silence.

In 1935, Himmler established a new arm of the SS, *Das Ahnenerbe* ('Ancestral Heritage Society'), staffed by high-profile Nazi academics. These men were tasked with organizing expeditions to many parts of the world – to Iceland in search of the Grail and to Iran to unearth evidence of ancients of pure Ayran blood. Three years later, the SS undertook in Tibet what was its most ambitious expedition. Film shot there survives and shows the bodies of Tibetans being measured and examined for vital indicators of racial identity.

Many were indulgent of Himmler's occultist obsessions but, as events later showed, behind it all lay a sinister motive – to inculcate into his SS rabid racist beliefs about the superiority of Aryan races. It was but a prelude to launch the programme of genocide against so-called inferior races.

but he was enough of a realist to recognize that the Bavarian SS still numbered fewer than 1000 men and was scarcely known outside the state. His pay of RM180 was meagre and the infrastructure needed to run an intelligence bureau almost nonexistent. From the cramped fourth floor of a house at Turfkenstrasse 23 in Munich, Heydrich operated with a team that consisted of Frau Heydrich as secretary and three helpers.

HARD WORKER

From the start Heydrich displayed the strength of three men, slaving day and night on what amounted to a mirror image of Göring's work in Berlin – drawing on existing SS records and amassing a card index, the matrix of any dictatorship, in which were recorded the intimate details of fellow SS members and anyone else who could present even the most distant threat. The outcome of all this industry was the *Sicherheitsdienst des Reichsführers SS* (SD), Heinrich Himmler's security service, but in fact controlled by Heydrich.

Some of those who observed Heydrich's zest for work, his seeming obsession, did not believe that this was due solely to his strongly affirmed dedication to National Socialism. A rumour began to circulate in certain Nazi circles that Heydrich was desperately striving to disown something from his past, nothing less, it was said, than a need to atone for an ancestry tainted with Jewish blood. An entry in a music lexicon was found to describe his father as 'Heydrich, Bruno, né Süss', possibly a Jewish name. This arose from a misconception. The second marriage of Heydrich's maternal grandmother, Ernestine Wilhelmine Heydrich, née Lindner, had been to a journeyman locksmith named Gustav Robert Süss. As the mother of a large family by her first husband Reinhold Heydrich, she had often chosen to call herself 'Süss-Heydrich'. The Nazi genealogist Dr Achim Gercke demolished the allegation decisively, by pointing out that Gustav Süss was 'in any case … not of Jewish origin'. The rumours reached Hitler, who took the cynical view that, if the claim were true, it would ensure Heydrich's loyalty, as well as being a handy instrument for blackmail should the occasion arise. The smear, as he regarded it, stuck with Heydrich throughout his short life, causing biographers and historians to speculate that here could lie an explanation for his savagery towards Jews.

Above: Three years after Hitler assumed power, Himmler, with the rank of *Reichsführer-SS*, had control of the entire German police apparatus, including the running of the concentration camps. All his activities were fuelled by the dream of creating a new elite of worldwide Aryan stock. By 1944, he had reached the pinnacle of Nazi power, assuming military status, initially as Commander in Chief of the Reserve Army.

Fortunately for Heydrich, the importance of the rumour paled against happenings on the wider stage. In the wake of Hitler's appointment as Chancellor, Germany's previously cherished institutions began their surrender to the Nazis. The country's numerous states (*Länder*), which had remained stoutly independent for generations, began dissolving without protest. A prominent exception was Bavaria, which Hitler intended to place in the hands of General Franz Xaver Ritter von Epp, the native of Munich who had been one of the most prominent members of a freebooter faction within the rightist *Freikorps* movement. In the early 1920s he had been area commander of the SA.

On the evening of 9 March, less than two months after the Nazi assumption of power, Ernst Röhm, backed by cohorts of the SA parading in front of the State Chancellery, requested a handover of power to von Epp and his creation as Commissar-General for Bavaria. The Bavarian Council of Ministers rejected the demand, denying that they had received any written confirmation of von Epp's appointment. This, however, had already been signed and sealed in Berlin, and a telegram confirming this was rushed from Berlin to the Munich telegraph office. An SS detachment under Reinhard Heydrich was present to ensure that no attempt was made to destroy the wire. Heydrich, with no time for niceties, broke into the office and seized the telegram at gunpoint. It was his first openly performed mission for the party and, in the remodelled Bavaria, it did his career nothing but good.

Right: Political prisoners await transportation to Dachau, the first of the Nazi concentration camps established in 1933 and situated a few kilometres from Munich. The camp was run and staffed by volunteer SS who formed the Death's Head units, with their skull-and-crossboned cap badges. The Gestapo had little say in the running of camps. It had a considerable say, however, in despatching to the concentration camps those they had arrested and interrogated.

CONSOLIDATION IN BAVARIA

Himmler meanwhile was preoccupied by his onward march to power. On 1 April, Adolf Wagner, Minister of the Interior and Deputy Premier of Bavaria, issued a directive that read in part, '… I appoint the *Reichsführer-SS* Heinrich Himmler … Political Police Commander of Bavaria. At the same time I charge him with the execution of all measures and the issuing of all instructions, in consultation with the competent authorities of the State of Bavaria, that are necessary for the establishment of the Bureau of the Political Police Commander in Bavaria.' The directive went on to enumerate the specific police units that formed part of Himmler's responsibilities, including, significantly, 'the concentration camps whether existing or those to be set up'. This reflected Himmler's determination to follow and eventually surpass Göring's Gestapo scheme of establishing camps in Berlin under the direction of Rudolf Diels.

The programme in Bavaria opened on the night of 9 March 1933, when action was taken against all known and potential opponents, based on reports by the party's 'intelligence experts'. Those arrested included Communists, members of the German Social Democrat Party, the *Stalheim*, sundry professional men, inevitably including Jews. They were taken to local prisons and to magistrates' gaols at the police and district headquarters. All too soon space was running out. Three days later Wagner, as the Bavarian Minister of the Interior, wrote to the state's Minister of Justice, Dr Hans Frank, with the information that '… the number of arrests by the police is likely to grow. Should the prisons at the disposal of the judicial authorities be insufficient for this purpose, I recommend using the methods that were formerly employed with regard to mass arrests of members of the National Socialist German Workers' Party. It will be recalled that they were locked into any old hovel, and no one cared whether the prisoners were left exposed to the weather or not.'

Himmler, however, preferred locations that were tidier, but by no means less brutal, commandeering a disused power station at Dachau, situated about 19 km (12 miles) northwest of Munich. At first this served as a detention centre for those arrested on 'suspicion of activities inimical to the state', but went on to become the nucleus of the concentration camp system throughout

Above: A member of the Nazi auxiliary police units – nicknamed 'Chained Dogs' – is seen patrolling with an SA man on a Berlin street. Both are keeping order during the elections of 5 March 1933, which gave the Nazis 44 per cent of the vote and 228 seats.

1933: THE CRUCIAL YEAR

30 January: Appointment of Adolf Hitler as Chancellor

22 February: 40,000 SA and SS men sworn in as auxiliary policemen

27 February: Reichstag fire

28 February: Hitler given emergency powers by a presidential decree

5 March: Reichstag elections – 288 Nazi deputies returned out of a total of 647

9 March: Himmler made police president in Munich

13 March: Appointment of Göbbels as Reich Minister for Public Enlightenment and Propaganda

17 March: Formation of the SS-*Leibstandarte* Adolf Hitler under Josef (Sepp) Dietrich

21 March: Communist Deputies forbidden to take seats in the new Reichstag

24 March: Adoption of the Enabling Act (Law to Remove the Distress of People and State)

31 March: Individual states of the Reich stripped of power

1 April: National boycott of Jewish businesses and professionals

21 April: Rudolf Hess designated Deputy *Führer*.

26 April: Gestapo formed

2 May: Labour unions dissolved

10 May: Book burning throughout Germany

17 May: Strikes banned

9 June: SD made the sole political and counter-espionage organization of the Nazi party

14 July: Law issued concerning the formation of new parties

20 July: Reich-Vatican concordat signed in Rome

22 September: Göbbels sets out Reich Chamber of Culture

24 October: Germany withdraws from League of Nations

12 November: Reichstag elections – 93 per cent of votes cast for NSDAP

the Reich – euphemistically classified as 'institutions for reform'. In addition, Himmler focused on two stumbling blocks to the successful creation of the SS state: the seemingly impregnable SA, primarily, but also Göring's role as Minister President of Prussia. The latter had appointed Kurt Daluege, another *Freikorps* veteran and blatant careerist, to a powerful post within the *Ordnungspolizei* (Orpo, 'uniformed police'), then promoted him to *Gruppenführer der Polizei* within the SS, despite Daluege's reputation as one of the crudest roughnecks in Berlin and his being dubbed 'Dummi-Dummi' ('stupid one') by his many detractors. A vast hulk of a man, Daluege made no attempt to conceal his contempt for Himmler, whom he regarded as a pedantic bore. Himmler, perfectly aware of the antipathy, became all the more determined to settle with Göring on where leadership of the SS should reside.

As well as the work of Rudolf Diels in establishing the fledgling Gestapo, Göring was able to draw on professional civil servants from the pre-Hitler days, as well as seasoned police and administrative personnel. There were nine fully operating desks, dealing with a multitude of subjects demanding political police scrutiny, the main emphasis being on all organizations on the left. Himmler nursed dreams of taking control of the entire operation for himself and opened his campaign. Heydrich, resplendent in the full uniform of an *SS-Standartenführer*, was despatched to Berlin with a request to meet Daluege, who pointedly refused to receive him. Telephone calls to the Prussian Ministry of the Interior, where Heydrich's quarry was installed, were ignored. From his base at the Savoy Hotel near the Berlin Zoo, Heydrich wrote an exasperated note to Daluege, although, as he recognized that Göring's man outranked him with the rank of *Gruppenführer*, it was couched in obsequious terms: 'Since Thursday I have been trying without success to penetrate the "protective screen". I have telephoned no less than six times.

Since I have to travel back today, I beg you to recognize this as a token of my visit and hope that the opportunity for a token visit will present itself in about ten days. I remain your most humble and obedient servant, R. Heydrich. Heil Hitler!'

Himmler and Heydrich thus had to be content with measures extending their power in Bavaria. On 9 March 1933, a group of SS and SA under Heydrich seized the building of the Munich Metropolitan Police. It was part of a general purge of the civil service. Within Munich itself Heydrich, in addition to being SD chief, became head of the political desk in *Abteilung VI* ('Department VI') of the Criminal Police.

HEINRICH MÜLLER

There were places for career policemen, many of whom were chiefly concerned with holding on to their jobs and had scant interest in either the National Socialist Party or indeed politics in general. Among these was Heinrich Müller, a thickset, bull-necked criminal police inspector who had been a member of Munich police headquarters and had headed the anti-Communist desk of the political section. Müller was forthwith put to work by Heydrich to winkle out members of the Communist Party of Germany (KPD) and to become broadly conversant with Soviet methods of infiltration. A formal enquiry into Müller's character destined for SS files declared, 'He is an elbow man. He tolerates none who might stand in his way. He knows how to display his efficiency.'

In March 1933, Müller's men searched a house belonging to a Munich couple and found Communist leaflets giving details of concentration camps and reception centres. The mere ownership of such material, Müller proclaimed, constituted 'high treason', an offence which, at the very mildest, meant incarceration. But, according to the pre-1933 law still in force, high treason could only be applied to passing military secrets. The leaflets in Müller's possession contained nothing to support the definition or merit the charge of high treason. In this case, he acknowledged defeat, but soon found means to close the loophole, ensuring that further revelations on camp conditions by outsiders fell within the new definition of high treason. Penal institutions began swelling their numbers with 'prisoners in protective custody' – increasingly, Communists and Socialists.

Below: Heinrich Müller, the Gestapo head, walked out of Hitler's bunker on 29 April 1945 and vanished. Originally an energetic Munich policeman, he had a keen instinct for self-preservation – sensing the time to quit and switch sides. Even as a Gestapo officer in 1939 he held left-wing views and is believed to have contacted the Soviet Union, where he eventually settled.

Above: Wherever the *Führer* travelled, he was under the protection of his very own black-garbed bodyguard, the SS-*Leibstandarte* Adolf Hitler, formed under that name in November 1933. The *Leibstandarte* had the status of an elite body, nominally headed by Himmler, but in fact under the direct control of Hitler himself.

PROTECTING THE *FÜHRER*

Progress towards the goal of power in Berlin still appeared to be beyond the Gestapo in Bavaria, so Himmler and Heydrich switched their attention to alerting Hitler to what they claimed were plots against his life and regime. When, for example, supplies were found to have been stolen from various arms dumps, Hitler was easily persuaded that this was the work of the SA, who had secreted them away in preparation for a planned insurrection. Soon there were whispers that agents of the Soviet Union were lurking on every street corner and that the assassination of leading Nazi figures was being planned from within. Every time he entered the building, the *Führer* was seen to stare nervously at the detachments of the *Reichswehr* who stood guard outside the Reich Chancellery. In such an atmosphere, Hitler became only too receptive to the idea that guard functions should be carried out by the trusty SS. The result was the foundation of a 120-strong unit, the elite SS-*Leibstandarte* Adolf Hitler (the Adolf Hitler Bodyguard), which Himmler regarded as a triumph for his SS, intended as it was 'to serve as the protector of the *Führer*'. By decree its sphere of duties was to be enlarged to include the internal security of the Reich, increasing Himmler's own powers.

All these changes were set against ever-escalating violence on the streets of Berlin and throughout Prussia, most of it fanned by the Brown Shirts.

Protests were voiced in cabinet, notably by von Papen, who provoked Hitler into crashing his fist on the table and promising to put an end to the obscenities *(Schweinereien)* of the SA squads. Himmler, seeing a fresh opportunity, put Heydrich to work, instructing him to let it be known in Berlin that a 'Trotskyist plot' had been uncovered to assassinate Göring. This assertion, whether true or not, was accompanied by the obvious question: if true, why had the Gestapo in Berlin, where Rudolph Diels was in charge of such matters, not uncovered this major threat to security? Given this lapse, surely it would be (in Himmler's words) 'just, opportune and necessary to pursue the enemy in the same manner throughout the Reich'.

THE *FÜHRER*

Führer ('leader') was the title used by Hitler to signify his role as supreme head of the Third Reich, equivalent to such designations as *Duce*, describing Benito Mussolini as supreme head of Fascist Italy; *Caudillo*, used by General Francisco Franco as chief of the Spanish state and Army commander in chief, and *Generalissimo*, the title assumed by Joseph Stalin as supreme commander of the Soviet armed forces.

A scapegoat had to be found for the lapse of the Berlin Gestapo. A dossier detailing Diels's heavy drinking, marital infidelities and other excesses reached President von Hindenburg. Diels was dismissed with the consolation appointment of Deputy Director of the Berlin police. But his continuing awareness of danger proved justified. While driving to work, he spotted two aides in front of the Ministry of Justice who waved him down and warned him that contingents from the SS and SD had occupied Prinz-Albrecht-Strasse 8, where his office had been searched, incriminating documents found and an arrest warrant issued. He hastily retreated and, in the company of a woman friend, decamped for the Czechoslovak resort of Karlovy Vary.

Göring's appointment of an old-guard Nazi as Diels's successor heralded pure farce. Paul Hinkler, the former Nazi Police President of Altona, was soon revealed as an alcoholic with a history of mental instability and was dismissed after 30 days of befuddled incompetence. Diels was traced and recalled, agreeing to resume his former post. But the position could only be temporary because his final removal came with the arrival of Himmler and Heydrich in Berlin. As a parting gesture, Diels was given the job of *Regierungspräsident* ('Head of the Regional Government') in Cologne. Göring had reached the end of the road as head of the Gestapo in Prussia and control passed to Himmler, who accepted the appointment on 20 April 1934, initially gaining the title of Acting Chief of the Prussian Gestapo.

At the end of July, the SS was made a unit independent of the SA, receiving Göring's blessing as Minister-President and Interior Minister; his decree stated that 'Himmler will be completely in charge and responsible only to me directly.' Himmler was to be headquartered at Prinz-Albrecht-Strasse 8 in charge of the political police, including the Gestapo. The SS men numbered three battalions. Added muscle came from the resources of Heydrich's SD. The foundations of a truly national police state had been laid.

CHAPTER 3

HEYDRICH TAKES OVER

Heydrich's ruthlessness in securing the destruction of Röhm's SA and the neutering of opposition within the old military order left Hitler free to pursue his ongoing preparations for war.

B erlin in the summer of 1934 was a city alive with rumours, not the least of which was that Ernst Röhm was heading a conspiracy to seize power. The army, the support of which Hitler so badly needed, claimed to have intelligence that Röhm favoured joining his SA to the *Reichswehr*, producing a left-wing 'people's army'. Yet it seemed that the *Führer*, loyal to old party comrades, was deliberately staying his hand. At the start of the year he had even thanked the SA leader for 'immeasurable services rendered to the National Socialist movement and to the German people'.

In a bid to neutralize the differences between the army and the Brown Shirts, Hitler had hit on a possible compromise. Colonel-General Werner von Blomberg, the Minister for National Defence, and Röhm, as Chief of Staff of the SA, were persuaded to sign a pact proclaiming the *Reichswehr* as 'the only official armed organization of the Third Reich'. The SA would be permitted to remain and was assigned a subordinate defence role. At a champagne reception before the signing ceremony, Röhm proceeded to blow the scheme apart. Fuelled by drink, he volubly denounced 'the military and the bankers', at the same time launching a diatribe against Himmler's racial preoccupations. Hitler was also vilified for betraying the revolution; what Germany needed, Röhm declared, was a socialist state.

This was exactly what Heydrich and his lieutenants had been looking for as they worked around the clock, sifting records for anything that might be

Left: An official portrait of *SS-Obergruppenführer* Reinhard Heydrich issued to all Gestapo offices, where display was mandatory. Heydrich reached this rank in 1941, by which time he had become chief of the SD and had organized the *Einsatzgruppen*, the SS murder squads that followed the German armies into the Soviet Union.

Above: Ernst Röhm, head of the SA, was originally one of Hitler's most committed supporters. On Hitler becoming Chancellor, Röhm demanded the reward of power, but his revolutionary beliefs had alienated the Nazis. On 30 June 1934, Röhm was arrested and two days later murdered in his cell at Stadelheim prison.

construed as subversion. Tapping telephone calls became the province of a special unit of the green-uniformed *Landespolizeigruppe General Göring*, retained by Göring for his own protection and which, based at the Cadet School at Lichterfelde, grew to several thousand. A sudden threat was presented by Franz von Papen, who as Vice Chancellor delivered a highly contentious address to students in the small university town of Marburg. He proclaimed that there were elements within Germany who were highly disturbed by the actions and threats of the Nazis – the persecutions, the arbitrary arrests and the end of free elections. He went on to condemn 'all the self-seeking characterlessness, untruthfulness, vulgarity and arrogance hiding under the cloak of the German revolution'.

To have arraigned so prominent a figure as von Papen, however, would have incurred the indignation of his old friend von Hindenburg, and this would have been unwise when Germany was striving for a measure of respectability beyond its shores. Heydrich looked for an alternative. The Gestapo soon discovered that the offending speech had been written by Edgar Jung, a young writer who was known to have conservative views and who had amassed a small but potentially subversive following. Swift action followed in the wake of the Marburg speech. Jung was abducted from his Munich apartment: the only clue as to the perpetrators was the word

'Gestapo' scrawled with shaving soap on his bathroom mirror. On 30 June, his severely dismembered body was found in a ditch outside Berlin on the road to Oranienburg.

DESTRUCTION OF THE SA

In Berlin that June, summer temperatures soared. Couples strode beneath the limes and chestnuts of the Unter den Linden, the less energetic slaking their thirst in the numerous pavement cafés. On one occasion activity was centred on the large mansion at the corner of Tiergartenstrasse, headquarters of the Berlin-Brandenburg SA, as a knot of its members in their brown uniforms emerged with their hands raised and were pushed and shoved into trucks by police touting carbines and submachine guns.

At the end of the month, the *Reichswehr* was put on alert by an article in the *Völkischer Beobachter*, the party newspaper, signed by Colonel-General Werner Freiherr von Fritsch, the Commander in Chief, which affirmed that 'the Army … stands behind Adolf Hitler … who remains one of ours … The German soldier is aware that he is involved in the political life of a unified country'. Here was a coded declaration that the army would be at the service of the Reich in every capacity, not just in military matters.

Hitler still clung to his faith in Röhm, stating in a speech before the Reichstag at the Kroll Opera House that 'at the beginning of June, I made a final effort with Röhm. I asked him to come to my office, and we talked together for nearly five hours.' In a bid to take the heat out of the situation, the SA was sent on leave for one month from 1 July and during that time was forbidden to wear uniform. The decision was greeted with consternation by Heydrich, Himmler, Göring and General Walther von Reichenau, Blomberg's Chief of Staff, who had given his approval to an armed uprising against the SA. How, it was declared, was Röhm to be despatched if the SA were allowed on leave?

Within days the draft text of a bulletin from Röhm and the General Staff of the SA, intended to be published in the newspaper *National Zeitung*, fell into the hands of

Below: A victim of the Röhm Purge – the Night of the Long Knives – in which Hitler ordered the killing of his enemies within the SA, most of whom were summarily shot. The true number of SA victims of the purge was never established, but the final figure is thought to have been more than a thousand.

Above: Kurt von Schleicher, the last Chancellor of the Weimar Republic, who, together with his wife, was assassinated during the Röhm purge at the instigation of Göring, following suspicions that von Schleicher had been intriguing to overthrow Hitler.

Heydrich's agents and was taken by many to spell out Röhm's intentions: 'I hope that on the first of August, a well-rested SA, filled with strength, will be ready to undertake the glorious mission it owes the people and the Fatherland. If the enemies of the SA think that it will not return from leave, or return only in part, let them enjoy their illusions as long as they can.'

When Hitler flew to Westphalia to attend the wedding of an old friend, Himmler took the initiative, warning of an imminent uprising in Berlin masterminded by Karl Ernst, one of Röhm's closest aides. The *Reichsführer* and his agents kept up the pressure with a flood of communiqués to Hitler reporting plans for an uprising in Munich. Hitler vacillated no more. He made for Bad Wiessee, south of Munich, where Röhm was ensconced in the Pension Hanslbauer with some personable SA youths. It was here that the blood purge began. Accounts vary, many agreeing only that the outcome was corpse-ridden and bloody. Röhm, who had been fast asleep, was dragged from his bed and hauled off to Stadelheim gaol. Two days later a gun was placed in his cell and he was ordered to take the 'honourable' way out. When he refused, a murder squad shot him down. In Berlin, under the direction of Himmler and Göring, some 150 SA leaders were rounded up and despatched by firing squads at the Cadet School at Lichterfelde.

A notorious instance of Göring's involvement in the violent deaths of what became known as the Night of the Long Knives was the cold-blooded killing on 30 June of both Kurt von Schleicher and his wife of 18 months at their house on the outskirts of Berlin. Göring was to claim that the shootings had been a mistake, that a breakaway group of *Landespolizei*, unauthorized by him, was responsible. Nevertheless he showed little remorse at a later press gathering and contradicted his earlier statements. In answer to a question from a foreign journalist, he said: 'General von Schleicher was plotting against the regime. I ordered his arrest. He made the mistake of attempting to resist. He is dead.'

Heydrich's agents from the SD were everywhere, including placing spies among the

> Accounts vary, many agreeing only that the outcome was bloody. Röhm, who had been fast asleep, was dragged from his bed and hauled off to Stadelheim gaol.

staff of Berlin's Hotel Adlon, a fashionable meeting place for politicians. Old scores were settled, motivated by naked revenge. Hans Bernd Gisevius, who had served in the Gestapo in the very early days and survived to become a witness in the post-war Nuremberg trials, testified that all documents relating to the Röhm purge were subsequently destroyed. Gisevius was a vivid witness of Heydrich's actions in his powerhouse at Prinz-Albrecht-Strasse 8 and described how orders were issued without pause. Heydrich was in possession of lists of intended victims who were referred to by the numbers accompanying their names. A stream of telegrams from throughout the Reich would provide information such as 'No. 8 has arrived. Nos 17, 35, 68 and 84 have been arrested. Nos 32, 43, 47 and 59 have been shot'.

DEATH OF STRASSER

Surviving documentary evidence of Heydrich's direct involvement in killings during the purge is sparse, but the link can be proved in at least one prominent incident. Gregor Strasser had been an early rival of Hitler for the leadership of the National Socialist Party. Along with his brother Otto, he remained dedicated to 'undiluted Socialist principles', a stance which served only to irritate Hitler in his pursuit of support from the country's industrialists. The writing was on the wall. The future Propaganda Minister Dr Paul Josef Göbbels, one-time protégé of Strasser as editor of the newsletter *NS-Brief*, sensed that power was shifting in favour of Hitler and

Below: A Gestapo contingent seen outside the headquarters at Prinz-Albrecht-Strasse 8 in June 1934. The very name of the street became a synonym for an organization that evoked fear in the ordinary German. Large parts of the area were destroyed by Allied bombing. A museum, the Typography of Terror Foundation, stands on the site today.

was prudent enough to change sides. Relations with the *Führer* – a title, incidentally, Strasser refused to use – deteriorated as well. The situation was certainly not helped when von Schleicher as Chancellor had suggested that Strasser should be made Vice Chancellor and Premier of Prussia. The link with Hitler's predecessor was enough to condemn him, a fate underlined by the terse entry in Göbbels's diary: 'A dead man'.

Strasser remained in political limbo until the time of the purge, when he was arrested and incarcerated in a cell at Prinz-Albrecht-Strasse, beaten up by his SS guards and shot. In his memoirs, *To the Bitter End*, Gisevius reported the testimony of another inmate: 'The prisoner heard loud footsteps in the corridor and orders being shouted. The guards clicked their heels. And the prisoner heard Heydrich saying, "Isn't he dead yet? Let the swine bleed to death." The bloodstain on the wall of the cell remained for weeks. It was the pride of the SS squadron, a kind of museum piece.'

After two days and following more shootings, Hitler put an end to further bloodletting, believing he had achieved his objective. Those who survived appeared to do so either from pure luck or, in the case of Rudolf Diels, from intervention by Göring, who retained an obstinate loyalty

Below: Hitler and Göring with Field Marshal Werner von Blomberg (left), supreme commander of the newly formed *Wehrmacht*, and Colonel-General Werner von Fritsch, army commander in chief (right). Both officers were opposed to Hitler's intentions of expanding the Reich by force and of increasing SS dominance.

towards an old associate. At 7 a.m. on 2 July, a memo was issued, 'To all subordinate police stations: All documents concerning the action of the last two days are to be burnt, on orders from above. A report on the execution of this order is to be made at once.' When it was all over, solid evidence of an intended putsch remained obscure, although much was made of Röhm's alleged plans for a shotgun wedding between the SA and the army to justify the events.

EXPANDING THE REICH

Relieved of the incubus of the SA, Himmler and Heydrich became unstoppable in their pursuit of power. By the summer of 1936, Himmler was Chief of the German Police, a formal expression as head of the SS. But it was not just the structure of the security apparatus that was preoccupying those with power in Berlin. Hitler was looking towards a broader canvas. By 5 November 1937, three years after the death of von Hindenburg had removed one of the last survivors of the old order,

the *Führer*'s confidence had grown sufficiently to summon a secret gathering to the Reich Chancellery. Present were the Minister of War, the Foreign Minister and the commanders in chief of the three services. The *Führer* held forth for more than four hours; from the verbiage emerged a single blunt analysis of Germany's situation – the country needed more living space, 'which could be solved only by force'. Targets, he declared, would be his birthplace, Austria, followed by Czechoslovakia and Poland. Preparations must be ready by the following year, 1938, and operations should be complete by 1943–5 at the latest. Although no effective opposition was voiced at the meeting, strong reservations were expressed afterwards individually to Hitler, but he had been in no mood to tolerate dissent. He was forced to recognize that the most serious opposition to his policy would come from the highest echelons of the army (the *Oberschicht*, or the 'upper crust'), principally von Blomberg, the War Minister, and from the Commander in Chief, Colonel-General Werner Freiherr von Fritsch.

THE BLOMBERG–FRITSCH AFFAIR

A convenient opportunity to remove von Blomberg occurred on 12 January 1938 with the announcement in German newspapers that he had married Fräulein Erna Gruhm in Berlin, a wedding witnessed by Adolf Hitler and Hermann Göring. The latter had been made aware that the new Frau von

Above: Gregor Strasser, a radical Nazi and talented organizer for the party during Reichstag elections, had been tipped for a bright future within the party. But as a convinced socialist in opposition to big business interests, he gained Hitler's enmity and rumours had circulated that he was plotting with Ernst Röhm to overthrow the *Führer*. These allegations led to his arrest and execution.

Below: A scene from the 1975 film *Salon Kitty*, which was based on events in the brothel of that name conceived by Heydrich and financed by the SD in the hope that its habitués, beguiled by compliant hostesses and luxurious surroundings, would reveal useful intelligence. Heydrich himself was known to make use of its facilities.

Blomberg's previous lover was Jewish, and Göring had persuaded him to quit the country. But matters were not to be as tidy as that: the Berlin police soon presented Göring with a file and photographs revealing that Erna von Blomberg had been a professional prostitute who posed for pornographic pictures; if necessary, Heydrich would be able to supplement the file. Von Blomberg was forced to resign and he retired with his bride to Capri. An apparent final twist to the story was revealed 38 years later in the biography of Heydrich by the veteran journalist Edouard Calic, who stated that he had interviewed von Blomberg's widow. She claimed that Heydrich had arranged for a set of photographs to be concocted by a Gestapo associate, superimposing her head on the body of a woman indulging in indecent acts.

In addition, a case of indecency in a public place was built up against von Fritsch when the Gestapo arrested a homosexual pimp and blackmailer named Hans Schmidt, who identified von Fritsch as the man he had observed committing a homosexual offence with a young boy at Potsdam train station. Rumours were circulated that von Fritsch, a confirmed bachelor, had homosexual tendencies, but he was acquitted by an army court of honour.

SALON KITTY

One of Reinhard Heydrich's more bizarre schemes was the setting up in 1939 of an SD-financed brothel named Salon Kitty. Its aim was to provide discreet entertainment for diplomats, civil servants and businessmen from within the Reich and beyond. Heydrich reasoned that, in the presence of suitably attractive female companionship, even the most cautious individual could be induced to relax and reveal useful information. A substantial four-storey villa was chosen in a fashionable district of Berlin. Microphones installed in specially built double walls were connected by automatic transmission to tape recorders. These picked up every word spoken throughout the building.

Strict instructions were given that no one was to know to whom Salon Kitty really belonged, least of all the hostesses who were recruited from the cream of the demimonde by Artur Nebe, chief of the Kripo. The ostensible owner of the house was able to call on the most experienced domestic and catering staff who served very superior – and very expensive – food and drink.

The clientele included Count Galeazzo Ciano, the Italian Minister of Foreign Affairs, who frequently brought parties of diplomats from Rome. To Heydrich's scarcely concealed delight, another habitué was Joachim von Ribbentrop, the Reich Foreign Minister. Heydrich himself paid the occasional visit to Salon Kitty, during which, needless to say, the microphones were switched off. Ultimately, though, he considered the brothel to be of limited value and the scheme was abandoned because, as he commented to a colleague, 'I am surprised how little emerged. Perhaps it is just a myth that secrets are given away in bed.'

Salon Kitty, a somewhat lurid film about events in the brothel and based in turn on a novel by Peter Norden, was made in 1975 by the Italian director Tinto Brass.

His career was nevertheless ruined. Eventually permitted to return to the army, von Fritsch was posted to Poland at the outbreak of war and, according to fellow officers, made it his business to be killed as soon as possible.

PREPARATIONS FOR WAR

With the fall of the two men, Hitler took over von Blomberg's office of Commander in Chief and abolished the War Ministry, creating in its place the High Command of the Armed Forces (*Oberkommando der Wehrmacht*, OKW). Under him he placed the compliant Wilhelm Keitel, who was to hold the position until the end of the war. Von Fritsch's position went to General Walther von Brauchitsch, who was regarded as a safe pair of hands. Sundry other generals were cleared away by transfers and retirements, until the snobbish clique of the *Oberschicht* had finally been removed. Hitler saw no reason to delay his plans for the creation of a Greater Germany.

All the signs suggested preparations for war. Austria was absorbed in March 1938, to be followed in October by the German-speaking regions of Czechoslovakia. The following summer Hitler had been due to hold the annual Nuremberg Rally, but it was abruptly cancelled; rumours of large-scale troop movements abounded. Plans were afoot to move army

Above: Alfred Naujocks, a former SA street fighter, was one of Heydrich's most trusted aides after joining the SS in 1932. Another of the born survivors, the chief protagonist of the Gleiwitz Raid was ultimately dismissed by the SD for disobedience and joined the *Waffen-SS* in 1943, where he was held responsible for murdering Danish Resistance members.

headquarters to Zossen, east of Berlin. On 15 August 1939, the pocket battleships *Graf Spee* and *Deutschland,* together with 21 submarines, set sail to the Atlantic.

CLANDESTINE OPERATIONS

Throughout this time Heydrich remained chained to his desk in Prinz-Albrecht-Strasse, immersed in the mountains of buff folders that poured in from the network of Gestapo agents. One of these was Alfred Naujocks, a former engineering student from Kiel University, whom the American reporter and commentator William Shirer defined as a typical Gestapo product – 'a sort of intellectual gangster' – who had joined the SD in 1934. One year into his apprenticeship, Naujocks had tracked down Rudolf Formis, a former Stuttgart radio engineer who had taken refuge in Czechoslovakia as an associate of Gregor Strasser's brother Otto. Formis had been transmitting anti-Nazi broadcasts for Otto Strasser's *Schwarze Front* ('Black Front') dissident movement. At the behest of Himmler, Heydrich's instructions to Naujocks and an associate had been to kidnap Formis and dispose of his radio transmitter. The operation was to be conducted swiftly and with minimum violence, so as to lessen any ensuing complications with the Czech authorities. However, a scheme to chloroform Formis and immobilize the transmitter with phosphorus went badly wrong. Formis had drawn a pistol and wounded Naujocks with three shots. An accompanying SD man, Gert Grothe, fired back, killing their quarry. A swift escape by a hotel window had thrown the whole area into chaos. Although the transmitter had been disposed of, the activities of the SD had been exposed. Back in Berlin, Heydrich had raged over what he regarded as a bungled mission 'straight out of a gangster film'. But his fears of incurring Himmler's wrath were unfounded, as Hitler had taken the broad view that important opposition had been removed; any complications were insignificant. The exercise had proved that the SD was able to work with some success beyond Germany's frontiers, and Himmler stressed to Heydrich that the SS intelligence apparatus should prove itself still further.

The next role assigned to the SD was to stage a series of incidents that could be used as a pretext for Germany to wage war. The most notorious of these was to fake an attack by 'Polish' troops on the radio station at Gleiwitz (now Gliwice), just inside the German border with Poland. In a sworn affidavit, presented at the Nuremberg war crimes trial, Naujocks related: 'On or about 10 August 1939, the Chief of the Sipo and SD, Heydrich, personally ordered me to simulate an attack on the radio station … and to make it appear that the attacking force consisted of Poles. Heydrich said, "Actual proof of these attacks of the Poles is needed for the foreign press, as well as for German propaganda purposes." I was directed to go to Gleiwitz with five or six SD men and wait there until I received a code word from Heydrich that the attack should take place.' His instructions then were to seize the radio station and hold it sufficiently long for a Polish-speaking German to deliver an inflammatory speech on air, exhorting the Poles towards a confrontation with Germany and urging them to take swift action. This would be the prelude to an imminent attack on Poland by Germany.

Naujocks made for the area of the operation, where he made contact with Heinrich Müller, who was involved in plans for a separate border incident in which it would be made to appear that Polish soldiers were attacking German troops. Naujocks's Nuremberg testament continued: 'Germans in the appropriate strength of a company were to be used. Müller stated that he had 12 or 13 condemned criminals who were to be dressed in Polish uniforms and left dead on the ground at the scene of the incident to show that they had been killed while attacking. For this purpose they were to be given fatal injections by a doctor employed by Heydrich. They were then also to be given gunshot wounds. After the assault, members of the Press and other persons were to be taken to the spot of the incident. A police report was subsequently to be prepared.' Heydrich had told Naujocks to secure one of the corpses – all carried the general code name 'Canned Goods' – to add verisimilitude to his own incident. Naujocks took charge of the body near the radio station. 'I received this man and had him laid in the entrance … He was alive, but he was completely unconscious. I tried to open his eyes. I could not recognize by his eyes that he was alive, only by his breathing. I did not see the shot wounds, but a lot of blood was smeared.'

THE ASSAULT

With two colleagues, Karl, the radio technician, and Heinrich, who was to deliver the crucial broadcast, Naujocks made an assault on the front entrance, while the rest made for the side. Their way was barred by a blue-uniformed security guard. Heinrich leapt on the man, thrusting him back against the wall and banging his head violently. In an office down the corridor, a man bending over a filing cabinet took the full force of

THE GLEIWITZ RAID (OPERATION HIMMLER)

On the evening before the German invasion of Poland on 1 September 1939, so-called 'Polish' troops carried out a simulated assault on a German radio station. The previous month Gestapo chief Reinhard Heydrich had called in Alfred Helmut Naujocks and outlined the details of a fictitious Polish attack on a small German radio station at Gleiwitz, just one mile from the Polish border. The purpose was to make it appear that the attacking force consisted of Poles. Naujocks, leading a force of SS Commandos in Polish uniforms, stormed into the radio station, fired a fusillade of shots and slugged the employees with pistol butts. A fake radio broadcast in perfect Polish called for Poles to 'unite and smash down any German, all Germans'. The following day an excited Hitler informed the German people that they were at war with Poland, citing 'the attack by regular Polish troops on the Gleiwitz transmitter'.

a pistol barrel to the head. His body keeled over with a crash, sending a chair and hatstand straight into the metal cabinet. Ahead of the trio was a green-painted door marked 'Silence'. Once inside the studio, Heinrich grabbed the microphone, fishing in his pocket for the prepared script. He delivered a spirited denunciation of Germany's leaders, who were pushing Europe into war, led by a bully who was prepared to sacrifice a small country in his boundless quest for personal ambition. By way of added colour, Naujocks pulled out his pistol and fired three times, shouting as loud as he could. Then he signalled Karl to kill the transmission. All three men teamed up with the rest of the party and lost no time in making their escape.

The party newspaper, *Völkischer Beobachter*, reported next day, under the headline 'Aggressors Attack Gleiwitz Radio': 'A group of Polish soldiers seized the Gleiwitz Radio building last night a little before eight. Only a few of the staff were on duty at that hour. It is obvious that the Polish assailants knew the ground perfectly. They attacked the personnel and broke into the studio, knocking out those they encountered on the way. The aggressors … read out at the microphone a propaganda speech prepared in advance, in Polish and German. They stated that the town and the radio station were in the hands of the Poles, who had insulted Germany, alluding to "Polish Breslau" and "Polish Danzig". The listeners, at first taken by surprise, notified the police, who arrived a few minutes later. The aggressors opened fire on the forces of order but at the end of a few minutes they were all taken prisoner. During the battle a Pole was killed.'

The Wehrmacht assault on Poland came at 4.45 a.m. on 1 September 1939; five German armies attacked from the north, west and south. Naujocks and his fellow SD agents had more than fulfilled Heydrich's desire for a role beyond Germany's borders.

ASSASSINATION ATTEMPT

There was no respite: Hitler was still in search of pretexts for further incursions in Europe. His endeavours were next concentrated on Britain and the Netherlands. On 8 November 1939, he travelled from Berlin for a celebratory gathering at a Munich hall to mark the sixteenth anniversary of the abortive 1923 Bierkeller putsch, using the occasion to deliver an anti-British diatribe. In a totally untypical move, however, the *Führer*, never given to short speeches, abruptly quit the platform after just eight minutes, pleading the excuse of a top-level military conference in Berlin. He had barely departed before the room was torn apart by a bomb, bringing the roof crashing down on the audience, killing seven and injuring 63. The *Völkischer Beobachter* blamed the incident on the British secret service. Himmler used the occasion to arrest some malcontents and proclaim large rewards for information leading to the capture of those responsible. The man ultimately charged with the bombing and confined to Sachsenhausen concentration

camp, a 36-year-old Communist sympathizer named Johann Georg Elser, later claimed that certain men, posing as Hitler's enemies and offering him freedom and money, had arranged for him to make and place the bomb. By no means everyone was convinced by claims of a British plot. William Shirer, for example, wrote in his diary: 'The thing sounds fishy to me … What Himmler and his gang are up to obviously is to convince the gullible German public that the British government tried to win the war by murdering Hitler and his chief aides.'

THE VENLO INCIDENT

Another piece of melodrama took place on the day after Elser's arrest, when the SD and Gestapo kidnapped two British intelligence agents who had been lured over the Dutch–German border at Venlo and accused them of encouraging the Resistance movement in Germany against Hitler. The fact that the Munich explosion and what became known as the Venlo Incident had happened so close together struck many outsiders as being altogether too convenient to be convincing. Heydrich's role in the pre-planning of the kidnaps was described after the war by one of its crucial figures, who was

Above: Each year, Hitler spoke at Munich's Burgerbraukeller, where, in November 1939, a time bomb was exploded. Although Elser was accused of being in the pay of the British, a fellow prisoner at Dachau alleged that he had been framed by the SS. Elser was shot on Himmler's orders, and the entire episode remains shrouded in mystery to this day.

Above: Following a speech to the Reichstag on becoming Chancellor, Hitler assembled his closest colleagues on the balcony of the Berlin Chancellery. Heinrich Himmler can be seen to the extreme left in the picture, while Göring, who had been the first Gestapo chief and was the future *Reichsmarshall*, stands to the left of Hitler.

destined to become a star performer and responsible for Gestapo counter-espionage in Germany and, eventually, the occupied countries. Like so many of his contemporaries, when the Nazis came to power Walter Schellenberg was a young man of 22 looking for a job. Three years at the University of Bonn, during which he changed from studying medicine to law, had left him with few qualifications and no money. Like thousands of other German university students, Schellenberg had to rely on his wits because decent jobs were hard to come by.

The ambitious Schellenberg set his sights on the SD and came to the attention of Heydrich. The attraction was understandable: both were young men on the make. For the Venlo operation Heydrich teamed Schellenberg with another bright SD talent, Helmuth Knocken, who was responsible for the creation of spy networks abroad. He was ordered by Heydrich to pose as a certain Captain Schaemmel, a real-life officer who had prudently been posted elsewhere. He then gained the confidence of two British agents, Captain S. Payne Best and Major R.H. Stevens, whom he had met during a number of meetings at Arnhem and The Hague, convincing them that there was a Resistance group of some strength in Germany. In the guise of Schaemmel, Schellenberg posed as its representative, begging to be treated seriously by London. He recognized though that matters would soon have to come to a head because, naturally enough, Payne Best and Stevens would expect concrete proposals from the people 'Schaemmel' claimed to speak for.

> The Nazi party was an obvious avenue to success; ideological convictions were irrelevant. In Schellenberg's own words, 'one met the better type of people'.

The pace was forced by the arrival of a familiar figure. Once again Alfred Naujocks prepared for action, mustering a group of SD men for a frontal attack on the café at Venlo where 'Schaemmel' and the British had agreed to meet. Payne Best and Stevens arrived outside the café in a large Buick, accompanied by a Lieutenant Coppins, and were met by a hail of bullets from an SS car crammed with Naujock's men. The British officers were scooped up by the Germans and driven at speed across the border, where they were held prisoner for the duration of the war. The most unfortunate victim of the whole affair was 'Lieutenant Coppins', revealed as an officer of the Dutch General Staff named Klop. He died in a Düsseldorf hospital of the wounds he received at Venlo.

The Venlo Incident left many unanswered questions. In his memoirs, Schellenberg claimed that the decision to seize Payne Best and Stevens was taken only after the bomb had gone off in Munich, but it was later revealed that Naujocks's team had been in position since 7 November, the day before the explosion. An irresistible conclusion was that both events emanated from the same source. On 27 November Himmler announced that he had found and arrested Georg Elser, who had collaborated with the two British agents. Whatever the truth, Hitler had his pretext for attacking in the west, notably the Low Countries – amply justified as the neutral Dutch had tolerated treachery towards the Reich on their own soil. The Gestapo had paved the way for the triumphant progress of the war both in the east and in preparation for the coming assault on the west. Throughout it all Himmler and Heydrich's forces had been progressively tightening their hold at home.

HE WAS INORDINATELY AMBITIOUS ...

'Not long after I had begun my work at Headquarters I was called to my first interview with Heydrich, the formidable chief of the SD. It was with considerable apprehension that I walked over to the Gestapo building where he had his office ...

'Heydrich was sitting behind his desk. He was a tall, impressive figure with a broad, unusually high forehead, small restless eyes as crafty as an animal's and of uncanny power, a long predatory nose, and a wide, full-lipped mouth. His hands were slender and rather too long – they made one think of the legs of a spider. His splendid figure was marred by the breadth of his hips, a disturbingly feminine effect that made him appear even more sinister. His voice was much too high for so large a man and his speech was nervous and staccato ...

'When I really got to know Heydrich during the years that followed, I never changed my first opinion of him. This man was the hidden pivot around which the Nazi regime revolved. The development of a whole nation was guided indirectly by his forceful character. He was far superior to all his political colleagues and controlled them as he controlled the vast intelligence machine of the SD ... He was inordinately ambitious. It seemed as if, in a pack of ferocious wolves, he must always prove himself the strongest and assume the leadership. He had to be the first, the best, in everything, regardless of the means, whether by deceit, treachery or violence. Untouched by any pangs of conscience and assisted by an ice-cold intellect, he could carry injustice to the point of extreme cruelty.'

Extract from Walter Schellenberg:
The Schellenberg Memoirs

CHAPTER 4

TIGHTENING THE GRIP

Hitler's incursions into Austria and Czechoslovakia created the conditions for the Holocaust's supreme technician, Adolf Eichmann, who stepped up the transport of Jews across Europe.

Throughout the lifetime of the Third Reich, thousands throughout Germany had their futures determined within an area of Berlin bounded by Prinz-Albrecht-Strasse (now Niederkirchnerstrasse), Wilhelmstrasse and Anhalterstrasse, forming what was to become the focal point for all the key security institutions of the regime. But it was Prinz-Albrecht-Strasse 8 that had the most sinister reputation, as the Gestapo's seat of power. Himmler, as chief of the entire German police as well as being *Reichsführer-SS*, headed a sprawling empire.

In September 1939, its various sections were brought under a single, highly effective instrument of terror created by Reinhard Heydrich. This was the *Reichssicherheitshauptamt* (RSHA, 'Central Security Office of the Reich'). In the words of the historian Alan Bullock: 'It concentrated under the control of half-a-dozen men … all the powers of spying and intelligence, interrogation and arrest, torture and execution on which dictatorship ultimately depends.'

Four of its seven sections were concerned specifically with police and intelligence matters. *Amt III* dealt with intelligence work in Germany and ultimately the occupied countries; its counterpart concerned with foreign intelligence was *Amt VI*. The Gestapo, designated as *Amt IV*, was, as we have seen, established under Heinrich Müller 'to combat opposition to the State'. It had many branches, notably its sub-section *Amt IV E*, which was in charge of counter-intelligence and the occupied countries.

Left: Heinrich Himmler (left) with his chief of personal staff, Karl Wolff (centre), and Reinhard Heydrich on their way to a film presentation at the 1935 Nazi party convention in Nuremberg.

SECURITY STRUCTURE

The structure of the RSHA ('Central Security Office of the Reich') from its formation was as follows:

OFFICE (*AMT*) I: Recruitment and assignment for the entire RSHA.

OFFICE (*AMT*) II: Logistical support – exclusive to the SD.

OFFICE (*AMT*) III: SD concerned with domestic intelligence within Germany.

OFFICE (*AMT*) IV: The Gestapo – political secret police with unquestioned powers of arrest.

OFFICE (*AMT*) V: The Kripo (Criminal Police), concerned with ordinary police matters.

OFFICE (*AMT*) VI: SD personnel concerned with foreign intelligence.

THE SD (*Sicherheitsdienst*, 'Security Service'): The intelligence branch of the SS under the leadership of Reinhard Heydrich, responsible for the security of Hitler, the Nazi hierarchy, the National Socialist Party and the Third Reich.

THE GESTAPO: A secret police force with the task of maintaining the National Socialist regime, affording the Third Reich protection by a political police who tracked down and eliminated all dissidents. For the most part, plain-clothed.

However, no clear-cut decision on the precise functions of the SD and Gestapo was ever established, and each constantly encroached on the work of the other.

In addition there was the SD, subject to the authority of Heydrich, who held the rank of *Gruppenführer*. *Amt V* took in the Criminal Police (Kripo), tasked with combating crime.

'THE GESTAPO IS EVERYWHERE'

The Gestapo, whatever the original intention may have been, was not a separate entity and was subject to constant scrutiny by the SD. This applied to all sections and sub-sections of the police apparatus, a source of bitter internal rivalry. The primary remit was to ferret out enemies of the state, a broad term that could cover those guilty of even the mildest dissent. Arrests, interrogations and house searches were carried out by the plain-clothes Gestapo, which recruited informers from a wide field, ranging from apartment block porters (*Blockwarten*) to shop assistants and office clerical staff, all of whom were recruited with dire threats as to the plight of their families if they were reluctant to do so. There were cases of children being indoctrinated at school and persuaded to pass on any unguarded remarks made at home against the regime.

Heinrich Müller's slogan, 'The Gestapo is Everywhere', was intended to strike widespread fear, but as a claim it was only partly true. There were areas of the Reich where his agents were thinly spread. But that did not stop industrious informers contacting Berlin from all over Germany. The very act of speaking could be dangerous; awareness of this led many Germans to find an outlet in *Flusterwitze* ('whispered jokes'), such as 'Do you know that in the future teeth will be pulled out through the nose. Why? Because nobody dares open his mouth.'

Müller, while concentrating largely on police matters, was plagued with schemes from Heydrich, who was forever restless and eternally keen to enhance his reputation. A proposal to Himmler that the SS should have its own weekly newspaper was eagerly accepted. The post of editor was passed to a shrewd populist journalist named Gunther d'Alquen, who launched the tabloid *Das Schwarze Korps* (*The Black Corps*). D'Alquen headed a staff of six who operated out of Zimmerstrasse 88 in Berlin. Within two years, *Das Schwarze Korps* was selling 189,317 copies per week, a figure that rose during the war to 750,000. Himmler was keen that the paper should carry a heavy weight of Nazi propaganda, but d'Alquen realized that this was not a prescription for sales. The columns were laced with the sort of items common to any tabloid, such as alleged profiteering by church leaders and instances of rampant homosexuality in monasteries. But the paper was far more than a propaganda organ with a populist slant. D'Alquen invited readers to voice any criticism of the regime through the letters page. Those naïve enough to fall into the trap soon found themselves engaging the attention of Müller.

Sneaks had a field day. An industrious Berliner named Paul Koch wrote that a certain butcher, Gustav Schiewek, was in the habit of handing 'his

Below: Dogs had an essential role when it came to SS surveillance and invariably accompanied a posse of Gestapo when they carried out lightning swoops on homes and premises. Here, dogs are being trained at the Gestapo School of Canine Intelligence at Rontengal.

customers their purchases wrapped in paper carrying an advertisement for a Jewish business'. The paper's advertisements provided further information for the Gestapo. Anyone so much as suspected of listening to foreign broadcasts was at risk. False 'for sale' advertisements were placed, offering powerful second-hand radios fitted with earphones. Those who attempted a purchase were promptly arrested and entered on a list of 'suspected persons'. Many were then paraded through the streets; behind them strode the Gestapo agents, ostentatiously displaying the offending radio sets.

Although born a Catholic with a fanatically devout mother, Heydrich had a burning hatred of any form of organized religion. With his strong encouragement, Gestapo attention was focused on all religious institutions and their members. Just what this could mean was brought home sharply to Chaplain Otto Graf, a teacher at Freiburg im Breisgau, who told a class of his pupils: 'In fundamental characteristics all men are alike, and there is a point of view that makes it possible to love and esteem all men. This is true even of Jews.' His remarks received due prominence in the press, bringing a swift riposte from the Minister of Church Affairs, who accused Chaplain Graf of 'misusing' religious instruction to express political opinions: 'His remarks were designed to raise doubts in the minds of his pupils as to the fundamental truth of the National Socialist world ideology in its racial theory, *Führer* principle and doctrine of absolute obedience to the state.' This was followed by a visit from the Gestapo, a sharp rebuke and the loss of his job.

Below: The Reverend Martin Niemöller, who was regarded by churchgoers as a kind of folk hero, provoked Hitler's fury. The *Führer* ordered his arrest, declaring that Niemöller would 'do time until he was blue in the face'. The Lutheran pastor survived the war and, in 1946, admitted Germany's war guilt in a speech in Geneva.

INTERNAL DISSENT

In the autumn of 1938, the most prominent figure in rebellion was the Reverend Martin Niemöller, a World War I submarine commander. In the early days he had sympathized with the Nazis, whom he saw as providing a 'national revival' for Germany after the country had endured 15 years of a shifting, rootless republic. His disillusion came with Hitler's declaration that the state had supremacy over religion and that Christianity was merely a transitional stage in the rejection of both Catholicism and Protestantism. In the wake of this, a host of provincial church organizations were suspended as the Gestapo arrested recalcitrant clergy and demanded that each pastor take an oath of allegiance to Hitler. It was also declared that: 'The National Socialist conception of life is the national and political teaching which determines and characterizes German manhood. As such, it is obligatory upon German Christians also.' An outspoken sermon of rebuttal to his congregation in the Dahlem district of Berlin led to Niemöller's arrest on 1 July 1937 and his confinement to Moabit prison. After eight months in gaol, he was arraigned before a *Sondergericht*, a 'special court' dealing with offences against the State, fined 2000 marks and sentenced to seven months' further imprisonment for 'abuse of the pulpit'. As he had already served more than this sentence he was released, but had reckoned without the Gestapo, whose agents seized him as he left the court. Eight years in the concentration camps of Sachsenhausen and Dachau stretched ahead before eventual liberation by Allied troops.

SURVEILLANCE

Surveillance remained a priority for Heydrich and the responsibility of SD *Amt II* (*Inland*), which worked closely with corresponding departments of the Gestapo. Of equal concern was SD *Amt III* (*Ausland*), with its host of foreign and counter-espionage agents. This brought him inevitably into contact with Admiral Wilhelm Canaris, head of the *Abwehr* ('Military Intelligence'), a shadowy, enigmatic personality whom Heydrich had first met during the course of his naval service. A further link between the two revealed another facet of Heydrich's complex character: he was an accomplished violinist. This attracted Canaris's wife, Erika, herself a keen amateur musician, and the two families enjoyed sporadic social evenings. These, however, did not prevent Heydrich from sensing a possible rival in Canaris; he saw the *Abwehr* as a symbol of old-fashioned thinking, peopled with a fair share of 'reactionaries' who could be a stumbling block to the fulfilment of the Nazi revolution.

But the power of the *Abwehr* in the field of intelligence could not be ignored; a working relationship had to be formed. The result was the so-called 'Ten Commandments', which, on paper at least, drew a line between the two intelligence services of the *Wehrmacht* and the SS. The Gestapo was to be concerned primarily with acts of treason, with the *Abwehr* granted the predominant role in espionage and counter-espionage. All might have seemed clear cut and reasonable, but to anyone who knew Heydrich it was clear that the agreement was shot full of holes. Slowly but surely the SD edged in against all enemies of the state, and that included surveillance of the *Abwehr* itself. Suspicious of everyone and forever watching his back,

Heydrich made no exception of Canaris and lost little time in ordering a Gestapo file on him, particularly when it was discovered in 1939 that the *Abwehr* chief had made tentative peace moves towards the Vatican, which he much admired. The code name of the file was quintessential Heydrich: *Schwarze Kapelle* ('Black Chapel'). Its presence meant that it could be produced at any time to bring about Canaris's downfall.

PERSECUTION OF THE JEWS

Meanwhile, the head of the SD allowed neither himself nor anyone else any peace. There were other ideological demons requiring attention – the offending presence of Jews, Freemasons, Bolsheviks. Above all, there were the Jews. At first, it appeared that those in Germany would have an easy ride. *Gleichschaltung* ('unification') – the total Nazification of Germany – had to be secured before the SS could feel confident that it was answerable to no one. Once that had been achieved the period of calm ended. In his second month as Chancellor, Hitler instituted a boycott of Jewish products and stores. With cries of '*Judah verrecke!*' ('Perish Judah'), the SA and SS rampaged through the towns and cities, inciting the crowds to beat up any Jews they encountered, as well as ransacking their shops and restaurants.

The heat was next turned on Jewish businesess and those who had dealings with them. On 1 August 1937, the office of the Munich Gestapo reported: 'Investigations were made in several government districts with the aim of finding out which peasants still have business contacts with Jewish dealers, particularly cattle dealers. These investigations produced shocking results. They showed that a large percentage of peasants still have business dealings with Jews. Thus it was established that in *Regierungsbezirk* ["administrative district"] Schwaben-Neuberg alone, over 1500 peasants had had commercial contacts with Jewish cattle dealers over the years 1936–7. It is suggested that the reason for this deplorable state of affairs is the fact that there is a lack of trustworthy Aryan cattle dealers with capital in the countryside, so that the peasants are compelled to do business with the Jews. Thus, for example, 80–90 per cent of the cattle trade of the Nördlingen market is in Jewish hands ... As a result of the regulations of the Reich and Prussian Ministry of Food and Agriculture, the Gestapo cannot do anything to control this evil. The deeper reason for it, however, lies in the attitude of the peasantry who show a complete lack of awareness of race. The investigations, which are not yet completed, already demonstrate that, particularly in those districts where political Catholicism is still in control, the peasants are so infected by the teachings of an aggressive political Catholicism that they are deaf to any discussion of the racial problem. The situation indicates further that the majority of the peasants are completely immune to the ideological teaching of National Socialism and that only material disadvantages will compel them to enter into a business relationship with Aryan dealers. The Bavarian state peasant organization in the Reich Food Estate was, therefore, informed of all those peasants who are known to buy from Jews so that all privileges of the Reich Food Estate can be denied them.'

> With cries of '*Judah verrecke!*' ('Perish Judah'), the SA and SS rampaged through the towns and cities, inciting the crowds to beat up any Jews they encountered.

Right: A wrecked and pillaged Jewish shop in Berlin's Friedrichstrasse, just one instance of the orgy of destruction that followed the unleashing of *Kristallnacht*. Passers-by either exhibited approval or, keen only on self-protection, studiously ignored the violence.

KRISTALLNACHT

Even more dramatically, the plight of the Jews was underlined on the night of 9 September 1938, with the launch of what became known as *Kristallnacht* ('Crystal Night', or the 'Night of Broken Glass'), when a series of terror attacks was made on Jewish synagogues and stores. These events could be traced to an order from Heydrich for the deportation to Poland of 17,000 Polish Jews, most of whom had migrated to Germany at the end of World War I. The Polish government had no wish to accommodate them and reacted by closing its borders and placing armed troops on alert. This left thousands of Jews not only stateless, but forced to wander without shelter and food as well. One of these was Zindel Gryszpan, a Polish tailor from Hanover whose possessions had been confiscated. News of his plight reached his 17-year-old son, Herschel, in Paris. On 7 November 1938 the teenager, touting a revolver, called on the German embassy. His precise motive remained obscure, but it is thought that his intended target was the Ambassador, Count Johannes von Welczeck. His enquiry was answered by a Third Secretary, Ernst vom Rath, who took the full force of five bullets. The victim, as it happened, was a sad choice because vom Rath had been a convinced anti-Nazi under surveillance by the Gestapo.

Nazi retaliation was immediate. An order was issued for the destruction of all Jewish places of worship in Germany and in annexed Austria: within just 15 hours, 101 synagogues were torched and 76 demolished. Some 7500 Jewish-owned stores were destroyed. Predictably, *Das Schwarze Korps* played its role, becoming progressively shriller in the days following *Kristallnacht*; on 24 November, the tabloid newspaper declared, 'No German should be asked to live under the same roof with Jews … we must expel them from our houses and living areas … The plan is clear: total removal, total separation!' Prime responsibility for the launch of *Kristallnacht* was later traced to Josef Göbbels, Reich Minister of Propaganda, who claimed that the murder of vom Rath had been a planned conspiracy. The Gestapo's role lay in a key message from Heinrich Müller in Berlin, transmitted at midnight on 9 November. Tagged 'Immediate and Secret', it read in part, 'Actions against Jews, especially against their synagogues, will take place throughout the Reich shortly … So far as important archive material exists in synagogues, this is to be secured by immediate measures … Preparations are to be made for the arrest of about 20,000 to 30,000 Jews in the Reich. Above all, well-to-do Jews are to be selected. Detailed instructions will follow in the course of the night.'

Evidence later emerged that the Gestapo had been involved even before *Kristallnacht* was launched. Joe Rose, a Jewish commercial artist living in Sudenburg, near Magdeburg, later recalled: 'Two members of the Gestapo approached Nosseck, a good friend of mine who was also Jewish and owned a menswear shop. Politely but in tones that left no doubt of their authority, they asked him to paint his name on the front of his shop. They were very precise. It had to be at eye level in identical lettering twelve centimetres high by one centimetre wide. Nosseck asked me to do the job. I charged him a nominal sum since I was tickled that the fee came indirectly through the Gestapo. As it turned out, I made quite a bit of money. Other shopkeepers who had received the same orders came to me and I was inundated with work. We put it all down to local bureaucracy and certainly didn't connect it with the killing of vom Rath. It wasn't until *Kristallnacht* that the real motive for it all became apparent.'

Hatred of Jews told only half the story. There were many cases of sheer greed overcoming ideology – legalized theft by the Nazis of just about everything the Jewish community possessed. Jews were subjected to a collective fine of one billion marks. Jewish businesses were sold to 'Aryan hands', personal silver and jewellery appropriated. In return, male Jews who had been seized by the Gestapo were later released.

Below: Lea Grundig, an engraver for a book called *Under the Swastika*, wrote: 'A house like millions of others, somewhere in Germany. Simple people, like you and me, live in this house: these people live in fear. Don't ask what they fear: they fear the Gestapo, of course. They fear the rampant denunciations … The fear is there: doors open furtively and the intimidated residents peek out to see who is affected.'

Deprived of their possessions and wealth, emigration was possible for those who could secure a permit, as the Heinrich family discovered. At the height of the onslaught, 13-year-old Joseph Heinrich from Frankfurt am Main, whose shopkeeper father was a Zionist sympathizer, was standing in the window of the family home watching the torching of the large synagogue across the street: 'Börneplatz was crowded with thousands of spectators who were making a circus out of this. Then suddenly the mob burst into our rooms, wielding axes and bars, and proceeded to smash everything. We managed to flee to the nearest police station but it did us no good. All they did was stare and laugh. Next we sought shelter with some friends but it wasn't safe to stay there and we took a taxi to my aunt's house. That was the Thursday and the arrests were going on all day long. The next evening came the knock on the door. They had come to arrest my uncle. My father protested, "I won't let him go alone." One of them shrugged, "Fine. You can come too." They took both of them away. A few hours later, my sister and I went to the police station, asking for our father. All they did was tell us to get lost. Several days later, my mother, my little sister Lorle, my younger brother Asher and me were put on a train for Holland. We went together with a group of about 25 children, organized by some Jewish women. When we arrived at the Dutch border, two SS men took us off the train, into a waiting room. Since we were Jews, we were pointedly segregated from German passengers. We were given no toilet facilities and no water, which made Lorle and Asher burst into tears. It wasn't until the evening that we were put aboard another train, the Rheingold Express. We crossed the border into Holland where we were crowded with journalists and photographers asking how things were in Germany. I remember that my feelings were mixed. I was a child and it seemed in some ways like a big adventure. I know I wasn't afraid. But then I realized that something had been irreversibly broken and I started to think what might be in store for us.'

The Heinrich children were looked after by a Dutch family who ensured that they wrote home every week. Joseph discovered that his father was imprisoned in Buchenwald concentration camp, which had not yet become an extermination centre. He managed to secure his freedom with a permit secured through another family member. Urged by his wife and under constant threat of re-arrest, he made for England. 'But my mother had no permit and I never saw her again,' Joseph recalled. 'My father was on the last civilian train to cross the Holland border and then on the last boat to England. On arrival he was promptly interned.'

PRINZ-ALBRECHT-STRASSE

Those who were wise decamped from the Reich. But by no means all were so fortunate; for those unable to buy their freedom there was the prospect of incarceration at Prinz-Albrecht-Strasse 8. Here Jews were joined by political prisoners, left wingers of all persuasions and outspoken critics of National Socialism. The large, imposing building covered around 62,000 square metres (15 acres). The interrogation and administrative offices were located on the upper floors, while on the first floor there was a communal cell into which 50 prisoners could be crammed. The cells had dim electric lighting or depended on daylight filtering through grilles from above. The cells were closely guarded by the SS, who added to a prisoner's sense of isolation by preventing all human contact; food was handed through a flap in the door.

An added misery for prisoners was the almost sure knowledge that their ultimate destination was either a concentration camp or another in the network of torture centres throughout Berlin. The place's baleful reputation dated from the early days of the power struggle between the SA and the SS. Rudolf Diels had not been above snatching prisoners from the Brown Shirts and bringing them to Prinz-Albrecht-Strasse. Interrogation was frequently brutal. The Communist politician Ernst Thälmann, for example, had been arrested the day after the Reichstag fire and was ultimately sent to his death at Buchenwald. He faced relentless interrogation. Four of his teeth were knocked out and a Gestapo official beat his buttocks with a whip of hippopotamus hide, which also slashed his face, chest and back. Wolfgang Szepansky, an artist of Polish-Latvian stock, was a Communist sympathizer and activist who had been arrested along with 15 others after street clashes and taken to Prinz-Albrecht-Strasse: 'On arrival a man in civilian clothes, so small he couldn't reach me to beat me above the head, booted me in the testicles, his face contorted with rage. That was his way of saying hello, I suppose. It is torture waiting in a cell for interrogation and when you know they're going to come and beat you, maybe to death. You hope the door won't open, hope they don't call your name, hope they'll just leave you … One of our 15 was beaten for hours and hours. He literally flew from one corner of the cell to the other. They took it in turns, it went on for hours. It's an indescribable torture to watch hopelessly as one of your comrades is beaten. The tortures get worse. They used thumbscrews, leg screws, nail under the fingernails, things I couldn't imagine if I hadn't seen them with my own eyes.'

Occasionally the outside world learnt something of what was happening in Prinz-Albrecht-Strasse. On 2 August 1934, the English newspaper, the *Manchester Guardian*, carried an

Below: Ernst Thälmann, who had been Chairman of the German Communist Party and an ardent Stalinist, later became a member of the Reichstag. Earmarked by Hitler for elimination, he was arrested following the Reichstag fire and, after hideous Gestapo torture, was eventually shot.

article on the treatment of political prisoners in Germany, one of whom had described his interrogation: 'I was taken to a room where I was searched, my notebook and some letters being taken from me. There was a table in the middle of the room and a writing desk in the background. Five officials sat down round the table. I was asked to sit down as well. I was closely questioned about persons whose names and addresses had been found in my possession (my rooms had been searched meanwhile, but nothing had been found save a few entirely harmless letters). Questions followed questions with extreme rapidity, hour by hour. It was after midnight and the officials began to hit me as they questioned me. My head ached. At about two or three in the morning, one of them read out a statement and told me to sign it. I was about to do so when I noticed that the sheet of paper had been skilfully folded, the edges of the folds being stuck together almost invisibly – when unfolded they left a blank space which could be filled in with words which would not have been signed by me but would nevertheless appear over my signature. Five pairs of eyes were fixed intently upon me. I put the pen down and said, "I'm

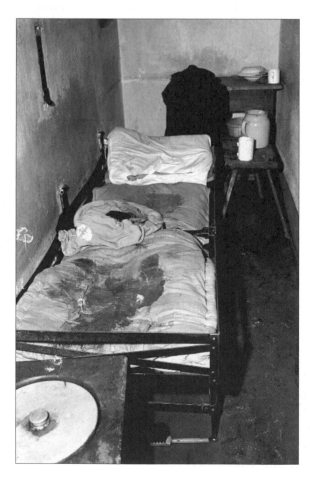

Below: Conditions in the cramped Gestapo prisons were harsh and humiliating, as this cell in Cologne demonstrates. Gaols were invariably crammed to capacity, and prisoners, who would have been kept standing for hours before being allotted a cell, could be hauled out at any hour for interrogation and beatings.

sorry, I can't sign a statement of this kind." "In that case we're unlucky," said one of the officials in a dry, matter-of-fact voice. I was taken down into the cellars and locked up in a cell. I was dead tired and fell asleep on some straw sacking.'

The interrogation and accusations – that, among other things, the prisoner had tried to get evidence to prove that the SS and SA were armed and organized in violation of the Treaty of Versailles – were resumed the next day. 'An official said to me, "So you know nothing, do you?" and struck me across the head with such violence that the room seemed to spin round and I fell down. I was kicked about as I lay on the floor. "Stand up!" one of them shouted. I had some difficulty in getting up. The same questions were again put to me, and I was again struck across the head until I collapsed, and again kicked about on the floor. This was done to me several times. Then they took me downstairs into the cellars. I sat down on the bench with other prisoners, men and women. Some had only just arrived, others had been cross-examined and were bruised and bloodstained. I kept on coughing and spat blood. I was in great pain.'

There came a time when the cells in Prinz-Albrecht-Strasse could take no more prisoners.

GESTAPO OFFICE SPACE

'It might interest the reader at this stage to take a look into the office I occupied as head of the Foreign Department of the German Secret Service. Entering the room, large, well furnished and covered with a deep, luxurious carpet, the visitor would be faced by my big mahogany writing desk. The most precious piece of furniture in the room was a big old-fashioned cupboard containing my personal reference library. To the left of the desk was a trolley-table covered with telephones and microphones connected directly with Hitler's Chancellery and other places of importance, one telephone providing a direct line to my home in Berlin, and my country house in Herzberg. Microphones were hidden everywhere, in the walls, under the desk, even in one of the lamps, so that every conversation and every sound was automatically recorded.

'The windows of the room were covered with a wire mesh. This was an electrically charged safety device, which was switched on at night and formed part of a system of photo-electric cells that sounded an alarm if anyone approached the windows, doors, safe, or, in fact, tried to get too close to any part of my offices. Within 30 seconds a squadron of armed guards would have surrounded the entire area.

'My desk was like a small fortress. Two automatic guns were built into it which could spray the whole room with bullets. These guns pointed at the visitor and followed his or her progress towards my desk. All I had to do in an emergency was to press a button and both guns would fire simultaneously. At the same time I could press another button and a siren would summon the guards to surround the building and block every exit …

'Whenever I was on missions abroad I was under standing orders to have an artificial tooth inserted which contained enough poison to kill me within 30 seconds if I were captured by an enemy. To make doubly sure, I wore a signet-ring in which, under a large blue stone, a gold capsule was hidden containing cyanide.'

Extracts from Walter Schellenberg,
The Schellenberg Memoirs

Those in euphemistic 'protective custody' found themselves in the police gaol at Alexanderplatz. Far worse was the Columbia-Haus, located near the Tempelhof airport and which had originally served as a military prison. Kurt Hiller, a journalist from the nonconformist weekly *Die Weltbühne*, was a Jew and therefore under Gestapo attention. After a severe beating at Prinz-Albrecht-Strasse, during which his nose was broken, he was sent to the Colombia-Haus, where he was taken to the basement. Four SS men from the party of guards grasped his wrists and ankles, pushed him down on a table and gave him 25 lashes by way of a 'greeting'.

ADOLF EICHMANN

As yet, the full horror of Nazi atrocities against the Jews was confined to Germany and, with their occupation in the shadow of war, Austria and Czechoslovakia. But itching to extend it was Karl Adolf Eichmann, for whom hatred of Jews had started early. He was born on 19 March 1906 and grew up in the Austrian town of Linz. Bereft of his mother at a very early age, he withdrew into a melancholy solitude. His shiftless father, almost perpetually jobless, regarded him with indifference. Dark and almost Semitic in appearance, the young Adolf had to endure schoolmates taunting him with the cry '*Der kleine Jude*' ('the little Jew'). When it came to earning a living he tried a number of jobs, the most significant of which was probably as a travelling salesman for the Vacuum Oil Company AG, covering Upper Austria, Salzburg and North Tyrol. This came with a motorcycle on which he made regular journeys between Linz and Vienna, and, eventually, into a Germany burgeoning with rallies, brown shirts and swastikas.

The appeal was instant. Back home, he joined the Austrian National Socialist Party and the ranks of what became its SS, already dutifully parroting Hitler's cry for *Anschluss* (union with Germany). Dismissed from his job on account of his party membership, he was able to seek a full-time post with the Austrian Nazis. This led to a useful contact through a meeting with a fellow Austrian, the fiercely ambitious lawyer Ernst Kaltenbrunner, who made no secret of his desire for power and held himself in readiness for the onset of *Anschluss*. Eichmann had an even more valuable meeting with Heinrich Himmler who, during a tour of inspection, swore him in as a member of the Upper Austrian SS. In February 1933, with *Anschluss* still five years away, the authorities in Austria had no love for the Nazis. They had already earmarked Eichmann as a likely troublemaker and, with the police literally knocking on his door, he decamped for the German border and contacted a branch of the SS to which he had been recommended. He was

Below: Adolf Eichmann travelled throughout occupied Europe to ensure that the efforts of various Nazi ministries responsible for the arrest, transportation and extermination of Jews were carried out. An efficient, emotionless bureaucrat, the five million or more deaths that resulted from the Final Solution were carried out on his orders.

assigned a period of military training in Lechfeld bei Passau on the German–Austrian border, followed by duty as a lowly *Rottenführer* (lance corporal) at Dachau concentration camp.

At 27 years old, Eichmann's application to join the SD was rewarded by a post to the department dealing with card indexes, where he was required to type out the personal details of Freemasons, a group considered to be dangerous because of their beliefs in liberal democratic ideas. The work in itself was not particularly taxing, neither did it promise advancement. Its value to Eichmann lay in the insight it gave him into SD procedures. In the manner of ambitious junior executives everywhere who seek to climb the company ladder, Eichmann lost no time in seeking out those of his superiors who were likely to be of the most use to him. On his own admission, whenever he came into contact with senior SS officers he was careful to spring to attention and click his heels.

He was also shrewd enough to decide on a special subject within the SD that had hitherto been neglected and which he instinctively felt he could make his own. He opted for the

'Jewish question', and early on he made it clear that its solution was his life mission in the Third Reich, taking upon himself the study of the entire Jewish social structure, in both Germany and every other European country, and the organization of Zionism. He even took lessons in both Yiddish and Hebrew. The result was that he found a secure niche in Section II 112 of the SD, the Zionist Organization desk. His status as an expert on Jewish affairs became such that he was included in a delegation sent to Palestine in 1937 to discuss with Arab leaders the possibility of large-scale immigration of Jews to the Middle East as part of their wholesale expulsion from the Reich. Agents working for the British Mandated Territory shadowed the visiting Germans and they were deported. The venture proved a failure – but not in the eyes of Reinhard Heydrich, to whom Eichmann remained both the dedicated anti-Semite and the industrious *Beamte*, the dependable bureaucrat. In recognition Eichmann was promoted to *Untersturmführer*, a commissioned rank.

Above: This photograph taken at Dachau appeared in the Nazi journal *Illustrierte Beobachter*. Its caption stated in part that these prisoners were, 'A group of political repeaters – persons who would not stop their agitation and subversive activity against the State even after a previous imprisonment'.

ANSCHLUSS

Events in Europe were unfolding fast. The move was towards war, prefaced by the Austrian *Anschluss* and the surrender of Czechoslovakia. The Austria Hitler dreamed of had been outlined in his *Mein Kampf* (*My Struggle*; 1925–6), the political programme he had begun while in prison following the abortive

Beer Hall Putsch. In it he had insisted that *Anschluss* between Germany and Austria was 'a task to be furthered by every possible means'. With Hitler's assumption of power in 1933 came the assurance from Berlin that the policy towards Austria was unchanged. The Austrian Chancellor, Engelbert Dollfuss, who had assumed office in May 1932, foresaw the threat presented to his country by Nazis both in Germany and Austria. The Austrian Nazis, with full encouragement from Berlin, unleashed a reign of terror in which government supporters were murdered. On 25 July 1934, a faction of SS *Standarte 89*, wearing Austrian uniforms, stormed the Federal Chancery; Dollfuss was shot in the throat and left to bleed to death. The intended putsch, though, was mistimed and badly bungled. To Hitler's fury, forces loyal to Chancellor Dr Kurt Schuschnigg, Dollfuss's successor, gained control. *Anschluss* would have to wait.

> On 25 July 1934 a faction of SS *Standarte 89*, wearing Austrian uniforms, stormed the Federal Chancery; Dollfuss was shot in the throat and left to bleed to death.

Hitler, however, remained determined. The crunch came in February 1938 when Schuschnigg was persuaded by Hitler to come to his mountain retreat at Berchtesgaden. The *Führer*, issuing dire threats, demanded concessions for the Austrian Nazis. Schuschnigg was introduced to three generals who happened to be there 'quite by chance': Wilhelm Keitel, chief of OKW (*Oberkommando der Wehrmacht*, the German armed forces), Walter Reichenau, commander of the German forces on the Bavarian–Austrian border, and Hugo Sperrle, *Luftwaffe* general for the border area. No hint could have been broader – if Schuschnigg did not give in to Hitler's demand, then there would be a solution by force. Austrian independence was on the line. The minutes of the meeting have survived. One outburst by Hitler sets the tone of the rest: 'I am telling you that I am going to solve the so-called Austrian problem one way or the other … Listen, you don't really think you can move a single stone in Austria without my hearing about it the next day, do you? I have only to give an order and in one single night all your ridiculous defence mechanisms will be blown to bits … After the Army, my SA and Austrian Legion would move in, and nobody can stop their just revenge – not even I.'

Back home, Schuschnigg attempted to steal a march on Hitler by announcing a plebiscite. But this was followed by German mobilization orders to three *Wehrmacht* Corps. On the morning of 11 March, Heinrich Himmler, his *Reichsführer*'s uniform garnished with two hand grenades dangling from the belt, left Prinz-Albrecht-Strasse flanked by aides and was greeted at Tempelhof airport by the most senior members of the SD, headed by Heydrich. Adolf Eichmann was by far the most junior of those present, but a significant role awaited him when the party arrived in Austria. Once there he lost little time in establishing the Central Office for Jewish Emigration, answerable to Heydrich. It possessed the sole authority to issue permits to Jews desperately seeking to leave Austria. As Germany was anxious to secure their wealth, Eichmann's attitude to the richest Jews was at times conciliatory, allowing synagogues to remain open and Yom Kippur to be celebrated. But the Central Office had another face.

It was also the section of the Gestapo dealing with religious enemies of the state, including those Jews whom it had not been able to fleece. After two months of house arrest, Schuschnigg was taken to Vienna's Hotel Metropole, which served as Gestapo headquarters. Incarcerated in a tiny room on the first floor, he was forced by his SS guards to clean out their quarters, including washbasins, slop buckets and latrines. This was a mere foretaste of his life for the rest of the war, which included spells in the concentration camps of Dachau and Sachsenhausen.

The British-born Oloff De Wett, who later became an agent for the French Resistance, was trapped in Austria at the time of the *Anschluss* and picked up under suspicion of being in touch with anti-Nazis. He also was taken to the Hotel Metropole, where he faced a brutish agent named Federmann. Despite the weight of questioning, De Wett attempted to stall. Federmann gave a slight nod to one of his henchman, who took a rubber mallet to the nape of the prisoner's neck just below the base of the skull, bringing intense pain to his ears and 'inside the cranium an evil hurt that expands and contracts in

Below: Troops parade on the Vienna Ring Road as part of the 1938 *Anschluss*. Seen saluting is Field Marshal Fedor von Bock, commander of the troops entering Austria. To his right is Arthur Seyss-Inquart, who went on to become *Reichsstatthälter* ('Regional Governor') of the renamed Ostmark.

time with the thuds'. All the while Federmann, smoking incessantly, blew smoke straight into De Wett's face. 'He blows on the burning end of his cigarette till it has a nice pointed red ember, poises the tip over my hand for a second, pulls his lips down at the corners, and pushes the cigarette slowly onto my skin … When he removes the extinguished stub he brushes away the ash and there is a neat little round leprous white patch, which in half an hour swells into a tiny shiny hemisphere. When Mr Federmann has three of these in a row they look not unlike three pinkish-yellow peas, till he hits them with a ruler, when they burst and the back of my hand is smeared with wetness from the fluid inside them.'

Below: After the annexation of Austria, Nazi hatred was turned on the Jews, who were forced to wash the streets of Vienna, many of which had been deliberately sprayed with acid.

Elsewhere, the Gestapo fulfilled what was to become their familiar role – arresting political opponents and decreeing which should be sent to concentration camps. The *Tagesrapport* (Day Report) No. 8 of 7–8 November 1938 from the *Geheime Staats Polizei* of the *Staatspolizei-leitstelle*, Vienna, reported: 'According to an assessment made at 6.00 p.m. on 6 November 1938, 6547 Jews were imprisoned during the *Judenaktion* in Vienna. Of those, 3700 Jews were sent to *Konzentrationslager* Dachau. 1865

were temporarily deferred and 982 were released. Two thousand Jews left behind after the inspection of those sent to Dachau were considered by a doctor to be too ill to be of use in a camp.'

OCCUPATION OF THE SUDETENLAND

The achievement of *Anschluss* and the subjugation of opposition within Austria left Hitler free to pursue his next pretext for conquest. In a speech to the Reichstag, he turned his wrath on Czechoslovakia with its ethnic chaos of Czechs, Slovaks, Ruthenians, Poles and Germans. No longer would the German people tolerate a situation where millions of their brothers lived in oppression, more specifically those living in the region bordering the German frontier and known as the Sudetenland, which virtually surrounded Bohemia and Moravia. Hitler's real aim, however, was the elimination of the Czech state, and preparations to bring that about had been in place since as early as 1933, when Konrad Henlein founded the *Sudetendeutsche Heimatfront*

('Sudeten German Home Front'), renamed the *Sudetendeutsche Partei* (SDP) in 1935, which received funds from the SS. On instructions from the steadily encroaching SD in Berlin, Sudeten Nazis edged their way into regional and local organizations, recruiting leading industrialists and business leaders.

The British Prime Minister, Neville Chamberlain, flew to Bad Godesberg on 22 September 1938, and the Munich Conference a week later determined the fate of Czechoslovakia, while German troops marched into the Sudetenland on 1 October. During the following March, Jozef Tiso, the Slovak premier, proclaimed the founding of the autonomous Slovak Republic, having previously agreed that it would come under German protection. German troops, without any prior warning, entered the rump of Czechoslovakia, where all resistance had been paralysed.

A decree created the Protectorate of Bohemia-Moravia, incorporated within the German Reich. The Czechs retained their own parliament and president, but there was a Reich Protector, a role filled by Konstantin Freiherr von Neurath, who had been German Foreign Minister between 1932 and February 1938. Henlein received his reward from Hitler: the position as head of the Civil Administration of Bohemia and Moravia. Supreme power in Prague rested in the hands of *SS-Gruppenführer* Karl-Hermann Frank, a one-eyed bookseller from Karlovy Vary (now officially known again by its German name of Karlsbad), whose adherence had been to the radical wing of

RACE TO HRADČANY CASTLE

Walter Schellenberg recorded Hitler's determination to reach Hradčany, Prague's historic castle district, as quickly as possible. 'Hitler, with his entourage and SS guards, raced through the night at breakneck speed over icy roads, passing the advancing German columns on the way. When we got there I had to select suitable offices and *Lebensraum* ["living quarters"] for Hitler in the castle.' The SD and German police at once took over control of the police, working very closely, however, with their Czech colleagues. 'The Czech police was an exceptional organization, the men having been most carefully selected and given excellent training. This greatly impressed Himmler. "Exceptional human material!" he exclaimed, "I shall take them all into the *Waffen-SS.*"'

MEIN KAMPF

Mein Kampf (*My Struggle*), which embodies Hitler's political philosophy, was published in two volumes. The first was written in the fortress gaol of Landsberg am Lech in Bavaria, while Hitler was serving a five-year sentence for his role in the abortive Beer Hall Putsch. In practice, he served only nine months in comfortable circumstances where he had ample time to dictate his book to his loyal follower Rudolph Hess. This first volume appeared in 1925 and achieved sales of 9400. By the time Hitler became Chancellor in 1933, more than a million copies had been sold of the completed book (issued in one volume in 1930).

Its thesis, predominantly racist, was that Germans had a duty to conduct themselves as a racially pure, superior Aryan people who, reinvigorated, must increase their numbers in order to fulfil their destiny of world supremacy. They would first, however, have to combat a Jewish-led conspiracy to spoil the purity of Aryanism through crossbreeding. One frequently quoted passage expresses his belief that 'the Jewish spirit' was working for the ruin of Germany: 'The black-haired Jewish youth waits for hours, with satanic joy in his eyes, for the unsuspecting [Aryan] girls, whom he shames with his blood and thereby robs the nation ... He seeks to destroy the racial characteristics of the German

with every means at his command ... It was the Jews who brought the Negro to the Rhine, always with the same thought and clear aim in the back of their heads – to destroy the hated white races through "bastardization", to tumble them from their cultural and political heights.'

Hitler went on to outline his remedy for destroying this 'bacillus'. A strong Aryan national state would be created through the suppression of all dissident parties, exiling all Jews and uniting all Germanic peoples. Expansion should come by conquering new lands from 'the lesser Slavs' and the settlement of German peasants in Eastern Europe and the Ukraine. Alliance with Britain and Italy would be necessary in order to destroy France, which was indicted as 'the stronghold of international Jewry'. His economic theories advocated national self-sufficiency and economic independence to replace international trade.

He had intended that the title of the book should be *Four and a Half Years of Struggle against Lies, Stupidity and Cowardice*. The publisher, Max Aman, who had served with Hitler in World War I, changed the title to the more commercial *Mein Kampf*. With considerable tact, Aman further persuaded Hitler that the book, which was turgid in style, should be heavily edited. The result paid off.

Henlein's movement that wanted union with the Reich and total German racial supremacy, fuelled by deep-seated hatred of the Czechs. The Gestapo came under the direct command of *SS-Gruppenführer* Franz Walter Stahlecker, so long a byword for his brutality.

The arrest of the son of a leading Czech politician was witnessed by a journalist who, posing as a German, had managed to penetrate the Petschek Palace in Prague, which became a notorious torture centre. The prisoner was at first slapped on both cheeks, then pushed into a corner and forced to keep his hands raised while the questioning began, only interrupted with slaps when he complained of cramp. The journalist filed his report to the British *Yorkshire Post*: 'Stahlecker ... entered the room and began questioning the prisoner, accompanying his words with slaps and blows, as well as insults to the Czech nation. When the examination was over, the prisoner was taken down to the basement of the palace … and thrown among 20 other prisoners, unshaven, white-faced and clad only in shirt and trousers. I asked my guide what would be the fate of the young man and he answered, "He will be beaten just enough not to die." He added that if the prisoner was lucky he would be freed in 16 days, and he would certainly not be kept in prison as there was no more room.' The Gestapo made wholesale arrests, so many that camps and prisons could not cope; those taken into custody were obliged to spend days and nights standing in the corridors of the Petschek Palace.

Also present from Germany were contingents of the *Einsatzgruppen* (SS 'Special Action Groups') – killer squads whose duties were to round up Jews and other dissidents. After the war, former SD and Gestapo protested that the action groups had been no concern of theirs and had operated separately. Documents drawn up at this time make no direct mention of the *Einsatzgruppen*, but in the light of future events their intention was clear. One such draft SD instruction read: 'The SD should prepare to start its activity in case of complications between the German Reich and Czechoslovakia … Measures in the occupied regions are carried out under the leadership of the senior officers of the SD. Gestapo officials are assigned to certain operations staff.' The blunt truth was that the Czech people were on the edge of an apocalyptic period of suffering, the extent of which could not even be guessed at this stage. As for Heydrich's forces, the charade of Gleiwitz and the invasion of Poland were imminent. The world was going to war.

Below: Hitler's motorcade swept triumphantly into Prague on 15 March 1939. Before leaving Berlin, the *Führer* had proclaimed to the German people: 'Czechoslovakia has ceased to exist.' SD and Gestapo initiatives followed swiftly. A joint draft document stated: 'The SD follows, wherever possible, directly behind the advancing troops and fulfils duties similar to those in the Reich, which are the security of political life and … all enterprises necessary to the national economy.'

CHAPTER 5

THE WAR BEGINS

At the Wannsee Conference in January 1942, Heydrich signalled the dire future of the Jews, as deportations were replaced by the gas chambers and the firing squads of the *Einsatzgruppen*.

O nce Hitler had secured Poland, his intentions were not in doubt. General Franz Halder, Chief of the General Staff of the *Wehrmacht*, summarized in a diary entry for 18 October 1939 a conversation with Eduard Wagner, the future Quartermaster General. The latter, fresh from a belligerent meeting with the *Führer*, had been told, 'We have no intention of rebuilding Poland. Polish intelligentsia must be prevented from establishing itself as a governing class. A low standard of living must be preserved. We must create total disorganization.' Even before this meeting, Wagner was made privy to Hitler's purpose. Reinhard Heydrich had been dispatched by Himmler to Army High Command to tell Wagner that high on the agenda was a programme of thorough 'house cleaning' – nothing less than elimination. Heydrich had even gone so far as to specify 'Polish Jews, intelligentsia, clergy and nobility'. The first stage would be the rounding up of Jews who would be confined in city ghettos.

The invasion itself had taken place at dawn on 1 September as a three-pronged, simultaneous attack. From the north, General Fedor von Boch had launched his 4th Army from Pomerania in the west and his 3rd Army from East Prussia in a vast pincer movement. Their prey was the base of the Polish corridor, the stretch of Polish territory between the two parts of Germany. This territory had been a source of extreme bitterness between Poland and Germany. Hitler had found it intolerable that the German province of East

Left: A triumphant Hitler takes the victory salute in Warsaw on 5 October 1939. German armies had overwhelmed the Polish forces, with the Soviets entering from the east. German-speaking Poles were welcomed into the Reich, while the remainder who were in what was known as the *Generalgouvernement* were treated as racially inferior.

Above: Murder of Polish Jews was a deliberate policy of Nazi rule. Theodor Eicke, who commanded the *Waffen-SS Totenkopf* Division for the invasion of Poland, had responsibilities extending to mass shootings such as these, mostly carried out by *Einsatzgruppen*, which followed the *Wehrmacht* into Poland.

Prussia on the Baltic was separated from the rest of the Reich by a land corridor giving Poland its only sea access at the Free City of Danzig (Gdansk) and the new port of Gdynia. He had intensified demands that Danzig be restored to Germany, giving the Germans the means to build road and rail links to East Prussia across Polish territory. The Poles had refused and now were paying the price. Farther south, under General Gerd von Rundstedt, the 8th and 10th Armies struck east for Warsaw from Silesia, while Cracow (Kraków) and Lwow (now Lviv in Ukraine, and known to the Germans as Lemberg) were to be the target of the 14th Army.

The plight of the Poles, unaccustomed to the ruthless character of *Blitzkrieg* ('lightning war'), was dire. There had been time to mobilize a mere 35 divisions, most of which were crushed in the vast pincer movements. Within 48 hours, the Polish air force had ceased to exist, most of its aircraft destroyed before they even had a chance to take off. The ground advance had been so rapid that the Russians, who had previously signed a 10-year non-aggression pact with Germany, agreeing to divide Poland, could scarcely keep up before moving in to grab their territory in the eastern part of the country. Germany incorporated within the Reich those frontier areas it had previously demanded. The rest of the territory in the southeast was designated a *Generalgouvernement* under the aegis of its Governor General, Hans Frank, a *Freikorps* veteran and former legal adviser to the Nazi party. On 23 September, Poland capitulated, and the following day Ribbentrop and his opposite number, Vyacheslav Molotov, signed a German-Soviet Boundary and Friendship Treaty and a number of secret protocols, declaring that they had fashioned 'a firm foundation for a lasting peace in Eastern Europe'. At the start of October, Hitler put his signature to a decree, which also carried the signatures of Göring and Keitel, giving still more power to Himmler, who became Reich Commissioner with the task of the 'Germanization' of Poland. He was ordered to bring back into the Reich 'true Germans' living abroad. The aim was to remove 'the sinister influence' of foreign sections of the populace who presented a danger to the security of the Reich and the German community, with a view to forming new colonies.

'GERMANIZATION' IN THE EAST

Hitler's demands for the 'Germanization' of Poland were interpreted by the *Reichsführer-SS* in the light of what he saw as SS racial principles: 'It is not our duty to Germanize the East in the old meaning of the term, that is to say to teach the people there the German language and law, but to see that only people of pure German blood live in the East … The cleansing of foreign races outside the incorporated territories is one of the essential aims to be accomplished in the German East.' He went on to order 'appropriate measures' to prevent the increase of the Polish intellectual elite. Once the liquidation of the Polish farmers had been achieved, the freed lands would be distributed to Germans.

This was by no means the full extent of Himmler's activities. By a decree of 12 December 1940, he was to establish a 'racial register', in which 'pure

Below: Hans Frank, Poland's Governor General, seen here in Crakow in 1941. Headquartered at nearby Wawel Castle, one of his most notorious actions was to send the entire teaching staff of Cracow University to internment or death. At Frank's instigation, concentration camps were swollen with Jews and intellectuals and Poland was made 'an intellectual desert'.

blooded Germans' or their descendants were to be re-educated and re-Germanized. Those who opposed such treatment were to be sent to a concentration camp. In the larger cities, the Jews were empowered to set up Jewish councils *(Judenräte)* to govern their communities under German instruction. Within these councils, power was in the hands of Governor General Frank. What this entailed was outlined by Lucy Dawidowicz, a widely quoted Jewish historian, two of whose family perished in the Warsaw Ghetto and in Treblinka. 'Jews were required to wear identifying arm bands; they were subject to seizure for forced labour in camps and other German

GHETTOES

The creation of ghettos in occupied Poland began in Warsaw, following the establishment of a *Judenrät,* first of the Jewish councils either appointed or elected to carry out Nazi orders. On 4 November 1939, armed Gestapo officers assembled *Judenrät* members and read them a decree ordering all Warsaw Jews to move within three days into an area designated a ghetto. The decree, issued by Governor General Hans Frank, specified that the *Judenrät* was obliged to accept and enforce all German orders. By the following month, the *Judenrät* had been made to erect large, wooden signs reading 'Danger: Epidemic Zone' at 34 street corners in the heart of the Jewish quarter. The area was then sealed off to enclose nearly half a million Jews. The penalty for those illegally leaving the 'Jewish residential districts' or for those aiding them was death.

Ghettos spread throughout Poland. In Lodz, more than 160,000 Jews were sealed off, and those in Cracow were encased behind high stone walls. In the Vilna ghetto, people in their own homes had their telephones removed. Incoming mail was heavily censored or withheld. Telegrams and cables could only be sent through the *Judenrät* and with Gestapo approval.

Ghettos were sited deliberately in rundown areas, with Jews from outside herded within. As the months wore on, homes fell into disrepair; street cleaning ceased along with sanitation facilities and adequate sewage. Dysentery, tuberculosis and typhus raged. The food ration for Warsaw was cut severely for the Jews, who received half the weekly maximum in grams for 'a population that does no work worth mentioning'. Inevitably, crime increased, with thieves stealing food from homes and shops.

To Himmler, the existence of Jews in Poland, whether in ghettos or not, was intolerable. In the summer of 1942, he ordered those in Warsaw to be removed altogether for 'security reasons'. By October, more than 310,000 had been transported to the extermination camps – most to Treblinka – for gassing.

Elsewhere in Warsaw, a clandestine Jewish army gradually set about acquiring what arms they could, opening fire on *Wehrmacht* and SS troops who, on 19 April 1943, marched in for the final destruction of the ghetto. The Poles held out for the next few weeks, while Germans reduced the ghetto to rubble. About 70 Jewish fighters escaped through the sewers to join the Polish partisans. But it was not until 17 January 1945 that the Germans forcibly withdrew from the twin pressures of the Red Army and the Soviet-sponsored First Polish Army.

The eventual destruction of the ghettos at the war's end left a legacy of bitterness, not just against the Germans, but sections of the *Judenräte.* Some believed that they betrayed the Jews by obeying the Nazi authorities, while others insisted they had gained time to save as many as possible.

installations being constructed. They were forbidden access to certain sections of the city; they were allotted smaller food rations than the Polish population. They were subject to arbitrary terror and violence; most synagogues were destroyed; thousands of Jews were killed at random.'

Events in Poland dropped from notice when, on 10 May 1940, German armies attacked in the west, overrunning the Netherlands, Belgium and France. With world attention elsewhere, Frank, with the full assistance of the RSHA and Gestapo, decided to deal with the Polish intelligentsia. He summoned his Secretary of State, Arthur Seyss-Inquart, an Austrian-born lawyer, and Joseph Bühler to draw up what came to be termed Action A-B (*Ausserordentliche Befriedigungs-Aktion*, 'extraordinary action of pacification'). This was aimed at those who allegedly were encouraging agitation dangerous to the security of the occupation army.

The directives of Action A-B were actually carried out by members of *Amt I* of the RSHA, under *SS-Brigadeführer* Bruno Strechenbach, a former chief of the Hamburg Gestapo and now also commander of the security police for the *Generalgouvernement*, and by *Amt IV*, the Gestapo, which had never previously enjoyed such power. Those 'intellectuals' who were seized, including a sizeable number from Cracow University, were tried by courts over which the Gestapo presided. There was no question of legal representation or reprieve from the sentences of summary execution by the SS. Frank, in a terse memo on 30 May 1940, stated that the trials were 'a simple operation of pacification which is necessary and must be done outside

Above: These Warsaw Jews are among those destined for the city's ghetto, set up in 1940 for some half million Jews. Two years later, the deportations began, reaching 6000 a day. This photograph and scores of others were filed away in SS archives by order of Himmler.

the frame of regular procedure'. Executions of the type associated with Action A-B were carried out by five *Einsatzgruppen* formed speedily by Heydrich for the Polish campaign. Each member wore the service uniform of the *SS-Verfügungstruppe*, later designated the *Waffen-SS* ('Armed-SS'), which sported the SD diamond as a cup band on the left sleeve.

OCCUPYING THE LOW COUNTRIES

During the six months following the conquest of Poland, it seemed that the mighty German war machine had gone into slumber. Officially, Europe was at war, but it was an unreal war – a 'phoney war' to the British, to the Germans a *Sitzkrieg* ('armchair war'). This inertia was soon to end. By 14 May, Hitler's bombers had pounded Rotterdam and The Hague, Stukas rendering unstoppable the German advance of 9th Panzer Division.

In both the Netherlands and Belguim, the aftermath of conquest was at first low key. Little seemed to change in the first few months of occupation. The press apparently enjoyed full freedom: Amsterdam's main newspaper, *De Telegraaf*, was slow to change beyond prominently displaying the exchange rate between the Reichmark and the Guilder. Restaurants, cafés and cinemas were reopened and the prohibition of alcohol lifted.

Below: Seen here is a summary execution of 64 Poles at Bochnia, near Crakow, in December 1939. At no time did the Nazis attempt to conceal their atrocities, and plenty of incriminatory evidence survived for the post-war tribunals.

Arthur Seyss-Inquart, the former architect of Action A-B, took over as *Reichskommissar*. His manner, albeit firm, was cordial. His announcement on his appointment was bland: 'From today, I have taken over as the highest civil authority in the Netherlands. The magnanimity of the *Führer* and the force of German arms have made it possible that after only a few days order is being restored to public life. Certain measures will be taken, but only in so far as the circumstances will make them necessary … We all know that the ultimate purpose of our *Führer* is peace and order for all who are of goodwill.' Then came the steel: 'It is expected that the population will show their appreciation for these favours by continued good behaviour.'

Above: After being appointed deputy to Hans Frank in the Polish *Generalgouvernement*, Arthur Seyss-Inquart went on to serve as *Reichskommissar* for the Netherlands, where he earned the hatred of the Dutch people. His avowed repentance after the war did nothing to prevent his death sentence and hanging at Nuremberg in October 1946.

From the beginning, the *Reichskommissar* revelled in his office. His inauguration address was delivered at The Hague in the imposing setting of the ancient Ridderzaal (Hall of the Knights), where Queen Wilhelmina used to open the government's winter session in solemn ceremony. To underline the changed circumstances still further, Seyss-Inquart imported the Cologne Radio Orchestra. For a while good relations appeared to persist. A Dutch administration was permitted to exist alongside that of the Germans. As the Queen and the Dutch government had fled to Britain, where they had set up a government-in-exile, the principal secretaries of the government ministries in The Hague constituted the highest Dutch authority in the country. They held regular meetings, acting as though they were a sort of cabinet. Since they were a mere façade, the Germans tolerated them; as time went on, however, they were replaced by Germans.

When it came to enforcing the will of the occupying power, there was an ideal practitioner in *Brigadeführer* Hanns Albin Rauter, an Austrian from Klagenfurt, whose links with extremist movements went back to the 1920s when he had been a member of the *Steierische Heimatschutz* ('Styrian Home Guard'), a fanatically anti-Semite paramilitary corps, the pan-German ideological platform of which moulded his future.

In the Netherlands, Rauter was designated *Generalkommissar für des Sichersheitswesen* ('Commissar General for Public Safety'). He also carried the title *Höhere SS und Polizeiführer Nordwest* (HSSPF, 'Higher SS and Police Leader') – *Nordwest* being the pan-German designation for the

Netherlands. This latter title was the most significant. It meant that Rauter was Hitler's personal lieutenant and as such commanded all SS organizations in the Netherlands, including the *Ordnungspolizei* ('Security Police'), the SD and Gestapo, as well as the entire Dutch police force.

PERSECUTION

Rauter lost no time in turning his attention to the country's Jews. On 7 August 1940, ritual animal slaughter was peremptorily prohibited: cattle were no longer to be killed by severing the arteries or bleeding. Only the generally accepted methods of stunning or shooting would be permitted. The next stage was for Aryan and Jewish butchers to be separated. Jews would no longer be allowed to serve Gentiles; overnight Jewish butchers lost 85 per cent of their trade. A decree later in the month was aimed at business enterprises with Jewish connections, however small. The effect was catastrophic on the roughly 140,000 Jews who lived in the Netherlands, 60 per cent of them in Amsterdam, as half were engaged in trade and commerce, ranging from the diamond industry and manufacturing to second-hand and street trade.

For a time strong-arm repression was kept to a minimum, until the occupiers were faced with protest demonstrations in Amsterdam's old Jewish quarter. Rauter sealed off the area, summoning the quarter's senior leaders and demanding the creation of what became the *Joodsche Raad* ('Jewish Council'). He faced further rebellion in the more prosperous area of south Amsterdam, where a clash with a Kripo patrol led to wholesale arrests. Some 400 Jews between the ages of 20 and 35 were rounded up and eventually deported to Mauthausen concentration camp. From then on, persecution worsened, with economic privation the next stage, as described after the war by Mrs Alfred B. Spanjaard, an Amsterdam Jew who survived two years in concentration camps: 'New decrees were issued daily. We were not allowed on certain streets. We couldn't ride in streetcars, our telephones and radios were taken away, we could shop only between 3 and 5 p.m., and we had to be in our homes at 8 p.m. All Jews were ordered to bring their money, jewels and insurance policies to the Lippmann and Rosenthal Bank in Sarphatistraat, where the Germans had taken over. There we had to make a complete accounting of our funds and valuables. We were allowed to keep 250 guilders and told we couldn't spend more than

Below: The eight residents of the secret annexe in Amsterdam, including the Frank family, were transported to Auschwitz. For Anne Frank (pictured) and her sister Margot, their final destination was Bergen-Belsen. The two girls both contracted typhus and died in March 1945.

ANNE FRANK

In occupied Netherlands, draconian anti-Jewish measures were directed from Gestapo headquarters in Amsterdam, resulted in mass deportations.

On 4 August 1944, the *Grune Polizei* ('Security Police'), under Gestapo orders, stormed a secret annexe behind a warehouse on Amsterdam's Prinsengracht canal. They arrested the eight people who had hidden there for almost two years, including the Jewish Frank family. All had been betrayed by informers and all were deported.

Throughout her time in the annexe, Anne Frank, the teenage daughter, had kept a diary describing her critical years of adolescence and the vicissitudes of people facing hunger, boredom and the inevitable emotional strains of the occupation. The diary had been thrown to the floor by the arresting team and was recovered after the war by Anne's father, Otto, the only survivor from the annexe. Anne herself had died in the Bergen-Belsen concentration camp at the age of 15.

The diary was eventually translated into more than 30 languages and moved people all over the world. One sentence has been widely quoted: 'In spite of everything, I still believe that people are really good at heart.' In Amsterdam, the annexe has been preserved and is visited daily by hundreds of people. Each year, young Germans journey to Belsen to pray for the soul of Anne Frank.

100 guilders a month for rent, clothing, food and medical expenses. It didn't matter whether rent alone amounted to more than that figure – that was the order. After the 250 guilders were spent, we had to draw on what was left of our funds at the bank. If we had nothing left, we were either supported by the Jewish community or we died.'

Prohibition had spread to the public services. Entry into the Civil Service was banned for Jews and for Gentiles married to Jews. This prompted Rauter to root out the background of all public servants, including adherents to pre-war political parties. The Gestapo and its ancillaries went on to carry out arrests, mass raids, deportations, action against strikes and executions. In all this they had the sinister assistance of Dutch turncoats-cum-undercover agents known as *Veteranensmänner* (V-men). There were plenty of them. Before the war, the National Socialist Party of the Netherlands (*Nationaal Socialistische Beweging*, NSB) had attracted few followers, but this did nothing to distract its founder, Anton Mussert, a village schoolmaster.

Life for the 90,000 Jews in neighbouring Belgium had seemed reasonably secure. As in the Netherlands, there were plenty of jobs to be had in the clothing trade and other small businesses, while Antwerp was also the focus of the diamond trade. In less than six months, all illusions of security were stripped away. With the arrival of the Germans, the Belgian tragedy of deportation began. Here also a Jewish council was set up, whose members were directly answerable to the Gestapo. It was up to leaders to negotiate for the release of individual Jews, and it was clear that the Gestapo would be sympathetic – subject to the price of 25,000 francs for each individual transported to Switzerland by the Belgian Red Cross. Reassuring letters were produced from those who had made the journey successfully as evidence that such an arrangement was possible. The council released scores of Jews, who paid an agreed fee to Gestapo or collaborating intermediaries and prepared for the journey full of hope, often obliged to leave behind their jewels and possessions. Many travelled no further than the deportation centre at Mechelen, a staging post for a final journey to the east. The presence of collaborators was pinpointed by Tos Haaker, a Jew living in Amsterdam, who wrote: 'The Jewish inhabitants were dragged outside and ill-treated. Ten minutes were granted to collect some clothes. Many of them, almost dead with fear, suffered themselves to be taken away without saying a word … vehicle after vehicle was loaded and driven away. No distinction was made: old and young, whether ill or healthy, everybody was dragged outside, many of them half dressed. First the victims were taken to the Gestapo where they remained a full day without food or drink. Then came large closed furniture vans … The human cattle were heaped up on them … The raids went on regularly.'

FALLEN FRANCE

By 10 June, the Germans were across the Loire river and Rouen had fallen. Without a fight, the French government abandoned Paris and moved to Tours, then to Bordeaux. Four days later, the triumphant *Wehrmacht* entered Paris and the Nazi swastika flag flew from the Eiffel Tower. On 20 June, Marshal Pétain, who had been a national hero during the Great War, sent a delegation to negotiate with the Germans. The Armistice terms signed two days later satisfied Hitler's deep hatred of the French, making France a truncated nation: the Germans were to occupy all the northern and western parts of the country, while Pétain was allowed to govern from the southern spa town of Vichy, destined to be the headquarters of collaboration.

'… many a cowardly compatriot was willing to point out houses where Jews were living or places where many of them were hidden.'
Tos Haaker, Amsterdam resident

Hitler, however, did not get his way entirely. Many *Wehrmacht* commanders, faced with Hitler's operational plans for the west, had right from the start protested vigorously about the activities of the SS and particularly the *Einsatzgruppen* throughout Poland. For once Hitler faced a solid wall of opposition and recognized that, if the occupation were to be a success, he would have to compromise. It was decided that no police unit or SD *Einsatzkommando* was to accompany the army in its advance through France. All police units would be subject to army command.

As might have been expected, none of this was to the liking of Himmler and Heydrich. The latter, however, saw a way round the problem. Among the forces of the *Wehrmacht* making for the French capital was a small knot of

men, wearing the uniform of the *Geheime Feldpolizei* (GFP, the 'Secret Military Police'), who drove into Paris in light, minimally armed vehicles with military number plates. They were scarcely noticed. Serving as Trojan horses, they were members of a specially formed *Sonderkommando* (an independent Commando) who, on Heydrich's orders, were to settle in unobtrusively and prepare the path for the Gestapo.

Indeed, the Gestapo, ensconced in the rue des Saussaies, was at first kept sparse. Müller's representative was an old crony, Carl Bömelberg, an experienced policeman who had the twin advantages of having previously lived professionally in France and being fluent in the language. His previous contacts with certain sections of the Paris police, particularly at the Préfecture, proved invaluable. Here he and his colleagues were without much difficulty able to lay their hands on the complete dossiers of German emigrés and Jews. Helmut Knochen, who had distinguished himself in Heydrich's eyes over his involvement in the Venlo affair, was Heydrich's representative on the spot, with instructions to build bridges with a frequently recalcitrant *Wehrmacht*. His most formidable opponent was General Otto von Stülpnagel, head of the *Militärbefehlshaber* ('Military Command'), with its headquarters in the Avenue Kléber, who made no attempt to disguise his detestation of Himmler, Heydrich and their agents. Jealous of the prestige of the occupation

Above: The treatment of Dutch Jews in the Netherlands was especially harsh and roundups by the *Feldgendarmerie*, who in addition to normal police duties were responsible for supervision and control of the civilian populace, were regular occurrences. Some 110,000 Jews were deported to Auschwitz, Sobibor and other camps. An estimated 75 per cent of Dutch Jews perished in the war.

85

Above: Members of the SS and Gestapo assemble outside the Ritz Hotel in Paris, making deliberate use of some non-service vehicles. Although intent on expansion, the SS and its offshoots initially sought a low profile in France in the face of allegations of interference from a resentful occupying army.

army, he had no intention of allowing Heydrich's men to jeopardize it. Furthermore, he refused all cooperation, pointing out that the *Sonderkommando* was interfering in matters of security and military intelligence, the joint province of the *Militärbefehlshaber* and the *Abwehr*, also established in Paris.

In the face of such intransigence, Knochen went out of his way to be conciliatory and to stress that he had no intention of antagonizing the occupation army. At the same time he was pursuing his own plans, which involved the assiduous courting of undercover movements sympathetic to the Nazis. These tactics were effectively under way in the second year of occupation. Prominent among these groups was the *Mouvement Social Révolutionnaire* (MSR), notorious for its anti-Semitism and the leaders of which were known to be increasingly impatient at what they saw as bureaucratic delays in implementing effective anti-Jewish measures. Such measures, they urged, should be dramatic, spearheaded by attacks on synagogues, the core of Jewish worship.

The most concentrated of these attacks took place throughout October 1941, beginning with a series of deafening explosions that ripped through Paris streets, gutting synagogues in the areas of the Rue Notre-Dame-de-Nazareth and the Rue de la Victoire. Von Stülpnagel reacted violently to what he regarded as blatant irresponsibility and directed his fury at *SS-Brigadeführer* Dr Thomas, the supervisor of the *Sonderkommandos*. He also attacked Knochen and *Obersturmführer* Hans Sommer of *Amt VI* of the RSHA, the latter required by Heydrich to liaise with the MSR and make the practical arrangements for the assaults on the synagogues. As von Stülpnagel wrote to Heydrich, 'the Commander in Chief of the German Army demands that *SS-Brigadeführer* Thomas be relieved of his post. The OKW takes it for granted the Berlin authorities are in agreement that Dr Knochen and *SS-Obersturmführer* Sommer should no long be employed in occupied territory.' By way of deflecting the row between the RSHA and the army, Heydrich made a single concession. Within days, *Brigadeführer* Thomas had requested 'to be relieved of his duties' and had been despatched to the newly occupied territories of Kiev as head of the Sipo-SD; Knochen and Sommer kept their jobs. Thomas was replaced by 27-year-old Theo Dannecker, a former lawyer of colourless personality who was nominally under the authority of Knochen as French head of *Amt IV AB*. In fact, his direction came from higher up the RSHA hierarchy, from Adolf Eichmann, who lost no time in pulling the strings of his puppet. On 22 August 1941 came the decree that all Frenchmen in detention were forthwith hostages and could be shot 'according to the gravity of their acts'.

TOWARDS THE 'FINAL SOLUTION'

Eichmann, by now an *SS-Sturmbannführer*, had other preoccupations: a major plan for the deportation of European Jewry, details of which were submitted to Himmler, via Müller and Heydrich. Originally Palestine was considered as a destination, but was ruled out by Himmler 'since it belonged to the Christians and the Muslims'. Instead plans were laid for the settlement of some 40,000 European Jews on the island of Madagascar, a French colony lying about 400 km (250 miles) from the coast of Africa and now under Vichy French control. The plan called for it to be ceded by France to Germany in a treaty. Money for the project would come from an international Jewish bank, which would take over the possessions of the deported Jews, who would be hostages in all but name and transported to the island by the German navy. It was intended that by the spring of 1941 the last Jew would have left the European continent.

Hitler had gambled on the war coming to a swift end so that Eichmann's plans could be implemented without delay. Events dictated otherwise. Operation Sea Lion, the invasion of England originally proposed for September 1940, had been postponed indefinitely. Göring's much-vaunted *Luftwaffe* had failed to subdue the Royal Air Force in preparation for the invasion, and there was no sign of Britain giving in after the defeat of France. The prospect of finding sufficient shipping in wartime to carry the vast number of Jews contemplated for Madagascar proved impossible. To

PÉTAIN AND VICHY FRANCE

In France, opinion is still sharply divided as to whether Henri Philippe Pétain should be regarded by history as traitor or patriot, although his heroic record in World War I remains indisputable. Born in 1856 to a peasant family in Cauchy-à-la-Tour, Pas de Calais, he acquitted himself with distinction while in command of an infantry regiment, and was promoted to command of first a brigade, then a division. In May 1915, he led his troops through German defences near Arras and the following February was assigned to halt the Kaiser's forces at Verdun, a task he achieved through organizational ability and energy. This was followed by promotion to Commander in Chief of the French armies in the field. At the age of 61, his place as a great French hero seemed assured.

By mid-1940, his reputation lay in ruins. In that year he had become deputy to the French Premier, Paul Reynaud, taking over when the latter resigned on 16 June. By that time he believed firmly that defeat was inevitable, urging immediate capitulation in order that France could secure the best possible terms from Hitler. On 19 June, he informed the Germans that he had formed a cabinet and asked Hitler for an armistice. The latter granted him an unoccupied zone in the south in which he was ostensibly free to govern.

Pétain was allowed to assume the title of Head of State. Together with Pierre Laval, who became first Vice Premier and then Foreign Minister, Pétain abolished the republican constitution and set up a dictatorship in conquered France. On 10 July 1940, the National Assembly, meeting at Vichy, awarded him a mandate for authoritarian rule within the unoccupied zone.

When German troops overran France in November 1942, following Allied landings in North Africa, Pétain became virtually a puppet of the Germans. Power shifted to Laval, who on Hitler's orders was made Premier. He collaborated enthusiastically, encouraging French deportations to Germany for hard labour.

As the end of the war approached, Pétain was forced to leave Vichy and accompany the Germans on their flight east. In April 1945, he returned voluntarily to France, where he was arrested. Most Frenchmen had come to detest him, even though he reiterated that collaboration with the Nazis had saved his country from an even worse fate. Tried for treason by the French High Court of Justice, he was convicted and received the death sentence, but was reprieved by General Charles de Gaulle. Pétain was exiled to the Ile d'Yeu and, after eventual compassionate release, died there at Port-Joinville on 23 July 1951 at the age of 95.

Pierre Laval, on the other hand, was shown no mercy. After arrest by American troops at Innsbruck, he endured an emotionally charged trial, facing abuse from spectators and even the jury. On the day of his execution, 15 October 1945, he took poison, which the doctors promptly pumped out of him. He was dragged retching and crying for water to the firing range, where it was later said he died with dignity.

Himmler and Heydrich there was only one alternative – what became known as the *Endlösung* ('final solution'), the physical extermination of Jewry.

Although Hermann Göring's prestige had suffered after failing to gain the advantage in the Battle of Britain, with his massive figure and seemingly tireless vitality he remained a popular figure with the German public, revelling in a lavish lifestyle as one of the leaders of the National Socialist hierarchy, with his second wife, Emmy Sonnemann, a former provincial

Left: Deliberate collaboration or the tired defeatism of an old man against a superior foe? Pétain sympathizers pointed out that he was the only Vichy survivor to request a return to France to stand trial. Seen here in the uneasy company of Hermann Göring, he justified all his actions as being in the best interests of France.

actress, playing the role of his consort. For all his surface bonhomie, however, Göring clung to every facet of his power and exercised it ruthlessly. At the end of July 1941, perceiving his most important office to be commissioner for Jewish affairs, he issued an order to Heydrich that all necessary measures should be taken 'in regard to organizational and financial matters for bringing about the total solution of the Jewish question in the German sphere of influence in Europe. I further charge you to submit to me as soon as possible a draft showing the measures already taken for the execution of the intended Final Solution of the Jewish question.'

The instrument of this directive was to be Adolf Eichmann, as the head of RSHA *Amt IV B2*. He announced at the end of May 1941 that all emigration from France and Belgium was forthwith banned. It was but a first step. The launch of Operation Barbarossa, the invasion of the Soviet Union on 22 June, meant a vast expansion of *IV B2* as an ingredient of the Gestapo. It had now gained the status of a Department of State, with a responsibility in every country occupied by the Nazis. Eichmann wasted little time. A mission was despatched to Bohemia and Moravia, which had been designated a Protectorate to provide 'autonomy and self-government' for the Czechs. In practice they were totally under the German heel, with Jews subject to German jurisdiction. The next stage was to set up a ghetto at Theresienstadt, formerly the Czech garrison town of Terezín, from where Czech Jews were to be deported to Poland.

Eichmann entrusted a particularly important role to an old crony of pre-war days, Dieter Wisliceny, who was active in Slovakia. There he was able to rely on the existing strength of German influence, including many of the 130,000 who were registered as racially German (*Volksdeutsche*). Particularly promising material was to be found among the black-uniformed Klinka Guard, a self-proclaimed elite with pretensions to be compared to the SS. By September 1941, the Slovak government had been pressured into promulgating a body of anti-Jewish legislation, containing 270 articles that redefined the Jews as a racial group, requiring them to wear the identifying Star of David, which made them liable to forced labour and eviction from towns and districts. *Wehrmacht* generals in western Europe, on the whole, held out against SS interference, in notable contrast to their Balkan counterparts. Lieutenant General Kurt von Krenzki, Commander in Chief Salonika-Aegean area, for example, did not hesitate to strike against the 55,000 Jews in the German occupation zone and rounded them up for work on fortifications and later for transportation to Auschwitz.

THE COMMISSAR ORDER

The uneasy relations between the *Oberkommando des Heeres* (OKH, the 'High Command') and Heydrich's cohorts had been of supreme unimportance to Hitler. In March, ahead of the launch of Barbarossa, the *Führer* had assembled 200 senior *Wehrmacht* officers in the Reich Chancellery and harangued them, screaming, 'We must abandon any thought of soldierly comradeship. Commissars and OGPU men are criminals and must be treated as such.' This was the origin of the notorious 'Commissar Order', which

Right: Executions of Soviet Resistance fighters and dissidents, such as these in Minsk, were characterized by extreme cruelty. Makeshift gallows often had no drops which meant that the victims slowly strangled to death.

EINSATZGRUPPEN

The *Einsatzgruppen* killer squads, organized by Himmler and Heydrich, were ready to follow the German armies into Poland in 1939. Once there, their orders were to round up Jews and place them in ghettos. By 1941, on the eve of the invasion of Soviet Russia, that remit had been expanded. On 2 July, a circular to the Chiefs of the *Sicherheitspolizei*, a fusion of the various state political and criminal police, spelt out their new duties:

'The immediate goal is the security-police pacification of the newly occupied areas ... All those search and execution measures that contribute to the political pacification of the occupied areas are to be undertaken. All the following are to be executed: officials of the Comintern, together with professional Communist politicians in general; top- and medium-level officials and radical lower-level officials of the Party; People's commissars; Jews in Party and state employment and other radical elements – saboteurs, propagandists, snipers, assassins, inciters etc, in so far as they are of special importance for the further economic reconstruction of the Occupied Territories.'

Each *Einsatzgruppe* and its individual detachment, the *Einsatzkommando*, varied in composition. In the Soviet Union, four *Einsatzgruppen* were known to be involved, each with a strength of between 1000 and 1200 men. Their spheres of operation were Group A, the Baltic States; Group B, Smolensk and Moscow; Group C, the Kiev region; and Group D, southern Ukraine. As for the *Einsatzkommandos*, out of around 1000 men, 350 could be members of the *Waffen-SS*, together with 150 drivers and mechanics, and perhaps 100 Gestapo. In addition there would be auxiliary police from the *Ordnungspolizei* (Orpo), the Kripo and the SD. Each *Einsatzgruppe* also went into action accompanied by its Executive – a mobile office of interpreters, radio operators, teletypists, office clerks and female staff.

On paper at least, each group was under the command of the relevant *Wehrmacht* force within the relevant area. This led some defendants at post-war Allied tribunals to disclaim any role for the SD or Gestapo. Although communications with the army group commanders were close, actual operational instructions were issued by Heydrich, and the army never saw their contents.

made it the duty of army formation commanders to treat political officers captured from the Red Army as criminals to be liquidated or handed over for execution to the *Sicherheitspolizei*. Heinz Höhne, in his book *The Order of the Death's Head*, succinctly points out that, as 'hardly a single general was prepared to offer active resistance to Hitler's ukase, the temptation was all the greater to leave the special treatment to Himmler's police'.

The 'Commissar Order' had barely been set out before Heydrich was faced with an agreement draft on the role of the *Einsatzgruppen* of the SS. In areas behind the front line, it was proposed that the army should be the authoritative voice 'for movement, rations and accommodation', and could only oppose the SS in areas where their activities might have an effect on military operations. The most significant sentence of the draft was not lost on Heydrich: 'The *Sonderkommandos* or *Einsatzgruppen* are authorized, within the framework of their task and their own responsibility, to take executive measures affecting the civilian population.' The draft was approved by Heydrich, giving the *Einsatzgruppen* almost complete freedom in their coming role in the Soviet Union.

Each *Einsatzkommando* within an *Einzsatzgruppe* came to be attached to a specific army group and moved with it, buttressed by other formations of the *Waffen-SS*. The following report, produced as evidence at the Nuremberg Tribunal, describes one unit in action: 'The head of a collective farm, in the vicinity of Bobruisk, was arrested because he had intentionally disorganized production by ordering the farmers to cease their work, and by giving instructions to hide the harvested shares in the forest. A total of 600 persons were arrested in Bobruisk and vicinity by a detachment of *Einsatzkommando 8*. Out of these, 407 persons were liquidated. The executed comprised, in addition to the above mentioned, Jews and elements who had shown open resistance against orders issued by German occupation authorities, or had openly incited to acts of sabotage … A large scale Jewish action was carried out in the village of Lachoisk. In the course of this action 920 Jews were executed with the support of a *Kommando* of the SS Division Reich. The village may now be described as "free of Jews".'

Below: A knot of bewildered, frightened Jews board a cattle truck, bound for concentration camps and almost certain death. Deportations to the east were arranged carefully so that the victims thought they were being sent solely to work.

REICH PROTECTOR

Adolf Hitler was meanwhile plagued by a new set of worries involving the designated Czech Protectorate of Bohemia-Moravia, which, apart from Germany itself, constituted the cradle of the Reich's armaments industry. Until the invasion of Russia, resistance within the Protectorate had been comparatively slight. Barbarossa changed all that, and Moscow played its part. A Pan-Slav Congress was convened in Moscow amid considerable publicity. All Slavs were called upon to undermine the occupiers whenever possible. Methods that were to become commonplace when the fortunes of war turned against Germany were now adopted: telephone and telegraph facilities were severed and trains derailed; factory machinery ground to a halt with 'temporary' breakdowns due to unexplained faults; there were minor explosions at supply dumps and unexplained errors in blueprints and tool patterns. Trains arriving with supplies for the occupying troops were unexpectedly delayed. In one 'accident', an SS man was injured when a broken piece of cornice mysteriously fell from a shop window. Within the Protectorate itself, propaganda was stepped up, not only with the wide circulation of Communist literature, but also through the publication of patriotic Czech poems. The spirit of Jan Hus, the Bohemian religious reformer and martyr, was evoked.

One man who watched the situation closely was Heydrich, whose attention focused particularly on the declining fortunes of the Reich Protector. It was common knowledge that Freiherr Konstantin von Neurath was regarded by Hitler as too soft and the process of undermining him was not difficult. He had a formidable opponent in *Gruppenführer* Karl-Hermann Frank, who had his eye on the post of Reich Protector and speedily marshalled support from within the most influential SS and police circles. Criticism of von Neurath hardened. Karl Böhme, commander of the Sipo and SD in Prague, was summoned to a meeting at Hitler's headquarters, the *Führerhauptquartier* at Rastenburg (now Ketrzyn) in East Prussia, where he outlined the successes of the resistance to Nazi rule within the Protectorate and von Neurath's patent failure to combat them. Von Neurath's dismissal followed. Even though the new holder of the post, Reinhard Heydrich, would be designated only as 'Acting Reich Protector', Frank's reaction was sour, as he received nothing. It was patently Heydrich's day.

After his arrival in Prague on 27 December 1941, the top-secret teleprinter in Berlin had rattled out an urgent message to Hitler, who was on the Russian front: '*Mein Führer*, I dutifully report that this afternoon, in accordance with today's *Führer* decree, I took over the Acting Leadership of the affairs of the Reich Protector in Bohemia and Moravia. The official take-over follows at 11 o'clock tomorrow, with the centre of operations in Hradschin [Hradçany]. All political reports and messages will reach you by the hand of *Reichsleiter* Bormann. *Heil mein Führer!* (Sgd) Heydrich, *SS-Obergruppenführer*'. The message had been dashed off in a mood of euphoria, but Heydrich tempered his enthusiasm with caution. At every phase of his political life he had looked over his shoulder, a reflex action. Perils were attendant in his new position and he was well aware of them. There were those in Berlin who matched him in intrigue and would not hesitate to take full advantage of his absences in Prague and seek to supplant him.

Heydrich had barely been installed in Prague Castle before he delivered a two-pronged attack. The first of his victims was the Czech Prime Minister, General Alois Eliás, who was known to be in contact with the exiled Czech government of Edvard Benes in London. The fact that he had also been a protégé of the discredited von Neurath was enough. Eliás was handed over to the Gestapo, who extracted a confession within hours, and he was then hauled before a German court and condemned to death. The execution was at first postponed and he was held as hostage for the good behaviour of the Czech people; he was finally executed on 19 June 1942.

> Heydrich ensured that all his links with the RSHA remained in place and that communication and transport to Berlin were to hand.

THE BUTCHER OF PRAGUE

The Gestapo went on to tackle known centres of resistance, following penetration by undercover agents of the SD. Heydrich frequently bypassed all legal processes and handed over prisoners for immediate execution, in some cases in public. A notorious example occurred on 15 December 1941 in the square beside Prague Cathedral, which since dawn had been under a soft, white carpet of snow. Normally it would have been a scene of Christmas-card festivity, save for a machine gun mounted on a low, squat dais pointing directly into the square. There was also a small wood and canvas pavilion containing five heavily carved chairs. The swastika flag flew from the roof. Those who were chosen to view the day's drama would look into a square cordoned off with red, black and white rope. Each corner of the cordon was dominated by a gigantic medallion on which was embossed the eagle and swastika of the Third Reich. On the ground had been painted one hundred yellow discs; a labourer from the Highways Department had been detailed to be on hand with a broom to keep the snow from obliterating them.

In charge of the day's proceedings was *Obergruppenführer* Kurt Schact-Isserlis, to whom Heydrich had handed more than a hundred dossiers on those the Gestapo and SD had been investigating since the invasion of Czechoslovakia. The contents were based on the reports of a network of informers placed in houses, apartments, factories and offices from the very moment that the Czechs had become the vassals of the Germans. Schact-Isserlis, whose detailed records of the day's work were to fall into the hands of the Allies at the end of the war, was able to recall many of those who had been condemned to death by the hastily assembled courts and were now on the edge of annihilation in the square. The event, moreover, was to be distinguished by the presence of Himmler, whose Mercedes flanked by outriders headed the party that drove to the pavilion.

It was then the turn of those who were about to die to enter the square: a cross-section of housewives, labourers, clerks and students. Schact-Isserlis waited until each of the condemned was standing on a yellow disc. The order was given at 12.15, as the clocks chimed the quarter. As the arc of fire swept steadily across the defenceless group, there was a momentary distraction; Himmler had slumped back in his chair in a dead faint. It was Heydrich who came to the rescue, as Schact-Isserlis later recalled: 'There was a look of contempt on Heydrich's face. Together with the chief of police he caught at Himmler's shoulders and thrust his head down between his knees. His glasses fell off and the clicking sound they made on the floor was simultaneous with the sound of the machine-gun as the executioner swept his gun from left to right again, from right to left ...' Immediately the killings ceased Himmler, groggy and deathly pale, and supported by Heydrich, was escorted to his

Below: Reinhard Heydrich, the Butcher of Prague, arrived in the Czech capital as Acting Reich Protector. Along with Karl Frank (to his left), Heydrich salutes in the forecourt of Hradçany Castle as the SS flag is raised.

Above: On 29 November 1941, Himmler, visiting Prague, expressed concern over Heydrich's arrogance and contempt for personal security. It was an arrogant stance that cost the latter his life.

Mercedes, where he was heard mumbling about 'Something to hang on to'. Then the cordon was dismantled and the corpses heaved into the back of lorries by Sudeten Jewish prisoners assigned to the task, who themselves were subsequently liquidated.

The very name of Reinhard Heydrich became enough to inspire hatred and fear; from then on he was known as the 'Butcher of Prague'. Himmler's devotion to the tenets of Aryan purity and hatred for what he saw as the bacillus of Jewry may have been total, but these beliefs had always been regarded with cynicism by Heydrich. This led to something of a clash between the two men over the progress of repression in the Protectorate. Heydrich recognized the blunt truth that the progress of the Reich war effort depended on industrial power: the output of the great Skoda armaments works, for example, had to be kept going. The problem was that the Resistance movement was concentrated there; any arrest meant a weakening of the work force.

It was this dilemma that impelled Heydrich to stand his previous policy on its head. He let it be known that, except in cases of extreme provocation, political persecution would be soft-pedalled; saboteurs, however, would be summarily shot. The fat ration was raised for two million Czech industrial workers. Luxury hotels in the smarter resorts, such as Karlsbad, were requisitioned as holiday homes. Heydrich's wife, Lina, was pressed into service as a social hostess, receiving a string of visitors to the Czernín Palace, while Heydrich himself listened politely to the petitions of various delegations. Inevitably, news of the change in policy reached the government-in-exile in Britain, who reacted with some alarm, particularly when their agents reported that Czech resistance had slowed significantly. London began implementing plans.

WANNSEE

Meanwhile, for Heydrich the office of Reich Protector was proving all-absorbing, and there was the old worry that his position as head of the RSHA could be under threat during his absences from Germany. The need to reassert his authority was one of the reasons for convening a conference on 20 January 1942 in a comfortably appointed villa, the former Interpol headquarters at Grossen-Wannsee, a pleasant lakeside suburb of southwest Berlin. Originally, it had been intended to hold the conference on 8 December, but at the last moment this was postponed owing to the Japanese attack on Pearl Harbor and the invasion of Allied territories in Southeast Asia, which had taken both the Allies and the Germans by surprise. The purpose of the conference – many of the minutes of which survived the war – was to review progress to date on the fate of the Jews and to give pointers for the future, notably in the light of Göring's directive of the previous July.

Left: Suspected resistance members are executed by an *Einsatzgruppen* firing squad. These executions were carried out during 1942 in Moravia, which, along with the area of Bohemia, constituted Heydrich's Protectorate.

THE FINAL SOLUTION

'One basic principle must be the absolute rule for the SS men: we must be honest, decent, loyal and completely comradely to members of our own blood and nobody else. What happens to a Russian and a Czech does not interest me in the slightest. What the nations can offer in the way of good blood of our type we will take, if necessary, by kidnapping their children and raising them here with us. Whether nations live in prosperity or starve to death interests me only in so far as we need them as slaves for our *Kultur*: otherwise it is of no interest to me. Whether 10,000 Russian females fall down from exhaustion while digging an anti-tank ditch for Germany interests me only in so far as the anti-tank ditch for Germany is finished. We shall never be rough and heartless when it is not necessary, that is clear. We Germans, who are the only people in the world who have a decent attitude towards animals, will also assume a decent attitude towards these human animals. But it is a crime against our own blood to worry about them and give them ideals, thus causing our sons and grandsons to have a more difficult time ... We can be indifferent to everything else. I wish the SS to adopt this attitude to the problem of all foreign, non-Germanic peoples, especially Russians.

'I mean the evacuation of the Jews, the liquidation of the Jewish race. This is one of those things that is easily said. Every party member says, "We will liquidate the Jewish race." Naturally: it is in the party programme. We will eliminate them. Easily done. Then your 80 million good German citizens turn up and each one has his decent Jew. Of course all the others are pigs, but this one is a splendid Jew. None of those who talked like this has watched, none of them has stuck it out. Most of you know what it means when a hundred corpses are lying side by side, or five hundred or a thousand. To have stuck it out, and at the same time – apart from exceptions caused by human weakness – to have remained decent fellows, that is what has made us hard. This is a page of glory in our history which has never been written and is never to be written.'

Speech by Heinrich Himmler, 4 October 1943

In the manner of a senior civil servant confining himself strictly to statistical facts, Heydrich, who had ordered the conference to be short, addressed leading personalities from the Ministry for the Occupied Territories, there under the authority of the Nazi's racial theorist Alfred Rosenberg. Heydrich revealed that there were only 131,800 Jews left in the original Reich territory, out of a quarter of a million at the start of the war. However, in eastern Europe, France and England there remained a total of 11 million Jews needing urgent attention. Wartime conditions had put paid to the policy of emigration but, as Heydrich told those present, 'there were other policies in the East'. This deliberately vague phrasing was subsequently revealed as a euphemism for deportation, ghettoization and mass killing of the kind committed by the *Einsatzgruppen*, although the minutes also suggest that Heydrich favoured the creation of a pool of Jews who would be available for slave labour.

This could scarcely have pleased *Hauptsturmführer* Dr Rudolf Lange, who has been described by Heinz Höhne as one of the 'Final Solution fanatics' who found 'this desire for Jewish labour highly disturbing, for it threatened to jeopardize their work of extermination'. Lange, as it turned out, was in the best position to know what such weasel words as 'evacuation' actually meant: his *Einsatzkommando* had murdered more than 35,000 Jews and countless other victims during the six months since the Nazi occupation of Latvia. Furthermore, within a few months of the Wannsee conference, he went to work with three gas vans at a deserted house set in the woods near Chelmno, 65 km (40 miles) northwest of Lodz in Poland. It was here that Jews were made to strip and climb into one of the closed vans, supposedly to use the showers. As soon as the door of the van was closed on them, gasses were fed into the van through a concealed pipe. Instructions issued by the RSHA on behalf of Heydrich stipulated that death should occur after 15 minutes, but in fact often took hours.

Eichmann, who was at Wannsee as the representative for the Gestapo, was careful to play down his role during his trial in Israel in 1961, presenting himself as the humble bureaucrat: 'My orders from my superior, *SS-Gruppenführer* Müller, were to ensure that the proceedings of the meeting were properly recorded and I spent most of the time sharpening the

Below: Prisoners from Dachau concentration camp are marched to work. The camp was staffed by volunteer SS who formed the Death's Head units, a designation based on their skull-and-crossbones cap badge.

stenographer's pencils.' At the end of the proceedings, Eichmann and Heydrich relaxed briefly over cognac, while others used the opportunity to ingratiate themselves with the pair and justify their own particular records. Heydrich, anxious to return to Prague, slipped away as soon as he could.

Within months a fresh worry arose. Himmler's latest obsession was France where he sensed that the influence and discipline of the Gestapo had withered through the ongoing rivalry with the army. He put this down to the absence of a sufficiently strong personality at the head of the SS and thought this deficiency could be remedied by the appointment of *Brigadeführer* Karl Albrecht Oberg, a former associate of Heydrich. The latter was anxious that Himmler's criticism of the RSHA's record in France did not reflect on him. Heydrich flew to Paris and arrived in style. The Ritz Hotel had been chosen for one of the most lavish social events that the capital had witnessed since before the war.

In such a setting the central figure presented something of an anti-climax: Oberg was pink-cheeked, outwardly benevolent and as self-effacing as any middle-rank civil servant. In fact, he was a classic career Nazi. He had fought on the Western Front in World War I and been awarded both the First and Second Class Iron Cross. The economic depression that followed the war wiped out the savings of the middle classes, and the Oberg family had proved no exception. By 1930 Karl, with a young wife, was struggling

Below: Here, prisoners arriving at Auschwitz concentration camp are divided into two groups: those considered strong enough to work and those deemed unsuitable, either through age or incapacity. An indication from the camp commandant (second from the right) signified the dispersal.

CONCENTRATION CAMPS

Concentration camps existed from the earliest days of Nazi power. On Adolf Hitler's appointment as Reich Chancellor in January 1933, Göring was named Minister President of the state of Prussia. As such, he was in charge of security and the police. Nazi sympathizers, both SS and SA men, held key posts in hastily set-up camps. Heinrich Himmler, as police supremo in Bavaria, formed his own 'model' camp at Dachau under SS control.

Arrest – the euphemistic *Schutzhaft* ('protective custody') – was the fate of anyone considered undesirable, including Jews, trade unionists, Communists, gypsies, homosexuals, petty criminals, Protestants and Catholics. Command was in the hands of an SS officer holding *Standartenführer* or *Sturmbannführer* rank, divided into companies in the charge of a *Haupsturmführer* or *Obersturmführer*. As was the case with most camps, members of the Gestapo were not directly involved in administration, although they had a powerful say in who was arrested and interned.

Early on, there were three main camps: in addition to Dachau, there were Buchenwald and Sachsenhausen. Camps at Belsen and Gross-Rosen in Germany, Mauthaussen in Austria and Theresienstadt in Czechoslovakia were soon developed. After a time, the camps established satellites, many used by industry as a source of labour, most notably in Russia where there were eventually as many as 500 satellite camps.

Following the Wannsee conference in January 1942, seeking to make the extermination of the Jews a systematically organized operation, camps sprung up in the east, notably Belzec, with a planned killing capacity of 15,000 a day, and Sobibor, handling 20,000 deaths. There were even more at Majdanek and Treblinka, where most Warsaw Jews were taken.

Final published figures for camp deaths must be approached cautiously because there is no documentation. Eleven million has been cited, although more recently historians favour six million. That figure, however, does not take into account deaths caused by disease or ill treatment.

With the impending collapse of Germany, approaches were made to leading Nazis to release Jewish prisoners and to permit the Red Cross to bring in relief. Most attempts were frustrated, and it was not until September 1944 that a Red Cross official reached Auschwitz. The following April food and medicines were brought to Theresienstadt, and prisoners on a forced march from Oranienburg received relief supplies. The incident that really brought the horrors of the camps to the world was the news of a Belsen typhus epidemic, where some 60,000 prisoners were crammed into space designed for 8000. The camp was handed over to the British on 15 April 1945.

to survive as the proprietor of a tobacco kiosk in his native Hamburg. By the following June, he had joined the National Socialists (as party member 575205) and was noticed by Heydrich for service in the SD. His rise in both intelligence and military work for the SS was rapid. By September 1941, he was SD *und Polizeiführer* at Radom in Poland, where he took part in the Jewish pogroms. Now, holding the same rank as Rauter in the Netherlands, he had come to France. Repression would now be stepped up throughout the Reich with a new ferocity that also had the effect of fuelling the activities of the Resistance. Heydrich, returning to Prague, was to encounter the resulting forces all too soon.

CHAPTER 6

THE OCCUPIED TERRITORIES

The Czech underground hit back with the assassination of Heydrich. Although it was hailed as a rallying call for resistance throughout Europe, it provoked fierce retaliation.

O ne of the highlights of the attendant ceremonial when Reinhard Heydrich had first arrived in Prague was a display of the ancient crown jewels of the Bohemian rulers in St Vitus's Cathedral. The centrepiece was the gold crown of St Wenceslas, studded with reputedly the largest sapphires in the world. Heydrich with cunning political calculation had already stressed that Wenceslas, who had been assassinated in the tenth century following a conspiracy by his brother Boleslav, had been a friend of Germany and had fallen to infamous partisans from the east. Hitler's creation of the Protectorate was thus righting an ancient wrong. The jewels when not on display had been secured by seven locks, a symbolic reference to the seven seals of the holy scroll from Revelations. Traditionally the keys were kept by seven different individuals, starting with the head of state himself. On this occasion, President Hácha handed the keys to Heydrich, who returned three of them with a flourish, declaring, 'See this as a token of our trust and also your obligation.'

But what Heydrich chose to ignore was that the tight security surrounding the jewels had its origins in a long-established legend. This declared that should anyone other than the true heir to the ancient kingdom put the crown upon his head, he was marked for death. It was perhaps typical of Heydrich that he should have scorned the superstition and reputedly donned the crown without hesitation.

Left: A company of German troops enter the courtyard of the Hradçany Castle in Prague on 15 March 1939, ahead of Hitler's arrival. Resistants were not slow to emerge but, as the picture shows, potential collaborators were already in place.

All ceremonial aside, it was soon apparent that the power of the Acting Protector and the SS was going to hold absolute sway. At his first official appearance, Heydrich addressed a gathering of army and party dignitaries at the Çernín Palace, his arrival greeted by Karl-Hermann Frank with an upraised Nazi salute. Note-taking during the meeting was forbidden. Nevertheless Heydrich's secretary, placed out of sight, recorded the speech in shorthand, the transcript of which survived. Heydrich made it abundantly clear that the SS, the SD and the attendant security police were inseparable from the conduct of business within the Protectorate and the Nazi party. The SS and SD were to be 'the shock troops … in everything that concerns the safeguard of our space from the standpoint of internal policy, as well as the safeguard of the National Socialist idea. As shock troops, we are always in the forefront of the army, we are particularly well armed, we are ready for action, and we know how to fight … Thus we act as an organ of execution, conscious of the mission of the *Führer* and the Reich, that mission that will take us from the Great German Reich to the Greater Germanic Reich. And since then the *Führer* has said to me, "Bear in mind that, wherever I see the unity of the Reich endangered, I choose an SS leader and send him there to

Below: Heydrich with his wife Lina, who fulfilled the role of consort and hostess during her husband's time as Acting Reich Protector. In fact, the marriage was under strain due to Heydrich's frequent absences in Berlin and serial womanizing.

preserve that unity." From those words of the *Führer* you can infer the overall task of the SS, and my special task here.'

The Gestapo's programme of terror was launched and extended all too soon. A new refinement was the introduction of 'protective custody' – the right to detain anyone without cause for an indefinite period. Lulled by inducements of cash and favours from Heydrich and Frank, there were droves of informers. The number of 'safe houses' set up by the Resistance shrank alarmingly as their ranks were penetrated either by the Gestapo or by traitors.

As the months wore on, Heydrich began increasingly to revel in his new job, and not just in the power it gave him. There were considerable fringe benefits, not least the acquisition of Panenské Brezany, a country estate outside Prague, which was infinitely more appealing than the formality of the Çernín Palace in Hradçany, although Lina Heydrich enjoyed acting as hostess there to compliant Czechs and visiting Germans. At first Heydrich had envisaged the life of a commuter, flying regularly between Prague and Berlin. But Lina, recalling her husband's previous

Above: Heydrich liked to be portrayed as the ideal family man and provided periodic photo opportunities with his wife and three children in support of the image. In this somewhat strained pose he is seen with his daughter, Silke.

absorption in work, and long absences for both official business and serial philandering, had rebelled strongly: the family, she decreed, was to make Prague its base. Heydrich himself responded by bolstering an image of the Protector with a human face. Photographers were encouraged to depict the couple in informal domestic bliss: Lina in skirt and flowered top with white knee-high socks, her husband in black shorts with a grey woollen jacket with brass buttons. To complete the picture of cosy togetherness, the couple's children, their two sons Klaus and Heider and his small daughter, Silke, were included in many of the pictures.

CODE NAMED 'ANTHROPOID'

Agents of Czech intelligence in Prague had warned London that Heydrich's 'carrot and stick' policy towards industrial workers was surprisingly successful in undermining resistance to the occupation. Yet the very word 'Protectorate' was anathema to Hitler. The *Führer* wanted the campaign of terror stepped up, fuelled by changing fortunes on the Russian front, a campaign that he had claimed with a grand flourish would be over in seven months. During the assault on Moscow, however, the iron winter had left troops frozen and immobile. Strong opposition, perhaps for the very first time in this war, began to show itself. Opposition of any variety had to be countered. By way of demonstration, on the day that Heydrich was due to leave for Berlin, Himmler sent a flash telegram to Prague, ordering the arrest of 10,000 hostages from among the Czech intelligentsia. Further orders were issued that a hundred of these should be shot that very evening. It was in response to just such an event that the government-in-exile had laid plans for the assassination of Heydrich, a move to put fresh fire into the belly of the opposition. Among the underground in Prague, however, conscious of the likely revenge by the Germans, there was horror at what was regarded as an excessive measure. Pleas were made to the British government to call off the entire scheme. These were ignored.

Until now the intelligence record of the government-in-exile had not been encouraging. Overtures, for example, had been made to the Royal Air Force (RAF) to fly a special agent into Prague to report on the situation within the Protectorate. The agent lasted just two weeks before the Gestapo picked him up. Matters then passed into the hands of Lieutenant Colonel Frantisek Moravec, who had been a foremost leader of the pre-war Czech Intelligence Service. In March 1939, he had fled to Britain along with 10 others, bearing valuable files which were made available to the MI6 arm of British intelligence. Before leaving he had bequeathed to the Czechs the nucleus of a Resistance movement, *Obrana Naroda*, which had access to a cache of 100,000 rifles and 10,000 machine guns, together with a sabotage section in charge of regular army officers. Much of it fell into the hands of the Gestapo, and the training of agents on Czech soil became virtually impossible.

Practical aid for the project to kill Heydrich was sought by Moravec from the Special Operations Executive (SOE), which had been established in 1940 to encourage, direct and supply Resistance groups in Nazi-occupied countries. Ten young men, all bachelors, were chosen for fierce, concentrated training in parachuting, surveillance, sabotage, firearm deployment and, above all, survival. For the actual task of killing Heydrich, codenamed 'Anthropoid', Moravec chose Warrant Officer Jan Kubis, a Moravian countryman, and Warrant Officer Josef Gabcik, a half-Slovak locksmith. Both were orphans in their late twenties and both were told frankly that, once their mission had been complete, their chances of survival would be slim. The pair had the assistance of Warrant Officer Josef Valcik, a member of another group, termed 'Silver A', which had been equipped with a strong transmitter for an intelligence role. As was so often the case with operations involving parachuting, a number of the subsequent landings were in different areas than those originally planned. The Gestapo picked up a number of agents and subsequently shot them.

The survivors, lodging in a series of previously designated safe houses, began shadowing the movements of the Reich Protector. For Gabcik and

Kubis, neither of whom had been to Prague before, the preparations for their task had been meticulous. The possibility of wrecking Heydrich's special train between Prague and the Czech border had been rejected because his travel patterns were found to be too irregular. It was clear that the attempt would have to be made on Heydrich's commuter route between his house and his Prague office. Moravec had traced out this route, pointing out a sharp bend at V Holesovice street leading down to the Trója bridge. At the bend was a slope by a tram stop; any car would be obliged to slow down there.

One of Heydrich's habits stood out. Although he was heavily guarded at the Çernín Palace and within the confines of his estate, he frequently dispensed with cover elsewhere, routinely travelling in his unescorted, 3.5-litre Mercedes open convertible, trusting in his driver, the bulky *Oberscharführer* Klein, and the pistols both men carried. Nor was the car reinforced with protective armour plating, as was the case with all vehicles used by the other Nazi leaders. Hitler frequently expressed his disapproval at Heydrich's cavalier attitude, but he paid no attention. Moravec's agents reported that Heydrich even declined the basic precaution of varying his route or ever changing his car with its highly distinctive number plate, SS-3. He also insisted on sporting two pennants on the mudguard – the SS flag and that of the Reich Protector. It was concluded that, in sublime arrogance, Heydrich simply refused to believe that anyone, given the repercussions, would dare to attack him.

Above: Jan Kubis, son of a Moravian peasant family, had served as a sergeant in the Czech army. He was one of the leading members of the 'Anthropoid' team, and it was his bomb that killed Heydrich. To evade capture, he took poison.

HEYDRICH ASSASSINATED

On the morning of 27 May 1942, Heydrich packed off his escort early, dawdled a while with his wife and children, and, ahead of leaving for Berlin, set off for his office, as usual sitting beside Klein in the Mercedes. At the agreed spot, Gabcik stood armed with his automatic weapon, Kubis with a specially designed bomb. Both men's nerves were jangling because the car was running late. Then at 10.32 Josef Valcik gave an agreed signal with a mirror as the Mercedes slowed down for the hairpin bend. A lone man standing on the pavement shifted his newspaper from one armpit to another: another signal. Kubis was momentarily distracted by the unexpected sound of a tram, which was likely to reach the corner at the same instant as the Protector's car. Withdrawal was impossible. Gabcik had already taken out his British-made Sten, taking aim as the Mercedes drew level. Kubis shouted 'Now' and Gabcik squeezed the trigger. To the horror of both men, the Sten malfunctioned.

Right: Kubis's bomb, which had been specially designed by SOE explosives experts, blasted a hole in Heydrich's car. The vehicle had none of the protective armour plating which characterized those used by other senior Nazis.

By then Heydrich had spotted his would-be assassin. If he had ordered Klein to speed off he would undoubtedly have saved his life. But his innate sense of self-preservation for once deserted him and he made two fatal mistakes: he not only shouted to Klein to stop, but stood up in the convertible as well, making a perfect target. As the car screamed to a halt Kubis lobbed his bomb at the nearside front panel, but the bomb fell short. Witnesses aboard the tram later testified that there was an enormous flash as the explosion from the bomb shattered the windows. Heydrich ran from the shattered car, firing as he went. Kubis, too, was running, catching a glimpse of his victim before darting between two tramcars and mounting the bicycle that had been placed earlier for speedy departure. He snaked away downhill, leaving Gabcik to run for freedom past the small group of people who had inevitably gathered. Then Heydrich was standing still, as if mesmerized, before his hand strayed to his right hip and he crawled back to the Mercedes. Klein, because of his ample bulk, had not been able to move fast enough in his pursuit of Gabcik, who was able to wing him before making off. Heydrich, an ominous dark stain spreading across his uniform, stood reeling. A blonde woman in the crowd recognized him and took charge, flagging down a cart carrying floor polish and ordering the reluctant driver to rush Heydrich to hospital. He managed to crawl out of the cab in a frenzy of agony and staggered round to the back, where he crashed to the floor.

As soon as the cart moved off, the spectators melted away apart from a few stragglers. First to reach the scene was a platoon of German infantrymen who had been on a field exercise. Before them was the wrecked Mercedes and, by it, the unfortunate Klein, incoherent with fear, babbling about the Protector being shot. A swift call by a doctor to the office of Karl-Hermann

Frank sent the SS racing both to the scene of the ambush and to the Bulowka Hospital. At the scene, Heinz von Pannwitz, head of the anti-sabotage section of the Gestapo, took charge. His men found a woman's bicycle, a man's cap, a light-coloured mackintosh, a Sten gun and some empty cartridge cases. There were also two briefcases, one of which contained a fused bomb, promptly identified as British.

At the hospital, patients were bundled out of their wards so that Heydrich could have a completely isolated room, plus accommodation for assorted SS and Gestapo. Preliminary investigation of the patient revealed lumps of wire, felt, leather and glass, all firmly embedded in spleen and liver. Serious though his condition was, the Nazi propaganda machine was soon issuing optimistic statements about the condition of Heydrich being 'promising' and 'responding to treatment'.

In Berlin, the one man who should have taken charge proved a total liability. Himmler, not unusual in times of crisis, was reduced to a state of first mental paralysis and then panic. Instead of allowing the Bulowka to carry on with the treatment, he contacted leading doctors and surgeons all over the Reich and the occupied countries, ordering them to rush to Prague. Heydrich clung to life for a week, but his condition weakened. Finally on

Below: Hitler, overcome with emotion, spoke only briefly at Heydrich's lying-in-state, preparatory to the body being taken in full pomp to the Invaliden cemetery in Berlin.

4 June 1942, following a final meeting with Himmler, he died. An anonymous hospital clerk wrote tersely in the register alongside the name of Reinhard Tristan Eugen Heydrich: 'Cause of death: wound infection'.

With Reich newsreel cameras in full attendance, Heydrich lay in state for two days. Draped in swastikas, the coffin was then conveyed across the Charles Bridge and taken to Berlin, first to RSHA headquarters and from there to the Reich Chancellery and its ultimate destination – the Invaliden Cemetery. *The Times* in London commented that one of the most dangerous men in the Third Reich had been given 'a gangster's funeral'.

REPRISALS

Immediately after the assassination, the Gestapo made more than 13,000 arrests, with some 600 executed for illegal possession of weapons. Death was decreed for those who expressed even the mildest criticism of the regime. The most notorious reprisal action (*Vergeltungsaktion*) was the destruction of the village of Lidice, northwest of Prague. The pretext given by Frank was that the villagers had assisted the parachutists. Every male inhabitant was killed in a massacre that stretched over 10 hours. The women were sent to Ravensbrück concentration camp. Except for a few whose appearance made them 'racially desirable', the children were deported to die in the gas chambers.

Below: The destruction of the village of Lidice, lying northwest of Prague, was in response to a demand from Hitler to show the Czechs and the rest of occupied Europe the consequences of defying German rule.

Fifteen days later another village, Lezaky, was torched. The village had concealed the radio transmitter of a member of the parachute group 'Silver A', who had taken refuge there and was later tracked down and killed. Nine houses surrounding a mill were encircled and the inhabitants driven out. All the adults were shot and 13 children transported first to Prague, where they were lodged with the surviving minors from Lidice. They were then sent to the concentration camp at Chelmno in Poland.

By now the assassins were activating the first of their escape plans. This was to make for Resslova Street across the river in the New Town, where a pastor gave them sanctuary in the crypt of the Greek Orthodox church of Sts Cyril and Methodios. It was an axiom among the intelligence chiefs of SOE that every group of agents carrying out an assignment ran the severe risk of containing at least one weak link. 'Anthropoid' proved no exception. Following the assassination bid and in the face of the inevitable manhunt, Sergeant Karel Curda of the 'Out Distance' group had broken one of the most important instructions they had all been given: they were forbidden to take refuge with families or friends because this ran the risk of betrayal. Curda, his nerves shattered by the extent of German reprisals, had made for his home in southern Bohemia, only too conscious that the Gestapo would surely trace him. Eventually he cracked and made for Gestapo headquarters in Prague to confess his link and, incidentally, claim the million crowns reward that had been offered. He paid dearly for his treachery. At first he

Above: After most of the women and small children had been taken away by a Sipo squad on 10 June 1942, Lidice village was burnt and an extermination squad shot 199 men and boys over the age of 15.

111

LIDICE

Although at his trial in 1945 Karl-Hermann Frank was condemned for giving the order for the destruction of Lidice and was subsequently hanged in public with relatives of the victims in attendance, the original idea came from Karl Böhme, head of the SD in Bohemia-Moravia, who was based in the industrial town of Kladno. The area, some 16 km (10 miles) northeast of Prague, was a spot favoured by parachutists and as such was under constant surveillance by the Gestapo. As for the village, it consisted of some 500 inhabitants, many of whom went to work daily in Kladno and had little interest in politics. Although there was no direct evidence, Böhme was convinced that the village was involved. On 28 May 1942, the black-uniformed SS and Gestapo, brandishing typewritten lists of names, cordoned it off and began their search, arresting eight men and seven women from the Stribny and Horak families, none of whom was ever seen again. The Germans then drove off, leaving the inhabitants to hope that the enemy had finished with them. But Böhme had no intention of leaving the matter there.

On the evening of 9 June, a squad of security police under *SS-Hauptsturmführer* Max Rostock returned to Lidice. What happened next was told to this author by Miloslava Kalibová, who was raised in Lidice, on the fiftieth anniversary of the massacre: 'The whole village was deafened by the roar of *Wehrmacht* trucks filled with military police. Lidice was sealed and roadblocks set up. The noise and arrests went on all night. They took away my father, Jaroslav, and my uncle Antonín and shot them both. Antonín's wife perished in Ravensbrück. We women were driven in our nightclothes into the main street. By then the village was a shambles, the houses gutted, the streets strewn with what was left of our possessions. We were told to collect a few things and some food supplies to last three days.'

Rostock marched the men, almost 200 in total, to the Horak farm, where mattresses were placed against the wall of the barn to prevent ricochets. There they were lined up for execution in groups of 10. As each group was shot, the bodies were left where they were and the next was lined up. Much of the activity was caught by the cameras of the *Schutzpolizei*, the film of which survived to become evidence at the Nuremberg trial. Some of the footage is still shown in the museum at Lidice.

The greatest lie was told to the women, who were informed on their arrival in the secondary school at Kladno that the children were going ahead in buses to a camp where they would await their families. In fact, 82 of the children went to the gas chambers. A few, considered worthy of Aryanization, were sent to foster homes. Miloslava Kalibová recalled seeing mothers giving up their children, some them pleading, 'Mummy, if you love me you cannot give me up.' 'In Ravensbrück we assembled in front of the camp hospital. A window opened and a voice asked us in Czech, "Where are you from?" "From Lidice. Are our children here?" "No, there are no children here whatsoever. This is a concentration camp."'

The village itself was systematically destroyed, carrying out Hitler's demand that no trace of Lidice should remain. It was burned, dynamited and rendered flat. Even its name was removed from the land registers. The community of Lidice may have been eliminated, but its name had not. News of the destruction soon spread. Villages in a number of countries took the name of Lidice, and many babies were named after it. On the third anniversary of the killings, some 140 women gathered in commemoration. Eventually 17 children were found and reunited with their mothers after a two-year search. In 1948, work began on building the first houses. The old site is preserved as a memorial and includes the common grave of the men of the village who were shot.

confined himself to betraying the names of Gabcik and Kubis, but his Gestapo interrogators were convinced he knew more. After beatings, they coaxed from him the whereabouts of the Moravec family (no relation to Frantisek Moravec). This married couple and their 21-year-old son Ata were active members of the Resistance and confederates of those responsible for 'Anthropoid'.

It was four in the morning when the black saloons screeched to a halt in Bishop's Road in the district of Zizkov. Gestapo inspector Oskar Fleischer led the rush to the front door of the Moravec apartment. Dragged into the corridor, the family was ordered to face the wall with their hands above their heads. Fleischer's men then set about the rooms, spilling out the contents of wardrobes and cupboards. When the interrogations began each member of the family knew it was only a matter time before torture would be used. As casually as possible, Mrs Moravec asked to go the lavatory, a request that was abruptly refused. When she pleaded again after an interval, a guard relented and accompanied her. As she walked ahead of him, she played casually with the medallion on her necklace. It was the work of a moment to extract a small poison pill and clamp it to her mouth. She fell to the floor, froth forming on either side of her mouth. All attempts at resuscitation were useless. Still in their pyjamas, Moravec and Ata were dragged to Gestapo headquarters. Fleischer reasoned that pressure on Ata, who had frequently acted as a courier for the Resistance, would prove the most productive action.

Above: In the museum, which is part of the new village of Lidice built after the war, is a tableau featuring photographs of victims either summarily shot or deported.

Above: Heydrich's assassins were cornered in the Prague church of Sts Cyril and Methodios and penetrated by an SS detachment on the orders of Karl-Hermann Frank (second from the right). Afterwards, the bodies were dragged from the church.

Relays of Gestapo thugs used fisticuffs, threats and bullying to break him, even ramming alcohol down his throat. He was also dragged to view his mother's body at all hours of day and night until eventually he became conditioned to tell the Gestapo everything he knew – including the hiding place at Sts Cyril and Methodios.

THE ASSASSINS ARE CORNERED

Nineteen officers, 740 NCOs and men were issued with guns and grenades and detailed to flush out the assassins and five others holed up in the church. Von Pannwitz, who was in command, was keen that all should be taken alive and interrogated. The area was encircled; von Pannwitz himself approached the church building, rang the bell and was admitted by a sleepy sexton. Weapons at the ready, his party edged towards the altar. In the prolonged battle that followed, those hidden in the upper nave and the crypt, although heavily outnumbered, refused to surrender, despite being urged by a handcuffed Karel Curda to 'Give up, lads. You'll come to no harm.' Tear gas bombs were lobbed in. When that seemed to have no effect, von Pannwitz summoned the fire brigade to flood the crypt using hoses thrust through a grille above a narrow ventilation shaft. Despite the rising water, SS troops were ordered to descend and pick out whom they could. The Czechs responded by shooting many of them down. Karl-Hermann Frank, growing impatient, ordered the siege of the church to be speeded up and, overruling von Pannwitz, sent in his own SS combat detachment.

The Czechs fought to the last or turned the weapons on themselves; two of them took poison. No one surrendered. In the ensuing silence, an SS party was detailed to make its way gingerly into the crypt. There was no answering fire. Soon came the shout: '*Fertig*' ('Finished'). The bloody, battered corpses were laid outside the church, Gabcik among them. Kubis had taken poison and was rushed to hospital where he lost consciousness and died. Identification of the other bodies was by the handcuffed Curda, who can clearly be seen in surviving photographs.

REPRESSION IN FRANCE

Elsewhere fortune was not smiling on the Germans. Previously unthinkable military reverses had begun to dog them in 1942 on the Eastern Front, where the *Wehrmacht* had lost more than a million men. Himmler required fresh recruits not just for the *Waffen-SS*, but also for the SD and Gestapo, who had to contend with a resurgence by underground forces. In France, the search for fresh manpower was the responsibility of *Gruppenführer* Karl Albrecht Oberg, who was based in Paris at 57 Boulevard Lannes.

He made overtures to the pro-Nazi representatives of Pétain's Vichy government, which nominally controlled the so-called Free Zone of France in the south. This was occupied in November 1942 after the Allied invasion of the Vichy territories in North Africa. The Gestapo swarmed into Vichy, launching a widespread dragnet for clandestine radio transmitters. Resistance cells were closed down in Lyon, Marseilles and Toulouse. *SS-Hauptsturmführer* Hugo Geissler, with his Gestapo headquarters at Vichy, was in charge of the *Einsatzkommando* that was soon installed in every capital of the military regions, notably Limoges, Lyon, Marseilles, Montpellier and Toulouse.

Combat, the largest and most effective of the non-Communist Resistance movements, did not hesitate to make life uncomfortable for those whose opposition was seen as lukewarm. Its power base was the University of Strasbourg, which had moved to Clermont-Ferrand in the Auvergne region and shared facilities with the city's own university. With the presence of students and faculty, the area became a powerful centre of dissent, from which Combat sent out letters, signed 'Centre Regional de Combat', ordering local shops and the proprietors of news-stands to cease displaying collaborationist publications. Refusal invited a quick response: bombs were set off in the homes and offices of suspected collaborators; tear-gas canisters disrupted meetings where speakers had the blessings of the Germans.

Arrests were inevitable as the Germans fought back. The most hated and feared man in Clermont-Ferrand was local Gestapo chief, Paul Blumenkamp, whose headquarters were in the Avenue de Royat. His colleagues included Ursula Brandt, known as 'the Panther' on account of the favourite fur coat she wore constantly, even during interrogations, beatings and tortures. One of the Gestapo's greatest coups came in the summer of 1943 when Hugo Geissler seized two agents in possession of weapons and radio equipment. Further arrests among members of ORA (*Organisation de la Résistance Armée*), one of the smaller Resistance groups, pointed to a cell within the university. On 25 November, all SD and Gestapo manpower was marshalled for an assault on the main campus in order to seize the files of leading academics. The SS detail, led by Georges Mathieu, a Vichyite who had thrown in his lot with the Germans, found its way barred by one of the professors, Paul Collomp, who promptly fell to a bullet. Further shots winged another of the staff.

> Combat, the most effective of the non-Communist Resistance groups, did not hesitate to make life uncomfortable for those whose opposition was seen as lukewarm.

Two students were wounded attempting to escape, while 15-year-old Louis Blanchet dropped from a window, only to fall victim to fire from German troops who had surrounded the buildings. Scores of students and members of faculty were arrested, and a total of 86 were deported to German concentration camps. By the end of the war, it was reckoned that more than 2000 were either executed within the regional *département* of Clermont-Ferrand or deported, with further incidents of torture and rape.

Gestapo rule in France remained absolute until the Allied landings on the coast of Normandy in June 1944. Paris was the centre of a web comprising some 130 separate Gestapo offices. In addition, there were the separate networks of the *Abwehr* and the *Geheime Feldpolizei*.

Himmler's obsession for gaining more power remained. By August 1943, he was Minister of the Interior and Public Health, supreme police authority in Germany and controller of the concentration camps throughout occupied Europe, while nursing a further ambition to gain an army command. His underlings, however, were stuck with the jobs they had, many of them plagued by the steadily growing forces of resistance.

In Paris, *Sturmbannführer* Horst Laube was approached by Oberg to head a department, designated Section II Pol, with the specific remit of surveying the most vexatious elements of French Resistance. Chief among these was an elite unit of guerrilla fighters or partisans known as the Maquis, a name derived from the brushland of Corsica where outlaws concealed themselves. When it came to ruthlessness, there were occasions when the Maquis could be the equal of the Germans: collaborators who were seized were often

Right: This sequence of photographs shows the execution of a French Resistance fighter. These scenes were repeated numerous times across occupied Europe.

summarily executed. Families who housed traitors within their ranks or who turned a blind eye to them received the broadest of hints from the Maquis – specially made miniature coffins were thrust through letterboxes. Resistance supporters within the SD and Gestapo also presented problems. Individuals were subjected to security checks, while all transfers, changes of station and promotions were closely monitored.

OPERATIONS IN NORWAY

Resistance movements in all the countries under occupation came to rely increasingly on the resources of the SOE, the members of which had received the memorable instruction from Winston Churchill to 'set Europe ablaze'. The Norwegians, who had been invaded by the Nazis on 9 April 1940 without declaring war, especially welcomed the resources of SOE. As far as the British were concerned, the Norwegians offered excellent material for resistance. A government-in-exile was established in London, while there was an outraged and resentful population at home. During the early stages of the German incursion, young Norwegians intent on becoming agents had arrived in England after braving the perils of the North Sea in an assortment of fishing smacks and private boats, under the noses of the Germans. From their ranks evolved a hard-trained force of subversives: 49 SOE agents had been landed back in Norway from fishing boats by 1942, together with 154 tons of arms and equipment. But 1942 was also a year of crisis. Pro-Nazi forces had penetrated deeply within the Norwegian Resistance, enabling the

Right: The Gestapo used a variety of torture methods when carrying out interrogations. Suspension from the feet was a speciality of the Paris Gestapo. After some 10 to 15 minutes in this position, loss of consciousness followed. The victim was then revived and, if information were not forthcoming, the process was repeated.

GEHEIME FELDPOLIZEI

The uniformed *Geheime Feldpolizei*, (GFP, 'Secret Field Police') originated in the months following the Nazis coming to power. They were originally members of the *Reichssicherheitsdienst* (RSD), an organization responsible solely for the protection of Adolf Hitler and other members of the hierarchy of the Third Reich. The RSD was the forerunner of the later *Reichsicherheitshauptamt* (RSHA), which was set up to bring into a single organization the State Security Police (Sipo and Gestapo).

Heinrich Himmler, however, was determined that the RSD should operate throughout the Reich and laid down what he saw as the essential credentials for members. They were required to be 'tried and tested National Socialists, and furthermore excellent criminal police officers of unconditional reliability, utmost conscientiousness in fulfilment of duties, good manners and physical dexterity'. The tasks of the RSD included Hitler's personal security and investigation of possible assassination bids. The RSD could also request assistance from other organizations and gained the right to take over all local police in circumstances requiring Hitler's personal protection.

Officers of the RSD were sworn in by Himmler and in Hitler's presence. All took the *Wehrmacht* oath until 1936, when it was changed to the oath of the SS. In May 1937, all RSD personnel were made SS members, provided they could prove Aryan blood to Himmler's satisfaction. There was considerable conflict between the SS and the *Wehrmacht* when it came to guarding Hitler in wartime conditions, with the *Wehrmacht* insisting that RSD officers should be designated *Wehrmacht* members. They were then given secret military police status and titled *Reichssicherheitsdienst Gruppe Geheime Feldpolizei*. Their power was considerable; they could 'request' help from any section of the police apparatus and could don the uniform of any of its branches.

The GFP was particularly active against Greek partisans in June 1944. In one characteristic incident while escaping from an ambush by guerrillas outside the village of Distomo, the GFP contingent unleashed 'atonement action' which included rape, looting and summary executions of locals. A Red Cross delegation that managed to reach Distimo subsequently encountered corpses dangling from trees.

In the post-war Nuremberg International Military Tribunal proceedings, the *Geheime Feldpolizei* was adjudged not to have been a criminal organization as defined 'within the charge of criminality contained in the Indictment'. The tribunal did, however, determine that GFP personnel committed both war crimes and crimes against humanity 'on a wide scale'. However, no senior GFP officials were ever prosecuted.

Germans to swoop on fishing vessels minutes before they set out from Ålesund. It subsequently transpired that information had been passed to the Nazis by Henry Oliver Rinnan, one of about 60 informers belonging to the so-called *Sonderabteilung Lola* cell of the Gestapo. Rinnan set an incredible record by handing over a thousand of his fellow countrymen to the Germans, hundreds of whom were killed or tortured. Captured after the war, he was found guilty on 13 counts of murder and sentenced to death.

It was also the turn of the Resistance group known as Milorg to suffer another of Norway's reverses. The scene was Televåg, a small fishing village on the island of Sotra, near Bergen, which was regarded as an ideal location because it was one of the nearest points to the Shetland Islands and had a staunchly pro-British population. Among these, however, were informers under the control of the local police chief, who was a known member of the *Nasjonal Samling* party headed by the notorious Vidkun Quisling, a failed pre-war politician who had formed his own government in Norway based on a pro-German, anti-British platform. The SD, under the ultimate control of Norway's *Reichskommisar* Joseph Terboven, closed in on the barn of the local Milorg leader's farmhouse, which was known to contain weapons, ammunition and radio sets. Two officers were killed by one of two Norwegian agents of SOE. In reply the Germans killed one of them, while the other was dragged away for questioning, along with the Milorg leader. Both were executed. All this was followed by vicious reprisals against Televåg itself, with 300 houses burnt to the ground and cattle killed. Almost the entire male population was deported, the rest interned.

> Norwegian Oliver Rinnan set an incredible record by handing over a thousand of his fellow countrymen to the Germans, hundreds of whom were killed or tortured.

Eighteen men from Ålesund, chosen at random, were arrested and under torture gasped out the names of Milorg leaders. During May and June, these revelations led the Gestapo to the main cells of the movement in Bergen, Stavanger, Oslo, Drammen and Kongsberg. Those whose lives were spared and who managed to escape to England testified to the government-in-exile what happened to their comrades who had been taken to the Gestapo headquarters in Oslo at 19 Møllergata. One witness told of a fellow prisoner 'taken down into the basement after having denied that he had been engaged in espionage. Here he was burned with a soldering iron on a couple of less sensitive points on the inside of the hand. Afterwards it was explained to him how much more painful it would be to be burnt in a more sensitive place. As he still refused to confess, he was first burnt on the inside of one of his wrists, and then burnt with the same iron on the other side of the artery.'

Gestapo units had then switched to the north, carrying out hundreds of arrests around Kristiansund, followed by mass shootings. Success for the Resistance in Norway was to be a long time coming.

DANISH TRIUMPHS

In Denmark, the Gestapo chief was *SS-Obergruppenführer* Karl Heinz Hoffmann. Serving with him were Gunther Panks and Otto Bovensiepen, who was a protégé of Ernst Kaltenbrunner, who became Heydrich's successor as head of the RSHA. Until the arrival of Hoffmann, Denmark had been able to maintain a degree of independence, remaining relatively prosperous owing to its self-sufficiency in food and increased agricultural exports to Germany. The 8000-strong Jewish community offered no threat to the occupiers, but predictably this cut little ice with Himmler or, especially, Eichmann, who activated his own *Sonderkommando* and sent one of his most trusted subordinates, Rolf Gunther, to Copenhagen to arrange for the deportation of the Danish Jews. An outbreak of strikes and increased activity by the Danish underground was seized on as a pretext. The sweep began overnight on 1–2 October 1943, the Friday night and Saturday of the Jewish Sabbath. To the frustration of Werner Best, who had been the first legal adviser to the SD and Gestapo, and was now Plenipotentiary to Denmark, the dragnet was only a partial success. A mere 472 Jews were found; most of the rest were saved through the swift action of Georg Duckwitz, one of Best's closest aides and a sympathizer with the Danes who had tipped off the Resistance. Fishing vessels had been mustered hastily and the Jews ferried to neutral Sweden.

The dying months of the war saw two triumphs for the Danish underground, one accompanied by tragedy. On the last day of October 1944, the Royal Air Force, with the help of SOE, mounted a successful attack on the Gestapo centre at Århus. The other target, nearly five months later, was the Shellhus in the centre of Copenhagen, which had been used by the

Below: Despite the approaching end of the war, the Gestapo hold on Denmark remained firm, and a decision was taken to immobilize the still active headquarters at Aarhus. This was housed in two buildings adjoining the university, which were attacked with pinpoint accuracy by Mosquito bombers of the British Royal Air Force.

Right: Two female partisan radio operators receive instructions from Red Army commanders in Belarus in 1944. Soviet partisans flourished from the start of the German invasion of 1941, quickly forming behind the Germans' swift advance. By the summer of 1942, many partisan groups numbered more than 1000 men and women. As the Germans retreated, partisans stepped up their activities, and by the end of the war they were estimated to number some 200,000.

Gestapo as its headquarters since the previous spring. The decision to destroy the Shellhus came at a bad time for the Resistance. Many of its leaders had been rounded up and a worrying volume of incriminating material had been filed away within the building. By December, Resistance leaders had contacted SOE in London, but circumstances were such that a proposed raid could not be contemplated until the following March. In the meantime, the plight of the Resistance became still more serious and a desperate radio message was sent to London urging the attack.

At 8.55 a.m. on 21 March, 20 Mosquitoes escorted by 30 Mustang Mk IIIs took off from Norfolk. Over a lake in western Zealand, the aircraft broke into three waves for the attack. Impaired visibility made pinpointing the target impossible: it was later reckoned that only two of the aircraft succeeded in hitting the Shellhus. Other bombs fell on the French school nearby and killed 123 civilians, including 87 children. One of the Mosquitoes from the first wave, flying low, hit an electric pylon and crashed near the school. Those bombs that did hit the Gestapo building fulfilled their intended purpose as, by striking the lower storeys, a number of the Resistance who were in their cells or undergoing interrogation on the upper floors were spared. Apart from the destruction of the building and its contents, the raid had another benefit, described by M.R.D. Foot, one of the leading SOE historians: 'One escaping prisoner, feeling it a pity to leave empty-handed, picked up a card index at random as he passed. It turned out to contain a complete list of all the Danes who were co-operating with the Gestapo, and to provide the base for a run of treason trials which took place after the end of the war.'

RESISTANCE IN POLAND

If many of the Resistance groups in the west were slow to form and become effective, many in the east, following the occupation of their countries, were up and running from the start. Poland provides a striking example. On 1 November 1940, the first anniversary of the outbreak of war, Nazi celebratory parades were held throughout the country. Not a Pole or a Jew turned out to watch, and all places of entertainment remained empty. It was not until early evening that the crowds appeared and began their slow and silent procession towards cemeteries and patriotic monuments. In Warsaw, the Tomb of the Unknown Soldier was a mass of red and white flowers. Although a mild protest by any standards, it was enough to inflame the Gestapo, whose forces carried out mass arrests and house searches in the capital and in Lodz. Underground newspapers and presses were seized: in Warsaw, for example, reporters and some 200 other clandestine workers of the *Dziennik Polski* (*Polish Daily*) were rounded up and shot.

At the core of the Resistance was the *Armia Krajowa*, the Polish Home Army, commanded from 1943 by the legendary Count Tadeusz Komorowski, widely known by his underground code name 'Bor'. This highly organized group, with its sabotage cells and production of forged documents, became feared by both the Gestapo and members of the collaborationist Green Police. There were many instances where it was hard to distinguish between conqueror and conquered. Often acting under radioed instructions from the government-in-exile in London, assassinations of Gestapo figures and Polish sympathizers were carried out with ruthless efficiency. Lieutenant Roman Leon Swiecicki of the Green Police was a leading collaborator, presiding

Left: Himmler ordered an end to the ghetto Jews of Warsaw in 1943 to be completed by Hitler's birthday on 20 April. Under the direction of *SS-Brigadeführer* Jurgen Stroop, some 2000 *Waffen-SS*, supported by *Wehrmacht* personnel with 7000 men in reserve, moved into the ghetto. In a month's fighting, some 60,000 Jews died, with opposition persisting until June. Only 100 Jews survived.

123

OTTO OHLENDORF CONFESSES

Probably the most notorious member of the *Einsatzgruppen* to be brought to justice was *SS-Brigadeführer* Otto Ohlendorf, former head of *Amt III* of the RSHA. Towards the end of the war, he was a specialist in foreign trade at the Ministry of Economics, but earlier he had commanded *Einsatzgruppen D*, a personal appointment of Heinrich Himmler. It is estimated that during its time in the Ukraine, attached to the 11th Army, Ohlendorf's *Einsatzkommando* executed 90,000 Jews. At his trial, Ohlendorf described a typical killing: 'The *Einsatz* unit would enter a village or town and order the prominent Jewish citizens to call together all Jews for the purpose of "resettlement". They were requested to hand over their valuables and shortly before execution to surrender their outer clothing. They were transported to the place of execution, usually an anti-tank ditch, in trucks – always only as many as could be executed immediately. In this way it was attempted to keep the span of time from the moment in which the victims knew what was about to happen to them until the time of their actual execution as short as possible.

'Then they were shot, kneeling or standing, by firing squads in a military manner and the corpses thrown into a ditch. I never permitted the shooting by individuals, but ordered that several of the men should shoot at the same time in order to avoid direct personal responsibility. Other group leaders demanded that the victims lie down flat on the ground to be shot through the nape of the neck. I did not approve of these methods ... because both for them and for those who carried out the executions it was, psychologically, an immense burden to bear.'

In the spring of 1942, Himmler ordained a change in the method of executing women and children. Henceforth they were to be killed in specially constructed 'gas vans', which the victims were induced to enter after being told they were to be transported elsewhere. According to a constructor of the vans, the change to gassing had a psychological effect on the Gestapo and SD men who were required to unload the bodies. Furthermore, their claims to suffer severe headaches slowed down the mechanics of execution. Ohlendorf testified that the vans could despatch only 15 to 25 persons at a time. As for adult male victims of the shooting squads, these included, it was claimed, 16,200 inhabitants of the Minsk ghetto who were mown down in one day.

Ohlendorf's judges at Nuremberg described him as a 'Jekyll and Hyde' figure whose actions suspended all belief. On 10 April 1948, he was sentenced to death along with 13 others. Of this group, four (Ohlendorf and three other group commanders) were executed on 8 June 1951.

over hastily convened courts that were little more than rubber stamps and the sole authority of which was to hand out death sentences. Home Army members carried out a thorough surveillance of Swiecicki's daily movements, concentrating on the journey from his Warsaw apartment to his office. One morning, as he stood at a tram stop, two men behind him waited until the tram approached before emptying their weapons into their target and melting into the crowds of commuters.

After every such assassination a set pattern was followed. Large placards and posters were printed and placed throughout Warsaw, or wherever the Home Army retaliation had been carried out, beginning with the words 'In the name of the Polish republic' and signed by the 'Directorate of the Polish Resistance'. In the case of Swiecicki, it was stated that a court had found him guilty of 'special crimes' and sentenced him to death. There was also a reference to the violation of laws instituted by the pre-war Polish government. The message was clear: the Home Army would not scruple to use measures that were a mirror image of those employed by the Germans. Traitors were executed without compunction or compassion. One dedicated Resistance member named Wojnowski (code name 'Motor') had made the cardinal error of telling his mother in Warsaw where she could get in touch with him. This gave the Gestapo a bargaining counter they could use to twist her son. Suspicious when it was singled out for a spate of attacks, his Resistance cell fastened on Wojnowski as a double agent. He was tried and shot.

The Home Army, via its courier and radio contacts, persuaded the BBC in London to broadcast news of Resistance executions throughout Poland. Critics argued, however, that such measures only encouraged reprisals against the civilian population. Indeed, Governor General Hans Frank instituted a system of *Standgerichte* ('exceptional tribunals') composed exclusively of Gestapo members, declaring: 'The exceptional tribunals of the security police must be composed of a *Führer-SS* from the security police and the SD and two other members of the same service.' Furthermore, the resulting executions were to be carried out 'on the spot'. This could only point to one conclusion: the process of annihilation was to be stepped up. By 1943, under Himmler's direction, the Gestapo had 60,000 agents throughout Poland, backed by half a million soldiers. The Home Army could not survive effectively on its own; links with the government-in-exile became even closer. Poles who had been trained to kill in England were parachuted into Europe and, through the Resistance networks, found their way to Warsaw.

Poland, of course, was far from the only victim of the continuing Gestapo menace. More than 40,000 Resistance fighters were seized in France alone during 1943, and the figures continued to mount. By the summer of 1944, however, things were very different. Europe was no longer the domain of the Nazis alone. Their reign of cruelty still had a while to run, but by now there was an added dimension. The Gestapo was facing more than resistance in its vassal states. Other enemies were stirring, and they came from within.

Above: *SS-Brigadeführer* Otto Ohlendorf made no attempt during his trial at Nuremberg to hide his role in the *Einsatzgruppen*, describing his close involvement in the mass killings with clinical detachment.

CHAPTER 7

STAMPING OUT RESISTANCE

In 1944, Hitler's personal nemesis threatened, not just from the remorseless advance of the Soviet Red Army, but also from within the highest echelons of the Nazi regime.

A dmiral Wilhelm Canaris of the *Abwehr* conducted business from behind a scarred, battered desk in his shabby Berlin office, where staff and visitors were obliged to tread a much-holed carpet regularly fouled by two wire-haired dachshunds. Books and journals were scattered haphazardly and were liable to fall from rickety tables. The unimpressive room was strikingly matched by the man who occupied it. At 5 feet 3 inches tall, Canaris was white-haired, slight, frail and with an air of perpetual fatigue, but a friend had once warned the unwary: 'The Admiral may not look much, but he's as sharp as they come.' Those on their first visit were invariably shown a statuette of three bronze monkeys. These, their owner was keen to point out, symbolized the tenets of his profession – 'See all, hear all, say nothing.' For this was Germany's key military spy, the man who had served in naval intelligence during World War I aboard the light cruiser *Dresden* in a celebrated action off the Falkland Islands. When the ship was scuttled, Canaris had made his dangerous way through Argentina and back to Germany, dodging British controls with a false passport.

Although he remained in the navy for a while after the war, Canaris's devious nature, love of intrigue and facility with languages had led him back to intelligence. Initially he had greeted the rise of the Nazis as a new dawn. His work within the intelligence community eventually brought him to the attention of Hitler, who wanted Germany to mirror the achievements of

Left: The head of the *Abwehr*, Admiral Canaris, (right in picture) is seen here with Göbbels and Himmler. Canaris maintained an uneasy working relationship with the SS chief, who did not scruple to spy on the *Abwehr,* which he succeeded in destroying.

127

Above: A long-standing opponent of Hitler's war aims, General Ludwig Beck retained strong links with others who opposed the Nazis, most prominent among them being Admiral Canaris. His role in the 1944 Bomb Plot was largely as titular head; however, it was sufficient involvement to seal his fate.

the British secret service. Canaris's rise was accelerated. On 2 January 1935, at the age of 47, he had taken over as head of the *Abwehr*. A loner with a loveless marriage, he revelled in his work and was perpetually on the move, travelling in his souped-up staff car from one end of the Reich to the other, a seemingly loyal, unquestioning servant to his master. But there was another Canaris, the man who was known to have confided to a colleague that Hitler and his associates were all 'a gang of criminals'. He had also been sickened by the killing of Ernst Röhm, the brutal culling of the SA and the sordid machinations that had accompanied the Fritsch-Blomberg scandal. His dogged loyalty to 'the new Germany' on the one hand counterbalanced his increasing loathing of its methods on the other.

THE PLOT TAKES FORM

Canaris's choice of subordinates reflected his opinions and served to transform the centre of foreign intelligence into a tool for the destruction of the movement it was pledged to serve. Colonel Hans Oster, his chief of staff and deputy controller, was a dapper and arrogant Saxon aristocrat of the old school, whose manner was in sharp contrast to his introverted chief. A Christian of deep conviction, he did little to conceal his detestation of National Socialism and of Reinhard Heydrich's SD in particular. When an Austrian intelligence officer reported for duty at the *Abwehr* and greeted him with the normally obligatory raised right arm, Oster snapped, 'No Nazi salute here, please!'

With the declaration of war, and particularly as military disasters began to set in, Oster developed the moral conviction that Hitler had somehow to be removed from office. Sufficiently realistic to accept that this could only be achieved through cooperation within the army, he made a bid to attract likely sympathizers. There could scarcely have been a better choice than Ludwig Beck, who had served as *Chef des Truppenamtes* (Adjutant General) in the *Reichswehr* and then as Chief of the Army General Staff. This position gave its holder an important role in all crucial military decisions. Hitler's proposals to conquer Czechoslovakia, however, had stuck in Beck's throat, and he compiled a document to prove that a Czech incursion as a prelude to a wider war had no chance of success on tactical and logistical grounds – the army simply did not have the resources. His objections were brushed aside and he resigned as Chief of Staff on 18 August 1938.

Oster's next move was to contact Carl Friedrich Gördeler, the Mayor of Leipzig and a hard-nosed administrator whose talents Hitler had badly needed in the early days. At that time, Gördeler had been attracted to Hitler's successes in reasserting national pride, apparently curbing profiteering and cutting unemployment. His support was rewarded with the post of Price Commissioner and Controller of Foreign Exchange. Hitler had even facilitated Gördeler's travel by letting him share his Ju 52 transport aircraft. Heydrich's agents, however, did not share this favourable view of Gördeler. His refusal to join the party was suspicious enough, but two other incidents found their way into his SD file. As Mayor of Leipzig he had been obliged to tolerate Nazis on the council. In the spring of 1936, these reported to Berlin that there was a statue of Felix Mendelssohn opposite the Gewandhaus concert hall; as he had been a Jew, this could only be regarded as offensive to all National Socialists. Berlin ordered a delegation to confront Gördeler with a request for the statue's removal. The delegation was rejected by the volatile mayor with the words: 'When that statue goes, then so will I.' Their next move was to present him with a swastika flag, which they required him to fly from the town hall. His reaction was to eject the Nazis from the building and lock the doors. Leipzig municipal police surrounded the town hall in anticipation of a fight with storm troopers. Even so, the Nazis went ahead and dismantled the statue. Gördeler resigned as mayor. Conscious of the danger he faced from the Gestapo, he next sought a useful cover, taking a job as financial adviser to the Stuttgart firm of Robert Bosch, the owner of

Below: Artur Nebe (seen to the right of picture with Reinhard Heydrich) combined being head of the Kripo with acting as a valuable conduit of information on Gestapo movements to German resistants.

which was a covert anti-Nazi. The main advantage was that, under the guise of legitimate business travel, he was able to make visits to Britain and the United States, during which he took the opportunity of dropping discreet warnings about the perils that Germany presented.

At home, though, Gördeler's machinations became progressively more risky, not just for himself, but also for Oster and Beck. This was particularly so when he succeeded in attracting a mole within Prinz-Albrecht-Strasse itself. As head of the Kripo, Artur Nebe, who before 1933 had enjoyed a senior position as a specialist in criminology with the old Prussian police, was understandably cautious in the material he was willing to release. It was nonetheless of considerable value: the seemingly innocuous private houses he listed, scattered throughout Berlin, were in fact Gestapo sub-stations. Another useful aide for Gördeler was Hans Bernd Gisevius, the one-time lawyer in the Prussian Ministry of the Interior who had witnessed much of the Röhm purge and later chronicled the brutal treatment of Gregor Strasser. An early witness of the effects of the Nazi takeover and the resulting police procedural irregularities encouraged by the Gestapo, Gisevius had long been compiling dossiers and calling for action against those who in normal circumstances would have faced criminal courts. With a healthy interest in self-preservation, Gisevius moved from job to job, not staying long enough

WILHELM CANARIS

Wilhelm Canaris was Director of the *Abwehr* (in full *Amt Ausland Abwehr*), the counter-intelligence department of the High Command of the Armed Forces. A former naval admiral, he was one of the main leaders in the 1944 conspiracy against Hitler.

Canaris was born in Aplerbeck, near Dortmund, on 1 January 1887. After active service, including at the Battle of the Falklands, in 1915 and 1916 he carried out a secret mission in Spain for the German navy. From 1924 to 1928, he was active in naval affairs and in 1935 took control of the *Abwehr* in the Reich War Ministry. In 1938, he headed the foreign branch of the *Oberkommando der Wehrmacht* (OKW), the High Command of the armed forces.

He gradually became an opponent of National Socialism and of Hitler's policies. He joined the Resistance movement, but was always against any attempt to assassinate Hitler. In cooperation with

General Ludwig Beck, Chief of the Army General Staff from 1935 to 1938, Canaris organized Resistance cells. He maintained a social relationship with Reinhard Heydrich, chief of the Gestapo, while trying to protect his own men who opposed Hitler. Faced with strong criticism of the *Abwehr* as an effective espionage arm, Canaris slowly broke down under the strain of his divided loyalties and was dismissed from office in February 1944. He was arrested along with several associates after the failure of the July 1944 bomb plot against Hitler and was hanged in the Flossenbürg concentration camp on 9 April 1945.

General resistance to Hitler failed primarily because it never extended beyond a small circle of conspirators and came too late to be of much practical use. Outside support was lacking, as the Allies insisted on unconditional surrender. Various proposals to assassinate Hitler were stillborn.

in any single ministry for an incriminating dossier to be compiled. Nebe and Gisevius set about drawing up a list of SS and SD locations that could be seized in a bid to topple Hitler from power. It soon became clear to Gördeler that the aid of the army would be essential, particularly when it came to seizing such locations as the SS barracks at Lichterfelde, together with radio and press centres in the Berlin area.

One of the most serious problems for the conspirators was how to tap the most likely sources within the army, as many of its senior officers preferred to press on with their service duties while shunning anything they regarded as politics. A typical attitude was that of Franz Halder, who was chief of the General Staff from 1938 until 1942: 'In the dictionary of the Germany soldier the terms "treason" and "plot against the state" do not exist. Thus I was in the position of one who has a soldier's duty – but also a duty that I consider higher, the duty to the flag. This is the worst dilemma a soldier can be faced

Above: One of the Third Reich's most enigmatic figures, Wilhelm Canaris combined his avowed dedication as spymaster for the 'new Germany' with his detestation of Himmler and his SS, whom he described as 'a bunch of criminals'.

with.' As it turned out, there was an exception: the conspirators' choice within the army was Erwin von Witzleben, a hardened professional who had scaled the career ladder to reach the rank of Lieutenant General of *Wehrkreis* ('Defence District') *III* of Berlin. As he was immensely popular with the troops of 23rd Infantry Division, it was reasoned that they could be relied upon to follow him in any circumstances. Gisevius supplied a pen portrait of 'a refreshingly uncomplicated man … a typical frontline general with his heart in the right place. Probably not too well read and certainly not inclined towards the fine arts, he was nevertheless a man firmly rooted in the chivalrous traditions of the old Prussian corps officers. He liked country life and was a passionate hunter.' His presence proved invaluable. Conscious that Gisevius was probably a marked man and certainly in fear of the Gestapo, von Witzleben provided him with a private office next to his own that it was hoped would be free from Gestapo wire taps, airily telling his adjutant that the newcomer was 'a close relative arranging the von Witzleben papers'.

When it came to treachery and conceit, the scenario for a coup that emerged was so Byzantine as to be worthy of the Nazis themselves. The first stage was to let it be known that Himmler was planning to arrange for his SS to replace the *Wehrmacht*. Von Witzleben and his followers were to take Hitler and Göring into protective custody on the pretext that Himmler's plans would place them in the gravest danger, after which Himmler and Heydrich

Above: Henning von Tresckow, another avowed opponent of the SS and Gestapo, was involved in a number of attempts on Hitler's life, most notably the Smolensk plot. While serving on the Eastern Front, he learnt of the failure of the July Bomb Plot and killed himself.

would be arrested on charges of treason. In such circumstances, *Wehrmacht* units outside Berlin would then be called upon to contain the remnants of the SS who had supported Himmler's alleged 'coup'. Once the *Wehrmacht* was in control, the true reasons for the takeover would then dramatically be revealed.

All the plans, however, were thrown by the announcement of the impending invasion of Czechoslovakia and the intention of the British Prime Minister, Neville Chamberlain, to fly to Germany 'to seek an accommodation' with Hitler. The news, flashed to every country in Europe, was greeted with relief by the bulk of Germans, who had little stomach for war. The conspirators sensed that the mood within the country had changed. If Hitler backed down, the whole impetus and support for a revolt would probably vanish. Following Hitler's meetings with Chamberlain at Berchtesgaden, Bad Godesberg and Munich, the *Führer* secured all he had demanded of the Czechs without firing a shot.

At von Witzleben's house, the conspirators tossed their secret plans into the fire. Only Oster retained his three-page, hand-written draft, which in a grievous blunder was locked away in the *Abwehr* office safe. As had been feared, when it became clear that there was a sporting chance of Hitler securing early victories in the west, the less single-minded of previous supporters lost interest and melted away. Originally it had been intended that Hitler should be arrested and put on trial, but by early 1943, as the war ground on and setbacks and casualties on the Eastern Front became more serious, it was becoming clear that Hitler was driving the country to annihilation. It was now time to think the hitherto unthinkable: there was no alternative to assassination.

OPERATION FLASH

The first significant attempt was termed *Smolensk Attent* (also called Operation Flash), plans for which were laid during January and February. It depended for its success on the work of a new group of conspirators who had joined in the wake of the reverses in Russia. Among these were General Friedrich Olbricht, chief of the *Allgemeines Heeresamt* ('General Army Office'), General Henning von Tresckow, serving with Army Group Centre with headquarters in Smolensk, and Fabian von Schlabrendorff, a junior officer on von Tresckow's staff. Canaris, aware of what was in the wind, remained personally aloof, but flew in two of his men, Hans von Dohnanyi and General Erwin Lahousen, ostensibly for a conference of *Wehrmacht* officers. At Smolensk, the conspirators met and evolved a plan to lure Hitler there and arrange his death. This would serve as the prelude to a rising in Berlin.

Hitler, who by this time was intensely suspicious of all his generals, was reluctant to leave his headquarters – the so-called *Wolfsschanze* ('Wolf's Lair') – near Rastenburg (now Ketrzyn). After a number of cancellations, however, he was persuaded to come to Smolensk on 13 March 1943. An attempt to draw Field Marshal Günther von Kluge, the commander of Army Group Centre, into the conspiracy failed; it was all down to von Tresckow and von Schlabrendorff, aided by Lahousen, who had brought along some bombs supplied by the *Abwehr*. The German explosives proved useless because their fuses emitted a low hissing that would betray their presence. Instead, British bombs, of a type that had been dropped by the RAF to Allied agents, seemed ideal, and it was intended to plant these in Hitler's aircraft during the return flight. It struck von Schlabrendorff that, when wrapped, two explosive packets placed in a single canister had a close resemblance to two brandy bottles. On the pretext of sending some liquor requested by a colleague at Rastenburg, General Helmuth Stieff, he managed to have the seemingly innocent packet placed aboard Hitler's aircraft.

> Forever indecisive, von Kluge, although he said he might join the conspiracy, relapsed into compliant obedience to Hitler.

The four-engined Focke-Wulf Condor had flown the *Führer* on a tour of the Russian front. This had taken him to Field Marshal Erich von Manstein's Ukraine headquarters, then on to Vinnytsya, followed by a return to von Manstein to offer congratulations on the destruction of a single Russian corps. On the flight to Smolensk, Hitler seemed tireless and conferred volubly with General Alfred Jodl, his operations chief of OKW. In the hold of the Condor the slow-burning fuse was working towards the wrapped canister. In a matter of minutes the firing pin would be released, crashing into the detonator and tearing the aircraft apart. The crash, according to von Schlabrendorff's post-war published account, should have happened shortly after leaving Minsk, some 30 minutes' flying time from Smolensk. It was reasoned that, once the attempt had succeeded, word would come from one of the escorting Messerschmitt 109s. As it was, a message was received only after the conspirators had passed an agonizing hour – the Condor, it reported, had landed safely at Rastenburg.

Von Schlabrendorff recalled: 'We were stunned, and could not imagine the cause of the failure. I immediately rang up Berlin and gave the code word

Above: Although the
Focke-Wulf Condor
containing the bomb
intended for Hitler on the
flight to Smolensk proved
an exception, the *Führer*'s
favoured fleet of Condors
was subject to rigid
security checks.

indicating that the attempt had miscarried. Then Tresckow and I consulted as
to what action to take next. We were deeply shaken. It was serious enough
that the attempt had not succeeded. But even worse would be the discovery
of the bomb, which would unfailingly lead to our detection and the death of a
wide circle of close collaborators.'

As luck would have it, a telephone call to Hitler's headquarters from von
Tresckow established that the parcel containing the 'brandy' had not yet
been delivered. It was then explained that there had been a mistake in the
bottles and von Schlabrendorff would be coming the next day on business,
bringing the good brandy. Once he had secured the incriminating package,
he rushed to catch the night train to Berlin and dismantled the bomb in the
privacy of the sleeping compartment, discovering that, despite the elaborate
preparation, the detonator had not fired.

Within two weeks there was another attempt. Colonel von Gersdorff,
another officer in von Tresckow's circle, had offered to sacrifice his own life
to kill Hitler. The idea was that while the *Führer* was opening an exhibition
at the Berlin War Museum, von Gersdorf, his overcoat stuffed with time
bombs, would throw himself at the dictator. As it happened, Hitler did not

stay long at the exhibition, nor had he turned up at the scheduled time. In any case, von Gersdorff noted that the place had been crawling with Gestapo. For the moment the *Abwehr* Resistance, consisting as it did of middle-aged plotters inhibited by past fears and prejudices that they could not conquer, waited for another opportunity. But elsewhere, and largely unknown to them, was another group of patriots who suffered no such inhibitions.

THE SCHOLLS

There had been a time when young people of Hans and Sophie Scholl's age, born in the years after the end of the Great War, would have looked back wistfully to events in the southern town of Nuremberg one day in September 1933, less than nine months after Hitler had come to power. They would have recalled a delirious, cheering and triumphant crowd that surged into the vast magnificence of the Zeppelinwiese stadium, the showpiece of the ancient city. Here was celebrated what Rudolf Hess, that devoted acolyte, had called the 'Congress of Victory'.

The day of the rally had belonged to youth – 60,000 of them in red and black or white vests and shirts, performing complex formation exercises for 90 extraordinary minutes, spelling out such slogans as 'Blood and Honour', 'Germany Awake', 'Youth and Labour'. They had moved faultlessly round and across the arena, the words appearing in red and black and white, in circles and rectangles and squares, and always somewhere in the centre of the design had been the dominant swastika. Overhead, towers of Klieg lights had supplemented the summer sun, and the forests of flagpoles surrounding the area had been draped with thousands of Nazi flags. Every movement of the tour de force had been greeted with a tumult of applause, which reached its climax when 60,000 polished steel knives were drawn as one and whipped head-high to simulate the effect of a blinding flash in the high afternoon sun.

For Hans Scholl, who had joined the *Hitler Jugend* ('Hitler Youth') movement in 1934, disillusion had been slow to form. He had found it difficult to understand why his father, Robert Scholl, did not share his dedication to the new Germany, calling its new leaders 'wolves and deceivers'. The assault on individual freedom under Nazism had been gradual; one by one, youth organizations that had long been a German tradition were outlawed, their members dragooned into joining the *Hitler Jugend*. The day came when the homes of Scholl and his friends were visited by the Gestapo, who ransacked books, photo albums and diaries, many of

Below: The only survivor among the senior opposition group of army officers opposed to Hitler, von Schlabrendorff (pictured) had recruited Klaus von Stauffenberg for his crucial role in the bomb plot. After arrest and torture, he escaped certain execution when the People's Court was destroyed by Allied bombing in 1945.

which were mere adolescent treasures and politically innocent. Hans was arrested and thrown into gaol before being released with a warning of the fate that awaited dissidents. Less lucky were the leaders of religious youth organizations, such as Adalbert Probst, who was shot by the Gestapo while 'trying to escape'.

After Hans's arrest, the Gestapo continued to shadow his family. His father had been unwise enough to denounce Hitler as 'a scourge' within hearing of a fellow council worker in Ulm, who lost no time in tipping off the local Gestapo. Then had come the inevitable knock on the door at two in the morning followed by the summary arrest. Herr Scholl was eventually released, with an assurance that the Gestapo would be back at the slightest provocation. The way his father was treated fuelled his son's indignation and his determination to take effective action, but at first he had been at a loss as to how best to proceed. After being called up for a period of military service, Hans was allowed to pursue his medical studies at the University of Munich. One of the most popular and liberal leaders there was Dr Kurt Huber, who had taken it upon himself to champion the cause of the persecuted Christian churches. Three priests in Lübeck had been arrested for distributing the text of sermons that specifically denounced the war.

> In the town of Lubeck, three priests were arrested for distributing texts of sermons specifically denouncing the war.

Another outspoken critic of Hitler had been the Bishop of Münster, Hans Clemens von Galen, who had deliberately stressed the role of the Nazis in corrupting youth through 'the illegal imprisonment, exile and expulsion of the innocent'. Huber collated the most inflammatory excerpts of the bishop's sermons and set about distributing them to Munich's influential citizens, including the Scholls.

It was not long before Hans discovered that many of his fellow students shared his zeal and, in the evenings, while free from their studies, a group laboured on what they regarded as their own testimonial of belief in the German people. Initially their leaflets struck a cautious note. Rather than directly condemning National Socialism, they cited classical writers with strong convictions on personal liberty and the evils of persecution. Alongside Göthe and Schiller, the leaflets made reference to the state of Sparta, which had abandoned love and friendship, making the individual totally subservient to the demands of the state. The implications were clear, nonetheless, and as time went on the tone, at first florid and romantic, changed to direct criticism of the Nazis. What had been a mere dissident group grew into a Resistance movement. Its name, *Die Weisse Rose* (the 'White Rose'), had been chosen by Hans Scholl from the title of a novel by the mysterious writer B. Traven, actually a German pamphleteer originally named Albert Feige, whose recurring theme was the basic inhumanity of large institutions, contained within a stirring adventure story of romance and mystery set against a Mexican background. Hans had long since joined forces with Kurt Huber, and both worked tirelessly to produce what became a veritable avalanche of leaflets.

Not surprisingly these fell into the hands of the Gestapo within hours of their distribution. At first Heinrich Müller regarded them as a mere irritant. There was no point in attempting to trace duplicating machines, which could be found all over Munich, or the cheap paper on which the leaflets were printed. As for surveillance, there was neither the time nor the manpower to organize dragnets of students' houses, apartments or rooms. But mild concern soon turned to alarm. The leaflets began to turn up in other parts of Germany, with cells springing up in the university towns of Hamburg, Bonn, Freiburg and Heidelberg. Younger members of the Gestapo were despatched to pose as students. To Müller's fury, valuable manpower was largely wasted on searching for nonexistent Resistance cells within these universities. In fact, it was the tireless Hans, his sister Sophie and a small group of friends who carried out most of the distribution. The couple journeyed to Linz, Vienna and Frankfurt, posting around 1500 leaflets, as well as scattering even more around the darkened streets of Munich, which emerged as the centre of the movement.

Below: Sophie Scholl (centre) with her Munich student brother Hans and Christopher Probst, a colleague in the White Rose movement. The organization spread to a dozen cities, highlighting the fate of the Jews and urging passive resistance and the sabotage of war industry.

THE WHITE ROSE GANG

Opposition to Hitler and the Nazi regime took many forms, intensifying as the war continued. One of the most prominent dissident groups among young people in Nazi Germany was *Die Weisse Rose* ('White Rose'), formed by students at the University of Munich in 1942. It proposed 'to knock down the iron wall of fear and terror'. Among those from the group hunted by the Gestapo were the brother and sister Hans and Sophie Scholl. Arrested and brought to hasty trial, they were both executed by beheading on 22 February 1943. Undaunted under Gestapo questioning, Sophie had declared, 'Thousands will be stirred and awakened by what we have done.'

In January 1943, as the broadsheets and wall slogans continued to spread, Himmler took a personal hand. He minuted instructions to an old colleague, *Obergruppenführer* Karl Freiherr von Eberstein, the chief of police in Munich, declaring that police searches throughout Germany were a waste of manpower. What was needed was covert surveillance by professionals centred in Munich: 'I assume these wire pullers are in Catholic and reactionary circles.' The clandestine task of rooting out those responsible was to be up to the SD alone. From the viewpoint of the Nazis, the need for action was paramount. Two weeks after Himmler's minute there came news of the fall of Stalingrad. It had proved impossible to conceal such a major disaster from the German people. Morale slumped and possibly for the first time in this war questions were being asked about the cost in human lives of the Russian campaign.

Early in the war Germans who perceived themselves as patriotic had not hesitated to report to the Gestapo examples of what they regarded as sedition. An SD report of 15 March conceded that there had since been a considerable change: 'According to our information rumours concerning the operations of opposition circles are spreading and are disturbing the population. Thus in many parts of the Reich talk goes on about "large demonstrations of Munich students". There is also talk of handbills and posters of Marxist content appearing in Berlin and other cities. Some sources for our information stress the point that the population is apparently no long reacting as it did before, removing these inflammatory writings and leaflets. Instead, they read them and hand them on.'

CAMPUS REVOLT

The change of mood was quickly perceived by *Die Weisse Rose*, which reacted by printing thousands more leaflets, which were left around the Munich University campus. One of the more florid of these read: 'Who has counted the dead? Hitler or Göbbels – to be sure neither. In Russia thousands fall daily … Grief enters cottages in the homeland and no one is there to wipe dry the tears of the mothers, but Hitler lies to those whose dearest treasure he has robbed and driven to senseless death. Every word that comes from Hitler's mouth is a lie. If he says peace, he means war, and if in the most sacrilegious way he uses the name of the Almighty, he means the power of evil, the fallen angel, Satan. His mouth is the stinking gate of hell, and his power is debased. Certainly, one must conduct the battle against the National

Socialist terror-state with every rational means, but whoever today still doubts the real existence of demonic powers has widely misunderstood the metaphysical background to this war. Behind the concrete, behind material perceptions, behind all factual, logical considerations stands the irrational, i.e. the battle against the demon, against the emissaries of Anti-Christ.'

The romantic trappings of idealism were still present, but it soon became clear that there could be no substitute for direct action. An opportunity was offered by Paul Giesler, Gauleiter for Munich and Upper Bavaria, who descended on the university in February 1943, flanked by droves of SS. He ordered all the students to gather in the assembly hall, where he began by ranting at them for their low morale. Any male students who were considered physically fit would be put to appropriate war work. As to the women students, they could fulfil a useful role by bearing a child each year for the good of the Reich. With a leer Giesler added, 'If some of the girls lack sufficient charm to find a mate, I will assign each of them to one of my adjutants … and I can promise her a thoroughly enjoyable experience.' This proved altogether too much for the students who rose as one, setting upon the speaker's bodyguard and known members of the Gestapo. Then they flooded out of the auditorium into the streets, which were soon the scene of anti-Nazi demonstrations on an unprecedented scale. Opposition hardened still further as the leaflet war was stepped up alongside the mood of rebellion coursing through Bavaria.

Shortly after dawn a few days later, and with Huber's latest leaflets stuffed in their satchels, Hans and Sophie walked eagerly towards the university. Once inside, they moved swiftly along the corridors, leaving packets at certain doors and lecture halls. The rest they scattered from the top floor of the main hall. Their content could not have been more inflammatory,

Below: A snatch squad of German infantry outside Gestapo headquarters at 8 Prinz-Albrecht-Strasse prepare to move off on another raid. Although most Gestapo raids were carried out by the SS or *Geheime Feldpolizei*, the Gestapo could draw on personnel from practically any arm of the *Wehrmacht* to carry out their bidding.

Above: Judge Roland Freisler (centre) gives the Nazi salute while presiding over the People's Court. He was known for his merciless hectoring of defendants and witnesses. He was killed in an American bombing raid on Berlin in February 1945.

urging the readers to mass action with such slogans as 'Resign from the Party Organizations', 'Fight the Party', 'The Dead of Stalingrad are calling you', 'The German name is dishonoured for all time if German youth does not rise now to take its revenge'. Unseen, Jacob Schmidt, a porter and handyman, and one of the countless *Blockwärte* who did not scruple to pass on snippets to the Gestapo, watched Sophie at work. He hurried away to raise the alarm and all the university exits were sealed. The roundup was swift. Brother and sister were seized, bundled into a black limousine and driven at speed to Gestapo headquarters, where they were locked in separate cells.

At first they held up well under interrogation, denying any involvement with leaflets or dabbed slogans, but brushes, stencils and duplicating equipment, seized from their homes, were now shown to them. Hans, sensing that denial would do no good, now admitted his activities, but attempted to persuade his interrogator that he alone had been responsible. As for Sophie, the method of interrogation adopted by the Gestapo functionary, Egon Mohe, was a choice example of how sophisticated the SD's techniques had become. Instead of releasing a barrage of questions, he offered coffee and cigarettes. His tone to the girl was one of sweet reasonableness. Surely she realized that she had done no service to young Germans fighting on the Russian front and who had desperate need of her loyalty. Were her actions the result of stupidity rather than malice? Sophie would have none of it, making it clear that she would follow the same path, if given another chance.

That evening Christoph Probst, another university music student and *Die Weisse Rose* adherent, was also arrested. He and the Scholls were charged with high treason. None was under any illusion as to their trial's outcome, despite formalities being observed with the engagement of a defence lawyer who, like all lawyers practising throughout the Reich, was a member of the Nazi Lawyer's Association. As for the judge, he was one of the Third Reich's most notorious figures, the intimidating Roland Freisler, a former Communist whose favoured technique was badgering and haranguing prisoners. As a State Secretary in the Reich Ministry of Justice, he was an ideal choice for President of the *Volksgerichtshof,* the People's Court, the proceedings of which were near farce and the sole purpose of which was to deliver predetermined rubber-stamped verdicts.

Predictably, the defence did not contest the judgment. Indeed, it would have been hard to so, as all three accused made no attempt to deny the charges and remained impervious to the rantings of Freisler, who all too soon was intoning the sentences:

'Hans Fritz Scholl, *Tod* (death).'

'Sophie Magdelene Scholl*, Tod.*'

'Christoph Hermann Probst, *Tod.*'

The condemned were then hustled into cars by the Gestapo and driven to Stadelheim Prison, on the southern outskirts of Munich, where they were put in separate cells and told to write their last letters. Hans and Sophie's parents were allowed a few last, harrowing moments with their children. Sophie, facing death first, was rushed into the execution chamber, where her hands were swiftly pinioned and she was stretched on the rack. It was calculated that the heavy blade was released within seven seconds of the victim entering the room. Guards were later to recall that Hans Scholl had cried out, 'Long live freedom!' That afternoon an account of the trials and executions was carried by the Munich newspaper *Neueste Nachrichten*; the text had been set in type while the trial was still in progress. The Gestapo did not let up its search for further members of *Die Weisse Rose*; Kurt Huber was among those taken and beheaded the following April. The fortunes of the anti-Nazi student movement had reached their lowest ebb.

THE FALL OF THE *ABWEHR*

The outlook for the *Abwehr* was scarcely better following the failure of Operation Flash. The next setback in the conspirators' fortunes involved Wilhelm Schmidhuber, a prosperous brewer and part-time *Abwehr* agent who had first become involved with the opposition to Hitler in 1940. One of the covert activities organized by Canaris's supporters had been to help Jews (often entire families) escape from Germany under the guise of employing them as counter-intelligence agents. Money was directed from the *Abwehr* budget to recompense them for ill treatment by the Nazis, not least the loss of their homes and possessions. The practice had Canaris's tacit approval; the organization was in the hands of Hans Oster and a deputy, Hans von Dohnanyi, a longtime anti-Nazi who, as one of his grandmothers counted as a 'non-Aryan', was already in Gestapo files.

The scheme had met with considerable success, but was placed under serious threat by the detention in Czechoslovakia of a Jew claiming to be an *Abwehr* agent and, unusually, found in the possession of 400 American dollars. Report of the detention reached Heinrich Müller, who decided to handle the matter personally. The suspect had promptly demanded his rights as a servant of the *Abwehr*, but Müller ignored the ploy and pressed on with his interrogation, learning among other things that the money had come directly from Herr Schmidhuber. The implications were too serious for delay and Schmidhuber was promptly arrested. He proved no match for persistent questioning laced with threats, and within hours Müller had uncovered the involvement and activities of Hans von Dohnanyi.

Müller's undisputed power within the Gestapo did not stretch to the *Abwehr*, which jealously guarded its position within the military. An appropriate authority was therefore required and Müller turned to Manfred Röder, Judge Advocate of the Reich military court. Röder's role within the *Abwehr* itself was impressive. He had successfully penetrated a group of around 100 pro-Soviet Germans who, under the code name *Rote Kapelle* ('Red Orchestra'), had set up a widespread espionage system operating for Moscow within the Reich. Müller, however, maintained his influence by persuading Röder to include a member of the Gestapo in the party of officials who arrived at the *Abwehr* on 5 April 1943. Röder announced bluntly that he had a warrant both to search the office and to arrest *Sonderführer* von Dohnanyi. Canaris, who believed that any incriminating documents would have been securely filed away, consented, but insisted that he must witness both search and arrest. Oster then protested that it was he who should be arrested because the activities of his subordinates were carried out under his direction. Röder, however, had anticipated such obstruction.

ROTE KAPELLE

One of the main achievements of the *Abwehr* in 1942 was unearthing a large number of prominent Germans running an elaborate espionage operation for the Soviets. Admiral Canaris's agents tracked some 100 clandestine radio transmitters, operating out of the Reich and occupied countries. Their initiatives were given the code name *Rote Kapelle* ('Red Orchestra').

A prominent organizer was Leopold Trepper, a Polish Jew and Communist trained by Soviet intelligence who contacted influential circles from a base in Belgium. His prime operator was Harold Schulze-Boysen, a left-wing Air Ministry employee with access to Goring's 'research' office, the *Forschungamt*, which specialized in tapping telephones. Schulze-Boysen and others succeeded during 1942 in sending vital information to the Soviet Union on German military supplies and plans, including the projected capture of Stalingrad.

The *Abwehr* pounced and there were 46 arrests, including Schulze-Boysen. From then on the SD and Gestapo took over. Equipment was seized and the operators interrogated and tortured, followed by mass executions. Trepper managed to survive, but there was no gratitude from the Russians. Flown to Moscow, towards the war's end, he was accused of collaboration with the Gestapo and imprisoned. After his arrest he emigrated to Israel.

He countered that the charge against von Dohnanyi involved not military matters, but a breach of currency regulations. Then, without further delay, he strode into von Dohnanyi's office and demanded a key to the heavy, green safe. This contained a weighty bunch of files, one of which was inscribed '*Z Grau*' ('Z Grey'). Von Dohnanyi attempted to remove three sheets of paper that projected from the file and was ordered to desist by Röder.

But when the latter's back was turned, Oster managed to seize them. Röder's subsequent report, the text of which has survived, describes what happened next: 'Major General Oster stood facing the chief investigator with his left hand behind his back, removed the said papers and concealed them beneath the jacket of his civilian suit. Having been observed by *Kriminalsekretär* Sonderegger, who was also present, and the chief investigator, he was promptly challenged and compelled to surrender the papers.' Oster was

ordered to leave the room. One of the three sheets was found to contain a memorandum alleging that military groups in Germany and certain elements in the churches were involved in bids to overthrow National Socialism. The memorandum's first sentence was enough in itself to constitute treason: 'For a considerable time now, a small circle of prominent clerics in the German Protestant Church have been debating how the Protestant Church can help in this war to bring about a just and lasting peace and construct a social system based on Christian foundations.' If this were not enough, another document outlined a territorial structure of a post-Hitler Germany.

Above: Graf Claus von Stauffenberg (far left) stands to attention in the presence of Hitler and Keitel outside the Wolf's Lair bunker on 15 July 1944, just a few days before the failed assassination attempt.

It was sufficient to lead to a crop of arrests. Von Dohnanyi was thrown into gaol, along with Josef Müller, the *Abwehr*'s man in Rome, and Pastor Dietrich Bonhöffer, a Protestant Minister who was also heavily involved. Hans Oster was relieved of his duties, cashiered by the OKW and forbidden to have any more dealings with the *Abwehr*. For a while Oster was able to retire to Leipzig, but the Gestapo had already marked his card; he was placed under arrest the following December. As yet Himmler considered there was insufficient evidence to hold Canaris, but the *Abwehr* was in its death throes.

News of the debacle stretched beyond Berlin. Not the least alarmed of the conspirators serving on the Russian front was Henning von Tresckow, who

THE KREISAU CIRCLE

The Kreisau Circle (*Kreisauer Kreis*) was a small group formed in 1933 to oppose Hitler and the Nazi movement and drawn from widely differing backgrounds, including army officers, academics, conservatives, liberals, socialists, Catholics and Protestants. Led by Helmuth James Graf von Moltke and Peter Graf Yorck von Wartenburg, it met at the Moltke family estate in Kreisau, Silesia (now Krzyzowa, Poland). Its members regarded Hitler as a catastrophe for the Fatherland, agreeing that it was necessary to bring their country back to Christian values by overthrowing the Nazi regime and establishing a new political and social ethic in its place. The group, however, was penetrated by the Gestapo. Many of its members were arrested and eventually executed after the bomb plot against Hitler on 20 July 1944.

promptly applied to von Kluge for sick leave. One of his first acts in Berlin was to contact Lieutenant General Friedrich Olbricht, the head of the supply section of the Reserve Army and a key opposition figure. Both men began to look for a suitable replacement for Oster. The need proved urgent. A decree issued on 14 February 1944 ordered the dissolution of the *Abwehr* and its two sub-sections, *Amtsgruppe Ausland* and *Abwehr Amt*. The former was merged with the *Wehrmachts Führungsstab* (the staff for the conduct of operations) of OKW, while the RSHA absorbed *Abwehr Amt* under the title of *Militärische Amt* ('Military Office'). Complete power in operations overseas was vested in Walter Schellenberg. For the conspirators it was nothing short of disaster. The protective cover of the *Abwehr*, the provider of fake alibis, falsified papers and explosives, was no more. And there were no longer the means to smuggle the more heavily compromised conspirators to safety in Switzerland.

OPERATION VALKYRIE

As Hitler led Germany more deeply into catastrophe, even those serving in the *Wehrmacht* who remained stubbornly loyal were experiencing crises of confidence. Among these was Claus Phillip Maria Schenk, Graf von Stauffenberg, a Swabian who could trace his lineage unbroken to 1298. His great grandfather, Franz Ludwig Freiherr von Stauffenberg, had been hereditary counsellor to the King of Bavaria and had been created Graf by Ludwig II in 1874. For all his aristocratic roots, von Stauffenberg had scandalized some of his fellow officers when, on the day Hitler assumed power, he had stood in his lieutenant's uniform at the head of a deliriously happy crowd marching through Bamberg. Unlike many of his contemporaries, he had seen nothing incongruous in wearing his full uniform when attending Mass each Sunday as a devout Roman Catholic.

An incident in 1938, however, when he was detailed as a young soldier to represent his 7th Cavalry Regiment at a Party Day demonstration in Bamberg, triggered a radical change of attitude. The main speaker was Julius Streicher, the gauleiter of Nuremberg and a dedicated anti-Semite, who had launched into wild, obscene invective against the Jews. This had proved too much for von Stauffenberg, military duties or not; he and a brother officer quit the parade. Ultimately, adherence to Nazism proved an impossibility: according to von Schlabrendorff, 'Von Stauffenberg's contempt for Hitler had a spiritual basis … It sprang directly from his Christian faith and moral convictions.' He had become ideal Resistance material. His change of heart did not go unnoticed by fellow officers of similar opinions. For a time he was attracted to another opposition cell known as the Kreisau Circle, a small group of officers and professional civilians deriving its name from the location of the estate of Graf Helmut von Moltke, a legal adviser to OKW. But the Circle's inherent pacifism made him impatient and he came to regard it as a mere talking shop.

Von Stauffenberg's army career took him first to Poland for service on the supply staff of the 6th Panzer Division and then with the Army High Command, where he remained, involved in long-term planning, until February 1943. This was followed by transfer at his request to active service and a posting to North Africa with the 10th Panzer Division, which in the following April came under heavy attack from American aircraft. The division's forces were widely strung out and vulnerable as tank crews tried to fire back with light machine guns. Von Stauffenberg's thin-skinned Volkswagen truck was powerless against .50 calibre bullets. The injuries he sustained were horrific, with the loss of his right arm, the third and fourth fingers of his left hand and his left eye.

It was a measure of his courage that he both refused the easy option of leaving the army and readily volunteered to place a bomb intended to kill Hitler during a military conference at the *Führer*'s Rastenburg headquarters. This would be possible because he was the sole member of the inner Resistance circle to attend the *Führer*'s staff conferences. Another advantage

Left: The Kreisau Circle met on the family estate of Graf Helmut von Moltke, one of its founders. What was perceived as his treachery occurred early in the war when he contacted the US ambassador in Berlin, who was alerted to the opposition movement. Von Moltke was arrested for treason and hanged in early 1944.

Above: Benito Mussolini views the damage in the ruined conference room of the bunker at Rastenburg, following the attempt on Hitler's life. During what was the final meeting of the two dictators, Hitler declared that his survival had been a positive intervention by God himself.

was that he was permitted to stand close to Hitler because his injuries had affected his hearing. As well as planning the actual assassination, von Stauffenberg and von Tresckow put the finishing touches to 'Operation Valkyrie'. This was, in effect, a remodelling of an existing plan that Olbricht and Canaris had presented to Hitler two years before as a means of tackling internal unrest. It had been pointed out to the *Führer* that by 1944 there would be roughly eight million workers and prisoners of war within the Reich, any of whom might organize rebellion. Olbricht and Canaris had argued the need for a plan to counter this happening. Hitler had given the scheme his blessing and the time had come to activate it.

THE BOMB EXPLODES

Rastenburg was an uninviting complex surrounded by lakes, swampy areas and thick forest. The buildings were topped with camouflage nets, artificial trees and fake moss. All three inner security zones were bolstered with checkpoints and guards on constant watch. A Polish labourer on his way home from work once attempted to cut his way through and was shot dead; thousands of mines covering some 50 metres had then been laid. Hitler's valets carried side arms at all times; every morsel of food was tested for poison. Personal searches were frequent.

But the die was cast. Von Stauffenberg, accompanied by Lieutenant Werner von Haeften, his ADC, flew from Berlin to Rastenburg with a time bomb in his briefcase. On the way to the conference hut after their arrival, von Stauffenberg used the pretext of having left his cap and belt in an anteroom to set the thin wire fuse. Then at 12.36 p.m. he placed the light-coloured briefcase on the floor against one of the heavy legs of the table. Claiming he had to make a telephone call, he slipped discreetly out of the room, much to the considerable annoyance of Field Marshal Wilhelm Keitel, who as Chief of Staff of the OKW was the most senior officer present and was conscious that von Stauffenberg was due to make his report next. Keitel went outside to find him, only to learn from the telephonist that Colonel von Stauffenberg had left. Keitel returned to the conference mystified, in time to hear General Adolf Heusinger's report outlining the serious situation prevailing on the eastern front. Colonel Heinz Brandt, the general's Chief of Staff, was keen to study the large military map spread in front of him, but found that von Stauffenberg's bursting briefcase was in the way of his feet. He leant down to edge it round to the further side of the table leg.

Heusinger was saying: 'West of the Dvina, strong Russian forces are driving northwards. Their spearheads are already southwest of Dvinsk. Unless, at long last, the army group is withdrawn from Lake Peipus, a catastrophe will …' At that point the bomb exploded. Black smoke and flame

Left: Friedrich Olbricht, formerly a career army officer, was the initiator of Operation Valkyrie, the intended military takeover of the Berlin administrative centre following Hitler's death. After the failure of the bomb plot, Olbricht was promptly court-martialled and shot.

147

poured from the hut, the table was torn to fragments, the ceiling fell in and the open windows were shattered. For the moment it was assumed that an air raid had been responsible. Four of those who had attended the conference were killed. But Hitler survived: his injuries were a bruised back and hands, burst eardrums and splinters in the left leg.

Shortly after 1.00 p.m. von Stauffenberg's aircraft took off for Berlin from Rastenburg. Asa it was not equipped with long-range radio, he remained in ignorance of what was happening at the *Wolfsschanze*, although he could not conceive that Hitler might have survived the explosion, which he had stayed long enough to witness before racing to the airport. All he could hope was that Olbricht, as Chief of Staff and Deputy Commander of the *Ersatzheer* ('Army Reserve'), had taken the agreed action, seizing buildings and setting troops on the move. To his consternation, however, von Stauffenberg learnt that Olbricht had done precisely nothing while he waited for confirmation that Hitler was dead. Still refusing to contemplate that the *Führer* could be alive and aware that valuable time was ebbing away, von Stauffenberg ordered Valkyrie to go ahead immediately. Olbricht promptly contacted General Friedrich Fromm, who had command of all *Wehrmacht* forces in Berlin at the old War Ministry building and was party to the conspiracy. Fromm, however, refused to move until he had positive proof of Hitler's death. Long regarded by some of the conspirators as a mere fair-weather friend, he now sensed trouble and a threat to his own survival.

Below: In the shattered Rastenburg bunker, Herman Göring (right) stands with (third from right) Julius Schaub, one of Hitler's earliest associates from the days of the abortive Munich putsch. This picture also shows *SS-Gruppenführer* Hermann Fegelein (fourth from the left), who was shot for attempted desertion in April 1945.

Indeed, doubts as to Fromm's loyalty had led to the nomination of Lieutenant General Erich Höppner as a possible replacement should Fromm turn against the coup.

The first confirmation from Rastenburg came when Keitel telephoned Fromm with the news that the attempt on the *Führer*'s life had failed. Von Stauffenberg's reaction when he arrived at the War Ministry was to declare stoutly that the coup should still go ahead and to plead for Fromm's support. When the latter refused, the conspirators seized him and confined him to his adjutant's room, cutting the telephone wires as a precaution. Some time later, Fromm pleaded to be allowed to return to his office, giving his word of honour as an officer that he would not try to escape. Inexplicably he was believed and his request granted. The conspirators were next faced with the unexpected arrival of three of his staff generals, who strongly refused to be associated with the putsch and demanded to be taken to their chief. Fromm quickly pointed out a little-used rear exit, ordering them to summon help, storm the building and put an end to the revolt.

EXECUTIONS

The events that followed were a series of disasters for the conspirators. A group of junior officers, hitherto loyal to Olbricht, sensed that the coup was falling apart and, fearing inevitable arrest, had smuggled some arms into the Bendlerstrasse headquarters. A deputation arrived to press Olbricht as to precisely what was happening. von Stauffenberg, attempting to intervene, was seized. As he attempted to break free he was shot in his good arm. Fromm now took matters into his own hands. He set up an impromptu court martial, declaring that General Olbricht, his Chief of Staff Colonel Albrecht Ritter Mertz von Quirnheim, 'the Colonel whose name I will not mention' (von Stauffenberg) and his adjutant Lieutenant Werner von Haeften were condemned to death. Ludwig Beck bungled an attempted to shoot himself and was eventually despatched with a shot in the neck.

Just before 12.30 a.m. the conspirators were led in front of a heap of sandy earth excavated during construction work in the courtyard. Drivers were directed to position their vehicles with their headlights fully on. Olbricht was shot first, followed by von Stauffenberg, who shouted, 'Long live our sacred Germany.' Then it was the turn of Mertz von Quirnheim. The signal despatched by Fromm covered up his own complicity: 'The putsch attempted by irresponsible Generals has been ruthlessly subdued. All the leaders have been shot. Orders issued by General Field Marshal von Witzleben, Colonel-General Höppner, are not to be obeyed. I have again assumed command after my temporary arrest by force of arms.'

Throughout 20 July, Heinrich Himmler had been at work in his special train, 14 carriages long, some 25 miles from Rastenburg. His initial reaction to the news of the assassination attempt threw him into a state of panic,

INTERROGATION

In the event of a prisoner holding out, the tortures would begin as they did with von Schlabrendorff: 'First, my hands were chained behind my back, and a device which gripped all the fingers separately was fastened to my hands. The inner side of this mechanism was studded with pins whose points pressed against my fingertips. The turning of a screw caused the instrument to contract, thus forcing the pin points into my fingers. When this did not achieve the desired confession, the second stage followed. I was strapped down on a frame resembling a bedstead, and my head was covered with a blanket. Cylinders resembling stovepipes studded with nails on the inner surface were shoved over my bare legs. Here, too, a screw mechanism was used to contract these tubes so that nails pierced my legs from ankle to thigh. For the third stage of torture, the "bedstead" itself was the main instrument. I was strapped down as described above, again with a blanket over my head. With the help of a special mechanism this medieval torture rack was then expanded – either in sudden jerks or gradually – each time stretching my shackled body. In the fourth and final stage I was tied in a bent position which did not allow me to move even slightly backwards or sideways.'

The torturers then fell on him with a series of blows from clubs, each of which caused him to fall forward, crashing full on his face. After each session he was flung back into his cell. But he told his interrogators nothing. Eventually he was bundled into a car and taken to the concentration camp at Sachsenhausen to await his appearance before the People's Court.

conscious that the days of his own power could be numbered. His masseur, Felix Kersten, found his employer preparing in high anxiety to descend on Berlin to deal with 'the reactionary brood'. First, however, Himmler went to congratulate Hitler on his survival, taking leave of him with the words, 'My *Führer*, leave it to me.'

One of Himmler's first actions was to order that there were to be no further executions. Those involved were to be questioned by every means at the disposal of the Gestapo, with prolonged torture where necessary. Only then would there be executions. Special fury was reserved for von Stauffenberg and his colleagues, as Himmler later related: 'They were put underground so quickly that they were buried with their Knights' Crosses. They were disinterred next day, and their identities were confirmed. Then I ordered that the corpses were to be burned and the ashes strewn in the fields. We do not want to leave the slightest trace of these people.'

Hurried orders were given to a group of Gestapo officials from RSHA *Amt IVE* (Counter-Intelligence) to make for the Bendlerstrasse. In charge was *SS-Standartenführer* Walther Huppenkothen, of the Sipo and the SD, known as a persistent and particularly brutal interrogator. Interrogations were also carried out by Josef Göbbels, whom the conspirators had intended to arrest. According to one of his press officers, questioned after the war, Göbbels's main object of suspicion was Fritz Fromm, who was by now badly scared. Göbbels snapped sharply: 'You seem to have been in a hell of a hurry to get inconvenient witnesses underground.' Fromm, who had simultaneously flirted with the conspirators while proclaiming his loyalty to his *Führer*, was to survive a little longer; the following March he was tried and executed.

CONSPIRACY IN FRANCE

At first it looked as if the conspirators who had been organized in France might succeed in their plan. On the orders of Lieutenant General Hans Freiherr von Boineburg-Lengsfeld, Commandant of Greater Paris, detachments of the second battalion of the 1st Guards Regiment had occupied buildings housing the SS, including the private residence of *SS-Gruppenführer* Karl Albrecht Oberg. The latter, along with Helmut Knochen, had been surrounded without protest. In addition, more than 1200 SS and Gestapo officers were confined to the *Wehrmacht* prison at Fresnes and inside the stone casemates of the old Fort de l'Est in Saint-Denis. Unfortunately a message reached Berlin from the one SD teleprinter station that had been overlooked. Nor had support for the plotters been quite as firm as had been imagined, as Admiral Theodor Krancke, the Paris naval commandant, had refused to contemplate a conspiracy; a thousand of his men were armed and formed into companies, ready to assault the prisons and release the captives. There was also a threat that a loyal armoured corps from the Normandy front, where Allied troops were consolidating their position, would be withdrawn to fall upon Paris.

Nonetheless, a successful if temporary effect of the actions in Paris had been to cut off all communication from France to Germany. The chief organizer had been Colonel General Carl Heinrich von Stülpnagel, France's Military Governor since 1942, who had always been openly critical of Hitler's war plans and had long been deeply involved in the conspiracy. But then came the blow of the defection of General Field Marshal von Kluge, commander in the west, whose devotion to the putsch had always been questionable and who had made it clear that his active participation would only be given 'in the event of the attempt being a success'.

In the hours following the death of von Stauffenberg and the others, von Stülpnagel and the other French-based conspirators gathered round radios listening to denunciations of the putsch and its perpetrators by Hitler, Göring and Admiral Dönitz. Plainly, there was little more to be done in Paris. Von Stülpnagel ordered all the 1200 prisoners to be released and returned to their headquarters. A staff car was despatched to fetch Karl Albrecht Oberg, who was also released. Von Kluge's final volte-face was to denounce von Stülpnagel, who was ordered to return to

Below: General Carl Heinrich von Stülpnagel, France's military governor, was at first highly successful as instigator of the proposed *coup d'état* in France on behalf of the German Resistance, but failed to win over Field Marshal von Kluge as Commander in Chief West. Hopelessly isolated, he attempted suicide but was arrested and, following his appearance before the People's Court, executed.

Berlin. As Himmler was now installed there in place of Fromm, that would mean instant arrest on arrival. With his mind made up, von Stülpnagel, accompanied by two sergeants, summoned a car for the journey, directing it to proceed above the desolate region of Verdun, where he had fought in 1916 as a captain of the Darmstadt Grenadiers. At one point he ordered the driver to stop, announcing that he would take a short walk. Then came the sound of shots. The sergeants discovered him floating in a nearby canal, one of his eyes blown away. An operation and blood transfusion at a nearby hospital saved his life, but not his sight.

> Von Stülpnagel ordered the driver to stop, announcing that he would take a short walk. Then came the sound of shots.

Heinrich Himmler was now in possession of powers of which even he had never dreamed. He was made Commander in Chief of the Reserve Army and put in charge of the Reich Ministry of the Interior, giving him control of 38 divisions of the *Waffen-SS*, where SD and Gestapo spies were planted in profusion. Meanwhile, Ernst Kaltenbrunner was implementing his 'Special Commission 20.7.44', where 400 of his staff tirelessly carried out interrogations around the clock. An *SS-Obersturmführer* Kielpinski was given the task of compiling 24-hour reports, which were sent to Party Secretary Martin Bormann and then passed on to Hitler.

The Gestapo's remit at this point was not merely to secure evidence against the collaborationists; Himmler went a lot further. As an obsessive reader of the myths and legends of a land too far lost in antiquity even to be called Germany, he resurrected what he believed to be an apposite ancient law. At a conference held in Posen (now Poznan) on 3 August 1944, he told the assembled gauleiters: 'All you have to do is to read up on the old German sagas. When they proscribed a family and declared them outlaws, or when they had a vendetta, they went all the way. They had no mercy. If the family were outlawed and proscribed, they said, "This man is a traitor, the blood is bad, there is bad blood in them, they will be eradicated." And in the case of a blood feud it was eradicated down to the last member.'

Even here, though, old habits died hard. The convention of circumlocution masked actual intentions: Himmler coined a new word *Sippenhaft* ('tribe liability') to describe his revived form of vengeance. But the resources of the Gestapo were stretched virtually to breaking point when it came to dealing with the actual conspirators. It proved physically impossible to detain all their families, but efforts were made. Von Stauffenberg's wife and new-born child were arrested and his other children dragged from their mother and placed in foster homes. Gestapo officials were frequently confused as to at whom *Sippenhaft* was aimed. Some of those hauled from their homes, bewildered and terrified, were totally unaware that there had been an involvement in a conspiracy at all.

THE PEOPLE'S COURT

All sections of the Gestapo were fully conscious of Hitler breathing down their necks, obsessively anxious to have proceedings hurried along. The People's Court finally opened on 7 August. Göbbels, as Propaganda Minister, arranged for copious coverage in the press and on radio, and a phonographic recording was made. A complete film record of the proceedings was secured by British and American forces at the end of war, and selections were used in evidence at the Nuremberg Trials.

In the dock were General Field Marshal von Witzleben and seven others who had been involved in one way or another with von Stauffenberg. All had been beaten and starved in the Gestapo cellars. Their plight was described starkly by Sir John Wheeler Bennett in *The Nemesis of Power*: 'Unshaven, collarless and shabby, they looked what they were, men physically and spiritually broken (had they not suffered the attentions of Walther Huppenkothen?), men who knew that their doom was sealed, who felt themselves to be upon the threshold of death and whose only prayer was for the boon of a swift ending … Those eight men could have had no illusions as

Below: Harangued and humiliated by Roland Freisler, Erwin von Witzleben faces the People's Court. He stood no chance with even his defence lawyer denouncing him as 'a murderer'. Totally unrepentant of his role in the bomb plot, he was executed by strangulation in August 1944.

to their position or their future. They knew when they entered the courtroom that they were already men condemned to death.'

Von Witzleben's dentures had been removed and he had not been allowed to shave. Decked out in the shabby clothes of a tramp, he summoned what dignity he could under Freisler's ranting, sneering tirade. Against a background of two busts of Hitler and Frederick the Great, the red-robed judge seized on a conversation von Witzleben had held with Beck the previous year. Both men had deplored what they had seen as Hitler's tendency to pick his senior commanders for their political reliability, rather than their military prowess. Freisler, playing to the cameras, bellowed, 'Did you think on that occasion who could do it better?' Von Witzleben replied unflinchingly, 'Yes!' 'Who, then could have done it better?' 'Both of us,' came the riposte. Freisler surpassed himself in hysteria: 'Both, both of you! This is an outrage that has never before been perpetrated here. A General Field Marshal and a Colonel General declare that they could do things better than he who is the *Führer* of us all … You profess to having said this?' Again

ERNST KALTENBRUNNER

The scar-faced giant *SS-Obergruppenführer* Ernst Kaltenbrunner succeeded the murdered Reinhard Heydrich as head of the RSHA ('Reich Main Security Office') – a role he exercised with singular brutality. He was born in Ried, Austria, in 1903, qualifying as a doctor of law and political economist at the age of 20. He joined the Austrian Nazi party in 1932, acting as its legal adviser. The next year, he was involved in the German-backed Austrian Nazis terrorist campaign against the state. When imprisoned with other Nazis after the 1934 attempted putsch in which the Austrian Chancellor Englebert Dollfus was murdered, Kaltenbrunner organized a strike, securing his own release and that of fellow political sympathizers. At the *Anschluss*, Kaltenbrunner formed his SS men into 'auxiliary police', conducting a violent campaign against Jews and prominent Austrians. His success earned him the post of Minister of State and command of the SS in Austria.

An industrious, obsessively ambitious networker with a special gift for seeing off potential rivals, Kaltenbrunner had long courted Himmler and his circle. The *Reichsführer-SS* had been impressed by his ideological commitment. By 1943, he had at Himmler's behest become chief of the RSHA, the Reich security office. The next year saw the collapse of Admiral Canaris's foreign intelligence organization, the *Abwehr*, by which time Kaltenbrunner had subtly shifted his allegiance from Himmler to Hitler. The latter gave him virtually a free hand in ordering atrocities on a vast scale, notably the elimination of Jews.

Many of those who came into contact with this huge, coarse man given to heavy drinking bouts found him repellent. Canaris remarked on his cold eyes and 'murderous paws'. Actively in charge of investigations following the attempt on Hitler's life, Kaltenbrunner decreed many of the executions. At the war's end, he was finally captured in Austria at the house of a mistress. During his trial at Nuremberg, it was obvious, given his appalling record, that no effective defence was possible. On the night of 15–16 October, he ascended the scaffold. His body was reportedly transported by train to Munich, where it was cremated.

came the reply, 'Yes!' The attitude of the defence was only too predictable, with von Witzleben's lawyer stating blandly, 'It will prove impossible for even the best counsel to find anything to say in defence or mitigation of the accused.' All in the dock were sentenced to death.

EXECUTION AT PLÖTZENSEE

There was no question of despatch by firing squad according to military precedence. Hitler had given the order: 'They are to be hanged like cattle.' And they were. Hans Hoffmann, the warder in charge of von Witzleben at the Plötzensee prison, whose account was supported by the testimony of another warder and the attendant cameramen, described the scene on 8 August: 'Imagine a room with a low ceiling and white-washed walls. Below the ceiling a rail was fixed. From it hung six big hooks, like those butchers use to hang their meat. In one corner stood a movie camera. Reflectors cast a blinding light, like that of a studio. In this strange, small room were the Attorney General of the Reich, the hangman with his two camera technicians, and I myself with a second prison

warder. At the wall there was a small table with a bottle of cognac and glasses for all the witnesses of the execution. The convicted men were led in. They were all wearing their prison garb, and they were handcuffed. They were placed in a single row. Leering and making jokes, the hangman got busy. He was known in his circles for his "humour". No statement, no clergyman, no journalists. One after another, all faced their turn. All showed the same courage. It took, in all, 25 minutes. The hangman wore a permanent leer, and made jokes unceasingly. The camera worked uninterruptedly, for Hitler wanted to see and hear how his enemies had died. He was able to watch the proceedings that same evening in the Reich Chancellery …

'The defendant went to the end of the room with his head high, although urged by the hangman to walk faster. Arrived there, he had to make an about-face. Then a hempen loop was placed around his neck. Next he was attached to the hook in the ceiling. The prisoner was then dropped with great force, so that the noose tightened round his neck instantly. In my opinion, death came very quickly. After the first sentence was carried out, a narrow black curtain was drawn in front of the hanged man, so that the next man to be executed would not be aware of the first one … The executions were carried out in very rapid succession. Each doomed man took his last walk erect and manly without a word of complaint.'

Above: Immediately following the bomb explosion at Rastenburg, Ernst Kaltenbrunner, who combined excessive brutality with heavy drinking, was ordered by Hitler to lay his hands on every last person involved in the plot, an order which he carried out with excessive zeal.

Right: Friedrich Graf von der Schulenburg, as a former ambassador in Moscow, was to have a prominent role in the direction of foreign policy in the post-Hitler regime, advocating a separate peace with the Western Allies while the war with Russia continued. But as a former diplomat with covert links to the Allies, he quickly realized that this was not possible.

Some of the doomed conspirators were able to survive a little longer. Notable among these was Von Kluge, whose defection from the conspirators ultimately did him no good. Relieved of his command by a distrustful Hitler, he took poison after being summoned to Berlin. The contents of the letter that he left proved that his heart had never been fully in the conspiracy: 'My *Führer*, I have always admired your greatness ... your iron will to maintain yourself and National Socialism ... You have fought an honourable and great fight ... I depart from you, my *Führer*, as one who stood nearer to you than you realized.'

The People's Court remained in session well into 1945. The sightless von Stülpnagel was led by the hand to the gallows on 30 August. Under torture his aide, Colonel Cäsar von Hofacker, let drop the name of the nation's hero, General Field Marshal Erwin Rommel. Although he had been in favour of Hitler's removal, Rommel had opposed assassination because he believed it would create a martyr. Instead he had suggested that it would have been better to place Hitler on trial to reveal his crimes. His involvement in the bomb plot had been minimal, but Hitler, when he heard of von Hofacker's admission, sent two officers to Rommel's home on 14 October, together with SS troops and contingents of SD. Rommel was presented with the choice of being arrested to appear before the People's Court or suicide. He took poison and, following his death from 'heart failure', was accorded a state funeral.

> 'Then a hempen loop was placed around his neck ... The prisoner was then dropped with great force, so that the noose tightened round his neck instantly.'

By this time the prospect of certain defeat lay ahead, but the process of revenge and recrimination wore on. Within Berlin's Tegel prison, Hans von Dohnanyi, knowing that he would be incapable of withstanding torture for long, toyed skilfully with his inquisitors, teasing them with a succession of wildly misleading statements and bogus leads. But the time came when he knew his tormentors could not be held off for much longer. As a drastic delaying tactic, he swallowed some diphtheria bacilli smuggled into the gaol by his wife Christine. These loosened his bowels and induced partial paralysis, but in the long run it made no difference. On Kaltenbrunner's orders he was sentenced to death at a court convened at Sachsenshausen on 6 April 1945. Carried into court on a stretcher, he was scarcely in a condition to offer any defence. Three days later he went to the gallows.

THE FALL OF CANARIS

In career terms, the greatest beneficiary of the downfall of Admiral Canaris was Walter Schellenberg, who gained still more power after the liquidation of the *Abwehr*, including responsibility for the whole of German Military Intelligence and with it a unified, if short-lived, Foreign Intelligence Service. Schellenberg received an order from *SS-Gruppenführer* Müller to arrest Canaris. At first the former head of the *Abwehr* was treated as a 'prisoner of honour' and was allowed to keep his uniform along with one of his beloved

Left: Bearers approach the gun carriage carrying the coffin of German hero Field Marshall Erwin Rommel in his home town of Ulm. Rommel was accorded a full state funeral because of his excellent war record.

157

Above: Unlike other Nazis who made overtures to the Western Allies, Hans Bernd Gisevius, a career civil servant formerly both of the Gestapo and the *Abwehr*, was trusted by American intelligence, but at the expense of the suspicious British. In 1948, he wrote *To the Bitter End*, a colourful account of the German Resistance.

dogs, but things changed radically with his transfer to Flossenbürg. He was clamped in chains and put in a solitary cell. Somehow he still hoped that the vengeance of the Gestapo would escape him, but the evidence was too strong, especially following the discovery of a safe in the basement of the *Abwehr* headquarters at Zossen. Among the damaging evidence were batches of files, memoranda and reports of negotiations with the Vatican, draft speeches by Ludwig Beck and sheets torn from notebooks in which Dohnanyi had outlined methods of undertaking a coup. There was also the revelation that Oster had betrayed plans for the German invasion of France and the Low Countries. Canaris was finally accused of being fully aware of plans for a *coup d'état* and had spared no pains to conceal the existence of a subversive group within the *Abwehr*.

At dawn on 9 April 1945, Canaris and Oster were herded across the yard to the gallows, where they mounted a small pair of steps that were kicked away. Death, according to later testimonies, was far from swift – according to one SS witness, 'The little Admiral took a very long time – he was jerked up and down once or twice.' The bodies were then hastily flung on a pyre and burnt.

THE SURVIVORS

Von Schlabrendorff's turn to appear before the People's Court had come the previous December when, along with five others, he had been hauled before Freisler. Owing to the large number of accused, the proceedings dragged on until the start of February 1945, when he was once again facing the judge's shower of abuse. But then came a dramatic interruption. The sirens wailed as bombs from American B-17s crashed in on the already shattered capital. The courtroom was wrenched apart, and its occupants rushed towards the basement cellars. Many did not make it, including Freisle – a heavy beam had sliced into his skull; in one hand he had been clutching von Schlabrendorff's file.

The latter had survived, but his ordeal was not yet over. He was hauled before another court where to his surprise Wilhelm Krohne, Freisler's successor, allowed him to speak in his own defence. He argued that the charges against him were illegal because his confessions had been extracted under torture, a practice abandoned by Frederick the Great two centuries before. The only result was an assurance from Krohne that he would be facing the firing squad rather than the hangman, and he was despatched to Flossenbürg, where the Gestapo were in control. As the Allies advanced into the Reich, however, the SS fled from the concentrations camps, often herding their prisoners along with them. With the American guns audible at Flossenbürg, von Schlabrendorff was transferred along with others to Dachau. On 4 May, he was among a group of prisoners abandoned by the SS in the village of Niedernhausen near the Brenner Pass, where they were found by an advance party of American troops.

A final figure for those executed following the bomb plot has never been established, although a minimum of 10,000 is quoted in many accounts. What is certain is that very few of the ringleaders escaped. Carl Gördeler, who had been tipped as Chancellor in a new regime, had already gone into hiding ahead of events at Rastenburg. For three weeks he had wandered through Prussia, relying on friends and relatives to shelter him. He knew the danger of staying too long in one place and kept on the move. In mid-August, exhausted and hungry, he stopped at an inn in a village near Marienwerder, site of his old home. Here he noticed that he was being watched by a *Luftwaffe* officer and swiftly made his getaway, only to be arrested. The following February he was executed.

GISEVIUS ESCAPES

As for the wily Hans Bernd Gisevius, who had joined the Gestapo under Göring and later thrown in his lot with the *Abwehr*, awareness of the way that the war was going in Germany led him to make overtures to British intelligence in Switzerland, where initially he was heartily distrusted and for a time suspected of being a double agent. He transferred his attentions to the Americans, where he briefed Allen Dulles of the Office of Strategic Services (OSS) on a genuine Resistance movement within the Reich. He convinced Dulles of his genuine credentials, but he had few illusions about his ability to remain free from the Gestapo for long. The value of his evidence to the Allies, particularly when it came to bringing Germany to account, was reckoned to be of such value that Dulles was determined to get him out of Germany and into neutral Switzerland.

Counterfeiters set to work to produce flawless copies of the documents Gisevius would need for his journey: a Reich passport with the necessary photograph, a set of orders from Gestapo headquarters, including a letter of authority for 'Dr Hoffman' with a forged Hitler signature, and the essential Silver Warrant identity disc of the Gestapo.

In his memoirs, Gisevius later described his journey from Stuttgart, where all was chaos at the station because Kaltenbrunner was due to board the Vienna express to his native Austria. The 'Dr Hoffman' who arrived at the tiny border crossing between Konstanz and Kreuzlingen two days later on 23 January 1945 was clad in the same summer suit he had worn on 20 July and presented a battered figure. The tired German border officials were unable to summon the will to examine his papers properly and waved him across. Gisevius duly responded with a tired Hitler salute before staggering into friendly Switzerland.

As a witness at the Nuremberg tribunal, he had little patience with those who maintained that it had not been possible for Germans to speak out against criminal acts. There could, he declared, have been more opposition, stoutly maintaining that 'Everything was possible in the Third Reich.'

CHAPTER 8

The End of the Reich

Amid the destruction of the Nazi regime, leading members of the Gestapo made their escape – some abroad, and some through suicide. Others were brought to trial in Nuremberg.

While Germany's fortunes of war declined, Himmler's power base expanded; following the abortive bomb plot he became the second most powerful man in the Reich. As commander in chief of the Reserve Army, he brought about the almost total humiliation of the old Army General Staff and its Command Organization. These became subordinated totally to the SS, which assumed control of the raising, equipping and training of no fewer than 38 *Waffen-SS* divisions under Himmler's command. Scraping the barrel for manpower, the *Reichsführer* cobbled together 15 *Volksgrenadier* divisions to wage 'a secret war of the people'. In an attempt to put fire into bellies, Himmler proclaimed, 'I give you the authority to seize every man who turns back, if necessary to tie him up and throw him in a supply wagon … Put the best, the most energetic and most brutal officers of the Division in charge. They will soon round up the rabble. Anyone who answers back will be put up against a wall.'

Just how impotent the Army General Staff had become was indicated when 'Bor' Komorowski, at the head of 35,000 Polish partisans, faced the German forces occupying Warsaw. These were not the *Wehrmacht*, however, but were under the command of one of Himmler's most brutal SS adherents, *Gruppenführer* Erich von dem Bach-Zelewski, well schooled by his service in the *Einsatzgruppen*. The atrocities committed under his orders by 4000 men of the Dirlewanger penal brigade and 6000 Russian defectors and

Left: Two Red Army soldiers fix the Soviet flag to a column on the Reichstag roof, followed by the firing of a triumphant salvo. The next day the flag was removed to fly proudly from the shattered dome.

prisoners drew protests from Colonel General Heinz Guderian, the last Commander in Chief of the *Wehrmacht*. The Warsaw rising was put down with savagery by the SS and, on 2 October 1944, the Polish Home Army of the Resistance surrendered.

Himmler soon had other worries, however, including rebellion in the small puppet republic of Slovakia, where a portion of the cabinet and army in Banská Bystrica declared against the government. The revolt lasted barely four weeks and was put down by *Einsatzgruppe H* and its Gestapo components under *SS-Obersturmbannführer* Dr Josef Witiska. Yet Himmler, despite his tenacious hold on power and its attendant grandiose titles (a typical example being Reich Commissar for the Strengthening of Germanism), had long since become a man divided. For as long as he could, he sought refuge in delusion.

> The atrocities committed under vom dem Bach-Zelewski's orders by 4000 men of the Dirlewanger penal brigade and 6000 Russian defectors drew protests from Guderian.

As much wedded to the past was Hitler himself. In November 1944, for example, he insisted on marking the anniversary of the beer hall putsch by extending to Himmler an invitation to make the customary commemorative speech in his place. Such irrelevant preoccupation was highlighted by Himmler's total ignorance of the true military situation. When told that there were no forces available to meet an impending Russian offensive, Himmler had replied to an appalled Guderian: 'You know, Colonel General, I don't really believe the Russians will attack at all. It's all an enormous bluff.' This

Right: By early August 1944, Polish insurgents had gathered all available partisans to fight the Germans on the streets of Warsaw. The crackdown came from the most brutal sections of the SS, notoriously the forces of *SS-Oberführer* Oskar Dirlewanger. It was composed of poachers, convicted criminals and various non-German police personnel – *Schutzmannschaften* ('defence forces') – created on Himmler's orders.

SECRET APPROACHES

Secret doubts and fears had crowded in on Himmler immediately following the July plot. He began putting out feelers among his own informers who might be able to identify surviving Resistance cells for him. A potentially useful figure was Carl Langbehn, a Berlin lawyer whom Himmler had known socially before the war through their daughters, who attended the same school. Suspected of left-wing sympathies, he was known to the Gestapo as being lukewarm towards Nazism, which made a useful cover for Himmler.

Another key Resistant known to Himmler and Langbehn was Professor Johannes Popitz, who harboured ambitions to become Finance Minister in an interim government should Hitler be overthrown. As early as 1943, Popitz had been arguing that the war would not be won by Germany and that the best course was to persuade Britain and the United States to negotiate, in order to prevent the ascendancy of Bolshevism. Himmler at that point had been noncommittal, but Popitz thought he detected some sympathy. He reported these feelings to Langbehn, who lost no time in travelling to prime his western contacts in Switzerland.

The Gestapo was also alerted; according to Schellenberg, it had picked up a radio message about Langbehn's activities, implicating Popitz at the same time. Fearing detection by Müller, Himmler hastily ordered their arrest. Trial by the Gestapo was obviously impossible. Langbehn was confined to a concentration camp far out of the reach of Kaltenbrunner and Müller, and executed on 12 November 1944. Popitz survived until the following February, when he was put to death.

was the man who was next to be assigned the post of Commander in Chief Upper Rhine to fill the need for an army group to be placed between Karlsruhe and the Swiss frontier, where British and American forces threatened a breach of the Rhine.

HOPES OF SURVIVAL

As for Himmler, his health suffered under the strain of commanding an army group, together with his numerous other responsibilities. Pleading an attack of angina and severe stomach cramps he retired to his favourite sanatorium, Hohenlychen, about 110 km (70 miles) north of Berlin. Here he was in the tender hands of his masseur, Felix Kersten, who had taken on the role of father confessor – Himmler called him 'his magic Buddha'. Göbbels paid a visit on 7 March, writing in his diary: 'He gives me a slightly frail impression … He uses strong language about Göring and Ribbentrop, whom he regards as the two main sources of error in our general conduct of the war, and in this he is absolutely right … Himmler summarizes the situation correctly when he says that we have little hope of winning the war militarily but instinct tells him that sooner or later some potential opening will emerge to swing it in our favour. Himmler thinks this more likely in the West than the East … from the East he expects nothing whatsoever.'

Hitler, who had scant sympathy for Himmler's health, summoned him to Berlin on 15 March to suffer a tirade and monologue about the 'general

Right: Carl Oberg (left) and Helmut Knochen were arrested by the American military police and handed over to the French in 1945. But the chaos of a shattered Europe meant that their trials had to wait. The military tribunal sitting at Cherche Midi Prison early in 1954 was faced with a 250-page dossier, while Oberg was subjected to 400 interrogations. It was not until October 1954 that both he and Knochen were condemned to death, a sentence later reduced to forced labour for life in April 1958.

conduct' of the war and the fact that his army could no longer be trusted to fight with vigour. Wilting from the experience, Himmler was in no mood to refuse when Guderian urged him, for the sake of his health, to give up command of Army Group Vistula, although he still retained nominal command of the Reserve Army and the *Waffen-SS*. His replacement was everything that Himmler was not. Colonel General Gotthard Heinrici was a seasoned professional with a wealth of experience. This grizzled veteran, impatient with anything approaching fantasy, was as appalled as Guderian had been at Himmler's military ignorance, declaring that he had failed to grasp the most basic elements of good generalship.

Himmler, in fact, had been dismissed for inefficiency, a move that delighted his detested rival Martin Bormann, who seized another opportunity to humiliate Himmler when elite SS divisions in Hungary failed to deliver the counter-attacks against Soviet forces that Hitler had demanded. The SS Division *Leibstandarte* was stripped of its special elite SS armbands, a degradation that further undermined Himmler's authority. Power, for what it was worth, now shifted to Ernst Kaltenbrunner as head of the RSHA.

HIMMLER SEEKS A WAY OUT

Himmler, as far as he was able, had steeled himself to face reality: he had taken personal steps to negotiate peace directly with the Western Allies. His visitors at Hohenlychen had included Count Folke Bernadotte, who served as Vice Chairman of the Swedish Red Cross. In addition, contact had been made with the World Jewish Congress and with Karl Wolff, Himmler's former liaison officer at Hitler's headquarters and later Military Governor of North Italy. Wolff had opened clandestine talks with Allen Dulles,

Roosevelt's envoy in Switzerland, about the surrender of German armies in Italy. Himmler had also been induced to sign an agreement that the concentration camps should be handed over intact with their prisoners still alive, while Dutch cities and the Afsluitdijk enclosing the Zuiderzee should be spared attack by V-2 rockets.

Next he sought contact with General Dwight D. Eisenhower, Supreme Allied Commander in Europe, hoping to use his post as commander of the Reserve Army to initiate peace negotiations, using Count Bernadotte as an intermediary. Winston Churchill and Roosevelt, however, turned down Himmler's proposal: they demanded Germany's unconditional surrender. That he was, next to Hitler, the most detested man in the Third Reich, with whom negotiation at this level had always been out of the question, never once crossed Himmler's mind. It was also a measure of his naïveté that he had previously confided to Schellenberg that Germany's war against the Soviet Union 'would, of course, go on'.

While Himmler still did not grasp cold reality, others prepared for the inevitable. In mid-August 1944, Karl Albrecht Oberg, who had already ensured that incriminating documents were evacuated from Paris, made preparations for departure along with Helmut Knochen. Making for Vittel in the Vosges, together with those members of the Gestapo they had managed to gather, they set up temporary headquarters in an area designated by OKW at that time as the stabilized frontier of eastern France. The move gained the fierce disapproval of Himmler, who nursed a deep-seated grudge against the pair for their behaviour at the time of the bomb plot when, as he saw it, they had put up little resistance against the conspirators. Oberg and his staff, forced to keep on the move, finally edged across the Rhine, where Himmler mustered him into the ranks of the *Waffen-SS*. As for Knochen, he received a peremptory summons to Berlin from Kaltenbrunner in order to explain his stance following the events at Rastenburg. Kaltenbrunner's strictures were comparatively mild: Knochen was stripped of his rank and posted as a private soldier to the *Waffen-SS*. Himmler, however, anxious even at this stage of the war to exploit the shadow of authority, countermanded Kaltenbrunner by giving Knochen a post in the SD of the RSHA, where he remained until the end.

BETRAYAL

Hitler had returned to Berlin on 16 January, its streets choked with three billion cubic feet of debris and its buildings pounded to rubble. Bombing by the USAAF in daylight and by the RAF at night was merciless. As the

Below: The most trusted member of Hitler's entourage, Martin Bormann had a rise which was unstoppable. In October 1944, he was appointed commander of the *Volkssturm* ('People's Army'), mustered as the Allies were invading the Reich. As his body was not positively identified until 1998, for years it was rumoured that Bormann had survived the war after quitting the Berlin bunker. He was tried at Nuremberg *in absentia* and sentenced to death. In 1973, the West German government declared him dead.

raids were stepped up, Hitler took the decision to move underground to what became his thirteenth and last FHQ. This was a two-storey bunker, buried 55 feet below ground, its exterior walls six feet thick, topped by an eight-foot thick concrete canopy beneath 30 feet of earth. Cramped rooms with low ceilings were grouped on either side of a central passageway where the daily conferences were held. Links with the outside world were restricted to a modest switchboard, one radio transmitter and one radio-telephone link with the OKW headquarters at Zossen, 24 km (15 miles) south of Berlin.

It was in this fetid concrete sarcophagus that the *Führer* suffered the second of two devastating blows. The first had been a communication from Hermann Göring sent on 23 April from Berchtesgaden. The *Reichsmarschall* had not forgotten tha,t according to existing *Führer* decrees, he had been designated to replace Hitler in the event of the latter's incapacity or death. Convinced the war was lost and satisfied that the provisions of the decrees held good, Göring dashed off a telegram: 'My *Führer*. In view of your decision to remain in the fortress of Berlin, are you agreed that I immediately assume overall leadership of the Reich as your Deputy, in accordance with your decree of 29 June 1941, with complete freedom of action at home or abroad? Unless an answer is given by 10 p.m. I will assume that you have been deprived of your freedom of action. I shall then regard the conditions laid down by your decree as being met, and shall act in the best interests of the people and the Fatherland. You know my feelings for you in the hardest hours of my life. I cannot express them adequately. May God protect you and allow you to come here soon despite anything. Your loyal Hermann Göring.'

In fact Göring, like Himmler, was seeking to contact Eisenhower for peace terms. As far as assuming the leadership was concerned, though, he had miscalculated badly. Hitler replied in fury: 'Your actions are punishable by the death sentence, but because of your valuable services in the past I will refrain from instituting proceedings if you will voluntarily relinquish your offices and titles. Otherwise steps will be taken.' Göring hastily concurred and was placed under house arrest by embarrassed SS men. Even so, he managed to despatch envoys on his behalf to the nearest American troops. Adopting a genial pose that temporarily beguiled a group of GIs, he then submitted to captivity, but his attempt to ingratiate himself and to treat 'man to man' with Eisenhower as one soldier to another was, predictably, a total failure.

For Hitler there came a further shock. Himmler's machinations to secure an accommodation with the Allies were somehow leaked to the Reuters news service in Washington, picked up in turn by Stockholm Radio and then by the Reich. Martin Bormann, his talent for intrigue undimmed, made sure that the news reached Hitler. One of the chief witnesses of his reaction was the celebrated aviatrix Hanna Reitsch, who proved an invaluable post-war witness because as a fanatical Nazi she was one of the last to visit the bunker. In a scene worthy of some grotesquely choreographed ballet, Russian shells

Left: An American private in the littered room in the Berlin bunker where Hitler and Eva Braun committed suicide. The room had been used by Hitler as an office where he was able to maintain his sole contact with the world outside via a radio-telephone link to Army headquarters at Zossen.

were devastating the walls of the Chancellery above, further poisoning the air of the bunker below. In a setting grown atrocious with human sweat and lack of air, Hitler erupted, screaming for vengeance, thrusting the text of Bormann's message into the hands of everyone he encountered, raging that his longest serving colleague – *der treue Heinrich* – had betrayed him.

SUICIDE

To those who were in a position to serve him at this time, Hitler, with his bent back and shuffling gait, presented an appalling spectacle. The face was drawn, the hair grey and the moustache flecked with white. By this stage he was unable to write, his signature forged by an aide. In a ridiculous move, as the appointment could just as easily have been made by telephone, and in conditions of considerable danger, he summoned Field Marshal Robert Ritter von Greim to fly to the bunker to take over as Commander in Chief of the *Luftwaffe* in succession to Göring. Badly wounded and stranded since the evening of 24 April, von Greim was then ordered to fly out of Berlin with Hanna Reitsch to arrest Himmler.

In the early hours of 29 April, Hitler married his devoted Eva Braun. After dictating his last will and testament, he directed that both Himmler and Göring be arrested as traitors. Unable to resist one last kick at the army, which had, in his view, deliberately let him down, Hitler ordered a message to be delivered to Field Marshal Keitel: '… my trust has been misused by many people. Disloyalty and betrayal have undermined resistance throughout the war. It was therefore not granted to me to lead the

THE END OF THE REICH

people to victory. The Army General Staff cannot be compared with the General Staff of the First World War. Its achievements were far behind those of the fighting front.' He then appointed Grand Admiral Karl Dönitz as President, Minister of War and Supreme Commander of the Armed Forces. In a grotesque gesture, the newlyweds threw an impromptu wedding reception during which, amid the clink of champagne glasses, Hitler rambled on about the glory days of the past. After finishing their farewells, the couple withdrew. In a few moments there was a revolver shot. Adolf Hitler's body was found on a sofa, dripping blood, while Eva Braun had swallowed poison. While Russian shells exploded within the gardens of the Chancellery, the corpses were carried outside and cremated.

HIMMLER FLEES

Established in his headquarters at Plön, between Lübeck and Kiel, Dönitz had taken it for granted that Himmler was Hitler's designated successor. So indeed had Himmler himself. It was not until the afternoon of 30 April that Dönitz received a signal from Berlin announcing his appointment – no mention was made of Hitler's death because that intelligence was supposed to have been conveyed to Dönitz via a message that never arrived. Himmler, an increasingly embarrassing irrelevance, haunted Plön, clinging to the Mercedes and SS escorts that provided the trappings of illusory power. It was Josef Göbbels who finally ended all doubts by sending Dönitz an unambiguous signal at 3.15 p.m. on 1 May, informing him that Hitler was dead and naming principal members of the new government, including the post of *Reichsführer-SS* going to Karl Hanke, the gauleiter of Breslau.

On the same day, an incident of black farce intervened. Himmler was contacted by the Belgian Fascist leader Leon Degrelle, who had served in the *Waffen-SS* and now came forward with a proposal that his men should join forces with Himmler's to set up some sort of Resistance group. A meeting was arranged at Malente, 10 km (six miles) west of Plön. Himmler, driving himself with his crash helmet rammed down on his head and followed by his bewildered staff, caught up with Degrelle, who was at the wheel of a Volkswagen powered by potato schnapps. The encounter was fatuous: Degrelle had no forces worth offering and his Belgian-SS sweepings had long slipped away. While the two men acted out their pantomime, Allied aircraft swept towards the column, sending both men diving into a ditch. Apparently drained of all resolution or interest, Degrelle made good his escape.

With the communication from Göbbels, Himmler was finished. May Day saw the beginning of the surrender of Germany; two days later, without any further consultation with Himmler, Dönitz began preparing for his surrender to Montgomery. Himmler, however, still clung to his fatuous illusions, the latest of which was the setting up of a 'reformed' Nazi administration in Schleswig-Holstein, which would negotiate with the Allies as a sovereign

Left: After being rounded up in Flensburg, three leading Nazis are paraded for reporters. Albert Speer (left), former Minister for Armaments and Munitions; Grand Admiral Karl Dönitz (centre), successively the commander of the German navy's U-boat arm, Commander in Chief of the German navy and the last head of the German government; and Colonel General Alfred Jodl (right), operations chief of OKW. All were convicted at Nuremberg. Speer and Dönitz received jail sentences, while Jodl, convicted of signing execution orders for prisoners of war, was hanged.

169

government. He then began distributing new titles to those who would serve him, a grotesque procedure watched with open-mouthed astonishment. On 6 May, Dönitz hammered in the final nail in a letter to Himmler: 'Dear Herr Reich Minister. In view of the present situation, I have decided to dispense with your further assistance as Reich Minister of the Interior and member of the Reich Government, as Commander in Chief of the Reserve Army, as chief of the police. I now regard all your offices as abolished. I thank you for the service you have given to the Reich.' It is not known whether Himmler received the message; an unsigned copy was found in Dönitz's desk, following the arrest and imprisonment of his government on 23 May 1945.

May Day saw the beginning of the surrender of Germany; two days later, without any further consultation with Himmler, Dönitz surrendered to Montgomery.

In any event, Himmler's retinue melted away one by one, save for two loyal companions. From now on his powers of decision deserted him entirely. With his motorcade reduced to just four vehicles, he took to the surrounding countryside with no plan or objective beyond some vague idea of making south and contacting the Americans. Eventually transport was abandoned altogether, and the men embarked on a long trek, blundering into a British control point near Bremervörde, halfway between Hamburg and Bremen. At first Himmler went unrecognized, as he had disguised himself by shaving off his moustache, donning an eye-patch and wearing the uniform of a sergeant in the *Geheime Feldpolizei* – a fatal error, incidentally, as that organization, originally part of the *Abwehr* and later incorporated into the Gestapo, was on Allied blacklists.

Together with others of whom the British were suspicious, Himmler was rounded up and taken to 031 Civilian Interrogation Camp at Lüneburg. There he was paraded before the commanding officer, Captain Selvester, who took up the story: 'The first man to enter my office was small and shabbily dressed, but he was immediately followed by two other men, both of whom were tall and soldierly looking, one slim and one well-built. The well-built man walked with a limp. I sensed something unusual, and ordered one of my sergeants to place the men in close custody, and not to allow anyone to speak to them without my authority. They were then removed from my office, whereupon the small man, who was wearing a black patch over his left eye, removed the patch and put on a pair of spectacles. His identity was at once obvious. He said "Heinrich Himmler" in a very quiet voice.'

HIMMLER IN CUSTODY

Himmler huddled in a blanket after he had refused the offer of a clean British uniform in place of his shabby, travel-stained clothes. A body search was undertaken, as Captain Selvester went on to relate: 'This I carried out personally, handing each item of clothing as it was removed to my sergeant, who re-examined it. Himmler was carrying documents bearing the name of Heinrich Hitzinger, whom I think was described as a postman. In his jacket, I found a small brass case, similar to a cartridge case, which contained a small glass phial. I recognized it for what it was, but asked Himmler what it contained and he said: "That is my medicine. It cures stomach cramp." I also found a similar brass case, but without the phial, and came to the conclusion that the phial was hidden somewhere on the prisoner's person. When all Himmler's clothing had been removed and searched, all the orifices of his body were searched, and his hair combed and any likely hiding place examined, but no trace of the phial was found. At this stage he was not asked to open his mouth, as I considered that if the phial was hidden in his mouth and we tried to remove it, it might precipitate some action that would be regretted. I did however send for thick bread and cheese sandwiches and tea, which I offered to Himmler, hoping to see if he removed anything from his mouth. I watched him closely while he was eating, but did not notice anything unusual.' Selvester was still worried, however, as he knew that the leading Nazis were in the habit of carrying poison with them against capture; there had already been an embarrassing incident where the authorities had not been sufficiently alert when a senior SS officer had crushed a cyanide capsule between his teeth.

Below: Arrested by troops of the British Second Army at Bremervörde on 21 May 1945, Heinrich Himmler, the former *Reichsführer-SS*, despite an earlier thorough physical examination to detect poison, managed to bite on a small phial of cyanide of potassium he had concealed. He took 15 minutes to die.

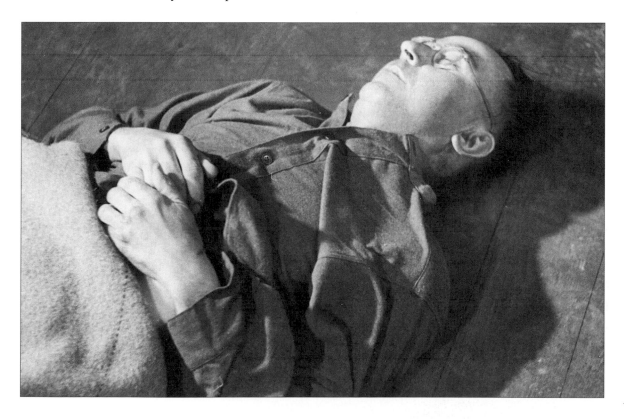

By now regarded as a prime catch among Nazi prisoners, Himmler was next handed over to Colonel Michael Murphy, Chief of Intelligence on General Montgomery's staff, who also believed that the former *Reichsführer* could, despite the previous searches, still be harbouring poison. At a special interrogation centre, Himmler was put in the charge of Edwin Austin, an archetypal British sergeant major in awe of no one, who brusquely ordered his prisoner to undress. Then Colonel Murphy and Captain C.J.L. Wells, an army doctor, carried out their search, after which the doctor ordered Himmler to open his mouth and immediately spotted 'a small black knob sticking out between a gap in the teeth on the right hand side lower jaw.' Under the light, Wells jabbed two fingers into the prisoner's mouth, whereupon Himmler suddenly turned his head aside and bit down hard on the doctor's fingers.

As the doctor shouted 'He's done it', Murphy, Austin and a Major N. Whitaker, also present, leapt on Himmler and rolled him over on his stomach to prevent swallowing. A needle and cotton pierced his tongue, while the cotton was threaded through to hold it out. Himmler was next upended and his mouth thrust into a bowl of water to try to wash out the poison. But, in the words of Whitaker, 'it was a losing battle we were fighting and the evil thing breathed its last at 23:14. We turned it on its

Right: Gestapo informers are herded together in a cell following the fall of Liege, Belgium, to the Allies in October 1944. It was estimated that by the end of the war some 24,000 Belgian Jews had been arrested, deported and murdered.

Left: The main
Nuremberg trials were
followed by indictments
issued to former members
of the SS. On the left of
the picture, one of the
most notorious of these,
Otto Ohlendorff, who
subsequently claimed that
he was 'conscripted' into
the *Einsatzgruppen*,
receives his charge sheet.

back, put a blanket on it and came away.' A request by an army dentist to
extract two of Himmler's teeth as souvenirs was firmly refused.

For the entire next day the body remained untouched, while journalists
and photographers crowded in, together with scores of British soldiers. Some
officers on Montgomery's staff deliberated as to whether the dead man
should be given military or Christian burial. The final decision – insisted
upon, some said, by Montgomery personally – was that there should be
neither. Instead, Himmler's corpse, decked out in British army trousers, a
military shirt and German army socks, was baled in an army blanket, secured
with camouflage netting and telephone wire. It was then tipped into the back
of a truck and driven to an unmarked grave, dug by three sergeants, on
Lüneburg Heath.

THE RECKONING

For the two surviving major figures in the history of the Gestapo, retribution
and punishment had to wait a while longer. At 10 a.m. on 20 November
1945, black-robed judges filed to their seats before the flags of four nations.
The International Tribunal at Nuremberg, authorized through a Charter set up
by the prosecutors of the four Allied nations, went into session as 21
prisoners were brought up from their cells; Ernst Kaltenbrunner, however,
was held in hospital with a head haemorrhage. The stark record of Nazi
crimes was set out in a document of 24,000 words. There were four counts:
'the Common Plan or Conspiracy', 'Crimes against Peace', 'War Crimes'
and 'Crimes against Humanity'. The indictment declared that the defendants

NUREMBERG TRIALS

It was said at the time that the choice of Nuremberg as the setting for the trial of the major war criminals was symbolic, highlighting the fall of a city which had staged the celebratory rallies in the days of Nazi ascendancy. The truth was more prosaic: although Nuremberg suffered much from bombing, it still had a working gaol and a Palace of Justice courthouse big enough to stage a major trial.

From the start, the trial was controversial, many claiming that it was an act of crude revenge. It was also pointed out that a 1927 League of Nations resolution, while condemning a 'war of aggression', had not proposed punishment or blame for individuals. However, those who supported the trial argued that the enormity of German war crimes was without precedent and called for exemplary punishment. The trial's legality was affirmed at a London conference of jurists from the four victorious nations, and a statute was signed on 8 August 1945.

The 21 defendants represented the German General Staff, government and Nazi party. Three more had been indicted, but Martin Bormann, Hitler's secretary, had eluded capture; Robert Ley, leader of the Labour Front, had committed suicide, and armaments magnate Gustav Krupp had been rendered unfit to stand trial.

Charges were grouped under four main headings: crimes against peace, war crimes, crimes against humanity and conspiracy. The trial continued, with some recesses, from November 1945 until the end of the following August. The judges' findings were delivered on 30 September 1946 and the sentences declared on the following day. In the early hours of 16 October, 10 went to the gallows in the Nuremberg gymnasium. Some of those who escaped the hangman were, after the corpses had been removed, mustered to clean up the detritus in the gymnasium.

had planned and waged wars of aggression in violation of international treaties, against countries and populations, and the rules and customs of war.

Charges against those associated with the Gestapo and SD involved 'the persecution and extermination of the Jews, brutalities and killing in concentration camps, excesses in the administration of occupied territories, the administration of the slave labour programme and the mistreatment and murder of prisoners of war'. The indictment covered a wide area, aimed primarily at key members of *Amt IV* of the RSHA, comprising the Gestapo and those sub-sections that had dealt with subversive, religious and political groups. In the frame also were '*Amts III, VI* and *VII* of the RSHA and all members of the SD, including all local representatives and agents, honorary or otherwise, whether they were technically members of the SS or not'. These sections covered such areas as domestic and international security and indicted their supervisors.

Conscious that he was the foremost defendant, Göring seized the opportunity in the witness box to dominate the proceedings, delightedly seeking with his formidable memory any opportunity to disconcert the prosecution lawyers, particularly when they were shown to be poorly briefed. Repentance, however, was not in his nature, and he readily declared that there had been a need to eliminate hostile political parties and to establish a secret

Right: Former SS officer Ernst Kaltenbrunner, the last head of the RSHA and Gestapo, stands to read a statement in the court at Nuremberg. Other defendants pictured include, from left to right, Hermann Göring, Rudolph Hess, Joachim von Ribbentrop and Wilhelm Keitel. In the trials, the Gestapo was indicted as a criminal organization, and its close interrelations with the SD and Kripo were revealed.

state police. Indisputably the most damaging question put to Göring was whether ill treatment of prisoners occurred when he was head of the Gestapo. The reply was evasive: 'At the time when I was still directly connected with the Gestapo such excesses did, as I have openly stated, take place. In order to punish them, one naturally had to find out about them. The officials knew that if they did such things they ran the risk of being punished. A large number were punished. I cannot say what the practice was later.' As for the concentration camps, they were Himmler's concern and he knew nothing of atrocities committed there in secret. What Göring could not deny was his order of 31 July 1941 tasking Reinhard Heydrich with 'organizing the final solution of the Jewish question in the German sphere of influence in Europe'. His conviction, which had always been highly likely, had become a certainty.

> 'At the time when I was still directly connected with the Gestapo such excesses did, as I have openly stated, take place.'
> Hermann Göring, Nuremberg

A distinctly more dislikeable figure, though, was Ernst Kaltenbrunner, the highest-ranking SS officer to survive the war. His responsibilities linked him directly to the Gestapo, the SD, the *Einsatzgruppen* in the Soviet Union,

and the horrors of the concentration camps. From a family of lawyers, his apprenticeship to Nazism and the SS had begun in his native Austria, when allying himself with Arthur Seyss-Inquart, the Austrian Chancellor following the *Anschluss*, he rose to the rank of *Gruppenführer*. Airey Neave, a future British Member of Parliament who as a young major served the indictments of the defendants at Nuremberg, wrote of Kaltenbrunner: '… a giant with massive hands … He had a long gaunt face with a deep scar that rose from the left of his mouth to his nose. There were gaps in his black teeth and he had huge ears.' He was described by the British novelist Evelyn Waugh, who attended some of the trial proceedings, as the only defendant 'actually to look like a criminal'.

Kaltenbrunner's attempt to find favour with the Allies by handing over the notorious Mauthausen camp to the Americans had proved unsuccessful. The basic points of Kaltenbrunner's defence were predictable: that he had been appointed RSHA chief solely to reorganize the Reich's political intelligence service and to amalgamate it with the former *Abwehr*. Control, he argued, had remained with Himmler and Müller. To Airey Neave, he protested: 'I

MÜLLER VANISHES

With his innate sense of self-preservation, allied with total ruthlessness, Heinrich Müller had managed to survive until the collapse of the Third Reich. Indeed, he managed to avoid standing trial for any war crimes.

Schellenberg, who had worked closely with Müller and with whom he had achieved a perilous rapport, felt that he knew the reason why. In his memoirs he describes a strange encounter in the spring of 1943. During a heavy drinking session, the Gestapo chief, much of whose work had been dedicated to countering Communist opposition, began to scorn his professed beliefs with disconcerting frankness. He went on to condemn not only the 'spiritual anarchy' of Western culture, but National Socialism as 'a sort of dung on this spiritual desert', comparing it with the moral superiority of Communism and the Soviet Union. All this was from the man who had been in charge of the anti-Communist desk in the political section of the Munich police headquarters during the last days of the Weimar Republic, and indeed who had

been praised by Hitler for deliberately basing a number of Gestapo methods on those favoured by the Soviet Union, which he had visited to carry out such a study.

Without providing any traceable evidence, Schellenberg postulated that Müller had been an undercover agent, possibly since as far back as the late 1920s, when the Communist Party in Germany had been at the peak of its membership. Whatever the truth, Müller vanished in 1945. Schellenberg claimed to have been told by a German officer that Müller had been seen in Moscow three years later and that he had died shortly afterwards. A 135-page file on Heinrich Müller, however, held by the US National Archives and Records in Washington, contains a shoal of reports and rumours that he was working after the war for the Czech, Argentine, Russian and Cuban governments. There are also claims he was killed in the last days of the war or that he killed himself and his family in 1946.

Müller was not the only servant of the Nazis to escape the justice meted out to others.

have only done my duty as an intelligence organ. I refuse to serve as an ersatz for Hitler'. Another plea had been made to Gustav Gilbert, the prison psychologist at Nuremberg, that he had nothing do with the mass murders, that he neither gave orders nor carried out any. He told Gilbert: 'You cannot conceive how secret these things were kept, even from me.' In court he was confronted with decrees he had signed personally, but he either disowned them or denounced his signatures as forgeries.

One of Kaltenbrunner's most notorious actions had been his dealings with Adolf Eichmann over the disposal of Jewish prisoners from Hungary. They had known each other for many years, and both had been members of the illegal Nazi party in Austria before the *Anschluss*. Relations had become closer following Kaltenbrunner's appointment as chief of the RSHA. On 15 October 1944, Kaltenbrunner ordered the despatch of Eichmann to Budapest with the suggestion that 50,000 Jews be deported immediately. Allied bombings and the advance of Soviet troops had made transit by train difficult. As the camp at Auschwitz was also under threat from the Russians, Eichmann suggested that the Jews should be marched on foot more than 193 km (120 miles) to the Strasshof detention camp near Vienna. Kaltenbrunner gave the necessary orders. Starting on 20 October, some 30,000 of the Jews, without food, clothing or adequate footwear, were marched from Budapest to Strasshof and other locations in the most appalling weather conditions. Many were later either abandoned or shot. Kaltenbrunner stuck to his monotonous abrogation of responsibility, a stance later flatly contradicted by one of his SS colleagues, *SS-Hauptsturmführer* Dieter Wisliceny, who declared: 'All measures taken in the field of Jewish affairs were submitted to Kaltenbrunner for basic decisions: first Heydrich, then Kaltenbrunner.'

On 1 October 1946, the International Tribunal found Kaltenbrunner guilty of committing war crimes and crimes against humanity. Eighteen days later, preceded by the Catholic chaplain, he was marched to the gallows. Asked if he had any final statement, he said: 'I have loved my German people with a warm heart. And my Fatherland. I have done my duty by the law of my people and I regret that my people were led, this time, by men who were not soldiers, and that crimes were committed of which I have no knowledge.' He reputedly took 15 minutes to die on the end of the rope. Sympathy was scant. Peter R. Black, historian in the Office of Special Investigations, US

Above: Executioner John Wood of the US Army stands on the scaffold erected in Nuremberg gaol for the executions on 16 October 1946. Von Ribbentrop was first to be executed, followed by nine others condemned during the trial.

Department of Justice, referred to 'the absence of any guilt, remorse, or even reflection on the millions of innocent people who had been murdered by the regime that he served or who died as a result of its policies. On the contrary, he appears to have been convinced that he had always done right, that his actions had been necessary, and that "history" would someday prove this.'

Ribbentrop was the first of the defendants to be executed, followed at short intervals by nine others – but not by Hermann Göring. Like Himmler, he had succeeded in concealing poison, which gave him the last laugh on his captors. Just how he managed it in a high-security jail was never determined. When the corpses of the hanged men were displayed, Göring's, as the result of the poison, was found to have turned bright green. All the bodies were cremated.

Others were more fortunate, not least Walter Schellenberg, who had found sanctuary with Count Bernadotte in Sweden and had busied himself with preparing a report on the negotiations in which he had been involved during the closing months of the war. His extradition was soon requested by the Allies, however, and he returned to Germany in June 1945 to stand trial, appearing first only as a witness in the chief Nuremberg proceedings. As a member of the SS, the SD and of his department, *Amt VI*, Schellenberg was found guilty and sentenced to six years' imprisonment, the relative leniency influenced by his efforts in the war's later stages to aid concentration camp prisoners, whatever his motives may have been. On release he settled in the little Italian town of Pallanza on the shores of Lake Maggiore, where he worked on his memoirs. His health deteriorated rapidly, however, and he died in March 1952.

BEYOND NUREMBERG

With the fall of Berlin, not only was Gestapo headquarters reduced to rubble, but also Prinz-Albrecht-Strasse was renamed Niederkirchnerstrasse in honour of a Communist Resistance fighter killed by the SS. The destruction of a building and a change of name, however, were not enough to expunge bitter memories and the desire for justice, especially in the former occupied territories.

On 25 March 1949, *SS-Brigadeführer* Hans Albin Rauter, convicted of his appalling record of Jewish persecution in the Netherlands, went to the gallows, a source of particular satisfaction to the Dutch Resistance organization Binnenlandse Strijdkrachten. But there were still intense recollections of events four years earlier.

On the night of 6/7 March 1945, Rauter had been shot and badly wounded by members of the Resistance near Apeldoorn. It was an unintended assault. On hearing the approach of a heavy vehicle, the Resistants, dressed in purloined German uniforms, had stood in the road in front of headlights piercing the darkness. They had been under the impression that it was a truck carrying food for the *Wehrmacht*, which they intended to hijack, but in fact they had brought Rauter's six-cylinder BMW convertible to an abrupt halt. As one they had opened fire, killing the driver and badly wounding Rauter in the jawbone, lungs and neck vertebrae – but he survived. Within hours, the local SD and Gestapo had taken over. On Rauter's orders, Resistance members, hostages and inmates from a nearby concentration camp were rounded up and shot by the *Ordnungspolizei*. A notice stuck by the abandoned bodies read, 'This is what we do with terrorists and saboteurs.'

As the years passed, various Gestapo, SS and RSHA personnel who had evaded prosecution felt that they were able to relax. For two men at least, such confidence was misplaced. It was somewhat ironic that after the war Adolf Eichmann had twice fallen into the hands of the Americans, on successive occasions giving the names of Otto Eckmann and Adolf Barth. As these were not on any wanted list, the Americans had shown little interest and in the chaotic conditions of the time it had not been difficult for Eichmann to vanish from POW camps. In March 1946, a man who gave his name as Otto Heniger appeared in the small village of Eversen, near Lüneburg Heath, at that time in the British Zone of Germany. This was just one of the many guises Eichmann adopted over the years. He explained that his home had

Below: The pyjama-clad body of Hermann Göring lies on a rough wooden coffin. This official picture was taken after his suicide in Nuremberg jail during the night of 15/16 October 1946. How he was able to secrete the cyanide in his cell only he knew. Along with the others who were executed, his body was cremated and the ashes scattered.

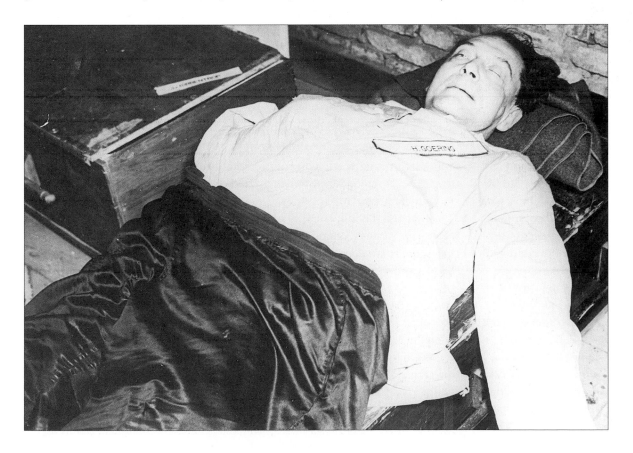

Above: The personification of prim bureaucracy, Adolf Eichmann, described by one observer at his trial as 'terrifyingly normal', stands in the glass-protected box during his trial in Jerusalem. As if he felt impelled to complete unfinished business, he made a full and frank confession, aiding his interrogators as if he were a prosecution witness at his own trial. He was hanged at Ramleh Prison on 21 May 1962.

been in Breslau and that he was anxious to join fellow refugees from the east. His papers were in order, which was scarcely surprising as at the time there was a flourishing black market in forged documents. He was allowed to share shanty accommodation with half a dozen ex-soldiers and managed to get a job with a timber firm.

Although the full extent of his Gestapo past was not yet apparent, Eichmann's name figured during the Nuremberg proceedings when Rudolf Höss, the commandant of Auschwitz, identified him as the bureaucrat who had been in charge of the mass murder of Jews, a testimony supported by others, including Dieter Wisliceny. The latter testified that during July or August 1942 he had been in Berlin to discuss the plight of Jews from Slovakia. There he met Eichmann, who proffered a top-secret document, edged in red. It was an order signed by Himmler the previous April, calling for the immediate implementation of the final solution of the Jewish question. Wisliceny stated in his testimony: 'Eichmann told me that the words "final solution" meant the biological extermination of the Jewish race, but that for the time being able-bodied Jews were to be spared and employed in industry to meet current requirements. I was so much impressed with this document, which gave Eichmann authority to kill millions of people, that I said at the time: "May God forbid that our enemies should ever do anything similar to the German people." He replied, "Don't be sentimental – this is a *Führer* order." I realized at that time that the order was a death warrant for millions of people and that the power to execute this order was in Eichmann's hands, subject to the approval of Heydrich and later Kaltenbrunner.'

Eichmann was only too conscious of the considerable risks he ran by remaining in Europe. In 1950, Eichmann fled to South America. It was apparent that Argentina had become one of the chief centres of the Nazi underground and that its dictator, Juan Perón, was willing to welcome important figures of the Hitler regime. There they received the help of a body called ODESSA (*Organisation des SS-Angehörigen*), which facilitated the escape of former Nazis and their sympathizers. By 1952, Eichmann was in possession of an identity card issued by the Argentinian police authorities under the name of Ricardo Klement. The card claimed that 'Klement' had been born in Bozen (known since 1918 as Bolzano) in northern Italy. Israeli agents, active in Argentina, were eventually led to a primitive brick house in a poor suburb of Buenos Aires. On 11 May 1960, Eichmann was seized on his way back from work at Mercedes-Benz, where he had a desk job, and taken to Jerusalem as the accused in the first televised trial in history.

In the dock of the Jerusalem courtroom, Eichmann's demeanour was marked by the same administrative pedantry and neatness that had characterized the running of his bureaucracy of genocide. Confession under intense interrogation was full and factual – it ran to some 3500 pages. Eichmann argued that he had not personally killed a single person and had only been obeying orders. These familiar refrains were both rejected. When he claimed that Rudolf Höss had made the decision to use Zyklon B at Auschwitz so that he could murder Jews at an accelerated rate of 9000 a day, the prosecution agreed – but lost no time in pointing out that Höss's decision could scarcely have been implemented without the delivery of the necessary human freight, Eichmann's sphere of responsibility.

> In the dock, Eichmann's demeanour was marked by the same administrative pedantry that had characterized the running of his bureaucracy of genocide.

Adolf Eichmann's appeal against the death sentence was rejected by the Israeli Supreme Court, and he was hanged at Ramleh Prison on 21 May 1962. He showed no remorse when escorted to the execution chamber by the pastor of Jerusalem's Zion Christian Mission, who said: 'He is the hardest man I ever saw. He seems unconscious of any wrongdoing. He seems to think he was eliminating a people who should be eliminated. If ever a trial by man was justified, this one surely is.' At Eichmann's request, his body was cremated and his ashes scattered at sea.

Above: Jean Moulin, one of the great heroes of the French Resistance, was seized by the Gestapo in Lyon and tortured under the direction of Klaus Barbie. On his enforced transfer to Berlin for further interrogation, he suffered a fatal heart attack in early July 1943. Numerous theories were advanced over the years as to who betrayed him, but no proof has ever been found.

THE FINAL TRIAL

The discovery of Eichmann and the subsequent trial caused a sensation at the time, but it could not compare with the high drama that led to the 1987 sentence of life imprisonment on Klaus Barbie, the 'Butcher of Lyon'. Memories of Gestapo terror bit deep in this corner of eastern France and, if those who had suffered were keen only to forget, they were not to be allowed to do so.

On the morning of 11 November 1942, an endless procession of German vehicles and uniformed columns of soldiers thundered through the suburbs and down the main boulevards of Lyon to secure the city. This followed Hitler's order, codenamed Attila, for the German occupation of unoccupied France (Vichy) in response to the Allied invasion of French North Africa, which was to secure for the Allies a favourable position for control of the Mediterranean. A few days later *SS-Obersturmführer* Klaus Barbie had driven into Lyon. At 29 years old, and still relatively junior in rank, he had secured a job of daunting responsibility – he was Gestapo chief of Lyon, the third largest city in France. He had done his homework well. As a fluent French speaker with little trace of an accent, he had previously visited Lyon in plain clothes and, mixing easily with the Lyonnais in cafés and bars, had built up a fair picture of its inhabitants. His brief from Helmut Knochen was to penetrate and break the Resistance movements, which were known to be particularly strong. He was also pledged to set up a 40-strong *Einsatzkommando*, a squad that was to become especially hated and feared throughout Lyon and its environs.

Throughout Barbie's regime of terror and intimidation, two events were to become notorious. On 2 June 1943, the afternoon peace of the northern suburb of Caluire was shattered by a clutch of black Citroëns, which roared into the Place Castellane, releasing a group of Gestapo. Acting on a tip-off, the origin of which was never to be confirmed, Barbie had learnt that a three-storey villa belonging to Dr Frédéric Dugoujon was a meeting place for prominent members of the Resistance, notably a Monsieur Martel, who was supposedly a patient suffering from rheumatism. The Gestapo began by kicking Dugoujon in the stomach, then set about hitting another man, using a leg ripped from a valuable antique table. But their main interest was in Martel – with good reason, as their captive was in fact Jean Moulin (cover name 'Max'), who had taken refuge there and was to become one of the great names of the French Resistance.

From the end of 1940, Moulin had toured southern France, linking Resistance groups to form the Combat movement. In 1942, after visiting

General Charles de Gaulle in London, he was parachuted back into France to establish, at de Gaulle's behest, the nationwide *Conseil National de la Résistance* (CNR). It first met in Paris in May 1943 and was one of Moulin's last initiatives before his arrest just weeks later. Although hideously tortured by the Gestapo, he kept silent and was put on a train bound for Germany. Somewhere on that journey he died; the death certificate received by his family from the registrar of the Paris Gestapo gave the cause of death as cardiac arrest.

Jean Moulin's reputation as an effective resistant and the likely identity of his betrayers became a subject of controversy over the years; however, as far as the city of Lyon was concerned, a later event was to be recalled with far greater poignancy. A signal dashed off by Barbie to Berlin on 6 April 1944 read: "In the early hours of this morning, the Jewish children's home 'Colonie d'enfants' at Izieu-Ain was raided. In total 41 children aged from 3 to 13 were taken. Furthermore, the entire Jewish staff of ten, five of them females, were arrested. Cash and other assets were not taken. Transportation to Drancy follows on 7.4.44 – Barbie." The children had been sent to the school by anxious parents all over France who had realized the danger posed to all Jews. A convoy of trucks and vans had made its way to the courtyard of the school. The staff were then held at gunpoint while the SS and the *Milice*, the armed force of the collaborationist Vichy, combed the house and drove the children out to be dispatched to Paris. On 30 June 1944, the children

Below: Tortures and killings carried out in Paris under Gestapo supervision were a grim feature of the occupation. This was revealed in September 1944 when the bodies of victims, many of whom had been burned alive or shot, were discovered in the Ministry of Aviation building where Germans had been quartered. Here, a captured German is confronted with scraps of cloth used to blindfold victims about to be shot.

were loaded into railway trucks and shipped to Auschwitz and death in the gas chambers. It was the atrocity of Izieu above all that motivated the famous Nazi hunters, the French Jewish lawyer Serge Klarsfeld, whose father had perished at Auschwitz, and his German-born Protestant wife, Beate, to track down Barbie and lead the long campaign for his forced return to Lyon.

At the end of the war, the 'Butcher of Lyon' received employment and protection from the American Counterintelligence Corps (CIC), which was keen to benefit from his police skills and reputed anti-Communist zeal, seen as valuable assets in protecting West Germany during the Cold War. Eventually, under the aegis of the CIC, Barbie decamped for Latin America, together with his wife and children, and established himself in Bolivia, gaining citizenship in 1957. He lived there in some comfort under the alias of Klaus Altmann, working for the dictatorships of both Peru and Bolivia. His identity was unmasked by the Klarsfelds in 1971, but the Bolivian government refused to extradite a man they declared to be one of their citizens. Neither was France particularly enthusiastic at the prospect of receiving this prominent ex-Nazi, who could well identify former Vichy collaborators, some of whom were holding respectable jobs. But the

DRANCY

An unfinished housing project in the Paris suburb of Drancy was chosen in December 1940 as the site of what was to become the largest assembly and transit camp (*Sammellager*) for the deportation of Jews from France. Sixty-two deportation trains carrying about 61,000 Jews left Drancy between July 1942 and August 1944. Most of these deportees perished in the concentration camp of Auschwitz-Birkenau. Until 1 July 1943, Drancy was administered by the French, although ultimate control rested with the *Sicherheitspolizei* (Sipo) and SD. The following day the camp was taken over by *SS-Hauptsturmführer* Alois Brunner, who was responsible for the final transportation to Auschwitz of the children from Izieu, near Lyon.

Before Brunner's arrival, French Jewish organizations and the Red Cross were permitted to send food and comforts to those held in Drancy, but Brunner refused to let the aid continue and reduced the food rations for prisoners. Until the Germans forbade religious observance, celebration of the

Jewish New Year (Rosh Hashanah) and the Day of Atonement (Yom Kippur) had been permitted, and a clandestine school for children had operated until the start of 1943 when it was discovered and forcibly closed.

As early as August 1941 there was Resistance activity. Up to August 1943, a total of 41 inmates escaped successfully and plans went ahead to build an escape tunnel with 70 prisoners digging in three shifts. The work was nearly completed when the Germans discovered the tunnel and sent many of the prisoners to their deaths.

On the night of 15/16 August 1944, just over a week before the Allies reached Paris, the Germans in Drancy burnt all incriminating documents and fled, leaving behind 1543 prisoners. Raoul Nordling, the Swedish consul general, took over control of the camp and approached the French Red Cross to care for the inmates. A monument to the deported Jews was erected in front of where the main gates of the camp had stood.

Klarsfelds persisted, and Barbie was finally extradited to stand trial in 1983.

The decision to hold a trial at all was criticized by those who argued that, as the bulk of Gestapo records had been dispersed or destroyed, what was the point of bringing one ageing man to court after so many years? Klaus Barbie had been no Eichmann, no architect of the Final Solution, but a mere Himmler underling who had never risen above the rank of *SS-Obersturmführer*. Thousands like him all over Europe had not been caught or tried, so why single him out? The doubts were countered by those who favoured a trial, pointing out that in Lyon, at least, it was going to be possible to bring justice to the memory of the murdered children of Izieu and the legend of Jean Moulin.

As had been intended, the parade into the courtroom of former victims, some of whom still bore the mental and physical signs of Gestapo interrogation, proved infinitely more telling than any documentation. Some witnesses, however, described the experience as particularly unnerving from the moment they caught sight of Barbie in the dock. His face bore the same remote stare and half-smile that he had adopted when carrying out his own interrogations some 40 years before. Obviously conscious that he had reached the end of the line and seemingly beyond caring, he made little attempt at a defence. Relief that the proceedings finally ended with a sentence of life imprisonment for crimes against humanity was by no means confined to his surviving victims. During the war, Lyon had produced its share of collaborators within Vichy, but those who suffered bad consciences during the trial need not have worried: Barbie named no names. No one, for instance, is ever likely to know for certain who betrayed Jean Moulin, although down the years there have been suspicions.

Klaus Barbie died in prison on 23 September 1991. It is unlikely that there will be another war crimes trial to compare with his. Even in the early days of a divided Europe and of the Cold War, memories had begun to fade. For the Gestapo itself there was to be no survival, but for Jews in particular, including today's descendants of victims of the Holocaust, the guilt of Nazism is not forgotten. For those anxious to trace the careers and activities of men such as Eichmann, Müller and Barbie there are books and documents in museums and archives worldwide. Their value is surely to provide ample evidence of the dangers and evils of dictatorship, especially with a repressive secret police in place to enforce it. The warnings remain as potent as ever.

Above: A young Klaus Barbie, seen here in *Wehrmacht* uniform, served as a junior officer during the invasion of France before joining the SD. The brief for his job in Lyon was clear: to penetrate and destroy the resistance movements. Alongside those of his victims who canvassed eagerly for his trial, there were past collaborators needlessly fearful of being exposed.

APPENDICES

NIGHT AND FOG DECREE

The notorious *Nacht und Nebel Erlas* – Night and Fog Decree – was an order issued on the *Führer*'s behalf by Field Marshal Wilhelm Keitel to the SD, Gestapo and Kripo on 7 December 1941. Carrying Keitel's signature, the *Führer Befehl* (Hitler Order) was directed against the inhabitants of the occupied territories of Western Europe. Its purpose was to seize persons considered to be 'endangering German security'. Their fate was to vanish into obscurity, hence the decree's title. No confirmation or denial of their whereabouts was to be given to relatives.

The decree had arisen from Hitler's abundant irritation at the security forces' policy of taking hostages – originally aimed at Communist resistance fighters and their families – which he considered counter-productive since it only encouraged the burgeoning resistance movements. Keitel, in a move that was ultimately to seal his fate as a war criminal at the post-war trials, went on to issue a directive explaining Hitler's order. The document, one of many produced at the Nuremberg tribunal under the general heading of 'Nazi Conspiracy and Aggression', declared: 'In principle, the punishment for offences committed against the German state is the death penalty. If these offences are punished by imprisonment, even with hard labour for life, this will be looked upon as a sign of weakness. Efficient intimidation can only be achieved either by capital punishment or by measures by which the relatives of the criminal and the population do not know his fate.'

Keitel later went further, declaring that if the death penalty was not administered within eight days of an arrest, 'the prisoners are to be transported to Germany secretly'. Other documents subsequently released and forming the bases for war crimes trials, revealed shoals of orders for 'NN' (as the order came to be known), including the sanctioning of torture and decapitation of male prisoners. In the dock, Keitel gave a lame apology for *Nacht und Nebel*, explaining, 'It was the will of the *Führer* after long consideration.' He went on to state that he had released the decree only reluctantly, protesting that it was the worst he had ever been required to carry out. Questioned closely as to why he had not refused to implement it, he claimed that he had repeatedly asked to be relieved of his OKW duties, but had never refused an order since all German officers and soldiers were legally bound by the sacred '*Führer* oath'.

The man known contemptuously by some of his colleagues as 'Lakeitel' ('Lackey Keitel') and 'Nickesel', after a children's toy donkey which never ceased to nod its head, remained staunchly loyal. Keitel was found guilty of aiding Hitler to commit aggressive war and of endorsing war crimes and crimes against humanity. His request to be executed by firing squad as befitted his rank was refused. He was hanged in October 1946.

UNIFORMS

The popular image of Gestapo personnel sporting black leather overcoats and broad-brimmed hats performing dawn arrests, followed by interrogation and horrible torture, tells just a part of the story. Not all Gestapo members wore plain clothes, neither were their duties by any means clear cut.

The *Grenzzolldienst* (Frontier Police Service) founded in October 1933 to police Germany's boundaries, was soon reinforced with the fledgling SS. Four years later, Reinhard Heydrich was made the sole authority on all frontier police matters, while executive authority was delegated to the Gestapo. While carrying out their border duties the latter were obliged to wear field-grey service uniforms and display the *Grenz-Polizei* arm band. Germany's frontier with Soviet-occupied Poland was controlled exclusively by the Gestapo.

The rapid entry of German troops into western Poland in 1939 prompted the creation of *Selbstschutz* (Self-Protection Units), who were responsible for defending German property and German inhabitants in Poland, maintaining custody of prisoners of war and guarding installations. Heinrich Himmler, forever sensitive to his authority, maintained strict control of what he stressed was a police organization. The staff of the *Selbstschutz* included rank and file Gestapo who initially wore civilian clothes, but progressively donned uniforms consisting of a black field cap with a white metal button at the front and the SS national emblem on the side.

Deeper entry into the Soviet Union brought new duties for the Gestapo. All members of the *Sicherheitspolizei* (Sipo), the security police unit consisting of the Gestapo and *Kriminalpolizei* (Kripo), were obliged to wear SD uniforms. Their special status was indicated by piping on the edges of their arm badges.

At the time of the invasion of Poland, Germany had at its disposal six *Einsatzgruppen* (Special Action Groups). *Einsatzgruppe* A had a strength of some 1100 personnel, including members of the Munich Gestapo. They were responsible for anti-resistance measures, which often meant the performance of mass executions. At first they stuck to wearing plain clothes, later switching to uniforms of field grey and army pattern shoulder straps. This led to much opposition from the *Waffen-SS*, who considered themselves a privileged elite and deeply resented what was regarded as encroaching on their territory. Consequently, SD and Gestapo members were allowed only to wear army and *Waffen-SS* shoulder straps if these incorporated the green piping of police units.

Later, entirely distinctive police pattern shoulder straps were introduced. Members of the SD and Gestapo wore general SS pattern field-grey overcoats edged in twisted cord according to rank. However, by the beginning of 1943, when the war had begun to turn against Germany and materials were becoming scarce, collar patches and cord were discontinued. Thus uniform embellishments became increasingly an unaffordable luxury and by the summer of 1944 uniform and equipment for officers, NCOs and men of the Sipo and SD became progressively standardized. In 1945, uniforms vanished altogether, hastily discarded by men who furnished themselves with false papers and scurried underground where possible to escape Allied justice.

RANKS

SS and Gestapo	British Army	US Army
Anwarter	Private	Private
Sturmann-Mann	—	Private First Class
Rottenführer	Lance-Corporal	Corporal
Unterscharführer	Corporal	Sergeant
Scharführer	Lance-Sergeant	Staff Sergeant
Oberscharführer	Sergeant	Technical Sergeant
Hauptscharführer	Staff Sergeant	Master Sergeant
Sturmscharführer	Regimental Sergeant Major	Warrant Officer
Untersturmführer	Second Lieutenant	Second Lieutenant
Obersturmführer	Lieutenant	First Lieutenant
Hauptsturmführer	Captain	Captain
Sturmbannführer	Major	Major
Obersturmbannführer	Lieutenant-Colonel	Lieutenant-Colonel
Standartenführer	Colonel	Colonel
Oberführer	Brigadier	Brigadier-General (1 star)
Brigadeführer	Major-General	Major-General (2 star)
Gruppenführer	Lieutenant-General	Lieutenant-General (3 star)
Obergruppenführer	General	General (4 star)
Oberstgruppenführer	General	General of the Army (5 star)
Reichsführer-SS	—	—

GLOSSARY

Abwehr: The central German military intelligence organization headed by Admiral Wilhelm Canaris, one of the leaders of the July 19944 bomb plot to kill Hitler.

Einsatzgruppen: Mobile armed units of police, consisting of Sipo, SD, SS and Gestapo personnel, used to round-up and execute enemies in the conquered territories in the East. Their main targets were Jews, communist officials – such as commissars – gypsies, political leaders, and the intelligentsia. Each unit was made up of a number of companies known as *Einsatzkommando*.

Gauleiter: The supreme territorial Nazi Party official, employed in Germany and annexed territories in Poland, Austria and Czechoslovakia.

Geheime Feldpolizei (**GFP**): Formed in 1939 at the request of Field Marshall Wilhelm Keitel, commander-in-chief of the OKW, the 'Secret Field Police' were essentially plain clothes military police. The functions of the *Geheime Feldpolizei* included counter-espionage, counter-sabotage, detection of treasonable activity and counter-propaganda. They also assisted the Army's legal system in investigations for courts martial.

Kriminalpolizei (**Kripo**): The 'Criminal Police' was tasked with combating non-political crime. Like the Orpo and Sipo, they were separate from the Gestapo and SD, although in reality personnel were increasingly controlled by Heydrich and tasked with Gestapo business.

Oberkommando der Wehrmacht (**OKW**): The High Command of the Armed Forces was set up by Hitler in 1938 to replace the old Weimar-era War Ministry. Commanded by Field Marshall Wilhelm Keitel, it was divided into three areas, and controlled all branches of the armed forces as well as military intelligence, including the *Abwehr*. The OKW was responsible for overseeing the individual military services and ensuring that the requirements of the political leadership were met. In essence, the OKW was seen by Hitler as a military staff responsible for issuing his commands to the various services.

Ordnungspolizei (**Orpo**): The Orpo were separate from the Gestapo and Sipo and handled civil matters such as traffic control, patrols and routine police business. In the occupied territories, however, the Orpo often became involved in the activities of the *Einstatzgruppen*.

Reichsführer-SS: Heinrich Himmler's title as supreme commander of the SS and Gestapo.

Reichsleiter: A member of the executive board of the Nazi Party. Martin Bormann was the best known.

Reichssicherheitshauptamt (**RSHA**): The Central Security Office of the Reich was created in 1939 as an umbrella organization for all the non-military intelligence agencies, including the SD, Kripo and Gestapo. The organization was originally headed by Reinhard Heydrich, and after his assassination, by Ernst Kaltenbrunner.

Schutzstaffel (**SS**): Meaning 'Protection Squad', the SS was originally the bodyguard of Adolf Hitler. Himmler transformed them into an army within the army. Up to 40 SS divisions were created, especially as the war on the Eastern Front accelerated.

Sicherheitsdienst (**SD**): Meaning 'Security Service', the SD was the intelligence organization of the Nazi Party, whereas the Gestapo was the 'Secret State Police'. In reality, the two worked so closely together as to be virtually indistinguishable.

Sicherheitspolizei (**Sipo**): Although nominally a part of the government rather than the SS, in reality the 'Security Police' worked closely with the SD and Gestapo in a fusion of the state and political police forces.

Sturmabteilung (**SA**): Known as the 'Brownshirts', Hitler's uniformed supporters were recruited as early as 1921 in Munich by Ernst Röhm to protect Nazi speakers and provide muscle on political rallies. The SA were destroyed as an effective force in 1934 after the death of Röhm during the purge known as the 'Night of the Long Knives'.

BIBLIOGRAPHY

ARONSON, SHLOMO. *Beginnings of the Gestapo System.* Jerusalem: Israel Universities Press, 1969.

BLACK, PETER R. *Ernst Kaltenbrunner: Ideological Soldier of the Third Reich.* Princeton, New Jersey: Princeton University Press, 1984.

BOWER, TOM. *Klaus Barbie: Butcher of Lyon.* London: Michael Joseph, 1984.

CALIC, EDOUARD. *Reinhard Heydrich.* London: Military Heritage Press, 1982.

DELARUE, JACQUES. *The History of the Gestapo.* London: Macdonald, 1964.

DAWIDOWICZ, LUCY. *The War Against The Jews, 1933–1945.* London: Bantam Books, 1975.

DESCHNER, GUNTHER. *Heydrich: The Pursuit of Total Power.* London: Orbis, 1978.

GALLO, MAX. *The Night of the Long Knives.* London: Harper & Row, 1972.

GISEVIUS, HANS BERND. *To The Bitter End.* London: Jonathan Cape, 1948.

GILBERT, MARTIN. *The Holocaust: The Jewish Tragedy.* London: Collins, 1986.

GRABER, G S. *History of the SS.* New York: D. McKay, 1981.

HEADLAND, RONALD. *Messages of Murder: a Study of the Reports of the Einsatzgruppen of the Security Police and the Security Service, 1941–1943.* Rutherford, New Jersey: Fairleigh Dickinson University Press, 1992.

HOHNE, HEINZE. *Canaris.* London: Secker & Warburg, 1979.

HOFFMANN, PETER. *Hitler's Personal Security.* London: Macmillan, 1979.

JOHNSON, ERIC A. *Nazi Terror: the Gestapo, Jews and Ordinary Germans.* New York: Basic Books, 1999.

MCDONALD, CALLUM. *The Killing of SS Obergruppenführer Reinhard Heydrich.* London: Macmillan, 1989.

MANVELL, ROGER AND HEINRICH FRANKEL. *The July Plot.* London: Bodley Head, 1964.

MASON, HERBERT MOLLOY. *To Kill Hitler: The Attempts on the Life of Adolf Hitler.* London: Michael Joseph, 1978.

NEAVE, AIREY. *Nuremberg: A Personal Record of the Trial of the Major War Criminals.* London: Coronet Books, 1978.

PADFIELD, PETER. *Himmler: Reichsführer-SS.* London: Macmillan, 1990.

REITLINGER, GERALD. *The Final Solution: the Attempt to Exterminate the Jews of Europe, 1939–1945.* Northvale, New Jersey: J. Aronson, 1987.

REITLINGER, GERALD. *The SS: Alibi of a Nation, 1922–1945.* New York: Da Capo Press, 1981.

RITCHIE, ALEXANDRA. *Faust's Metropolis: A History of Berlin.* London: Harper Collins, 1998.

SACHS, RUTH. *Adolf Eichmann: Engineer of Death.* New York: The Rosen Publishing Group, Inc., 2001.

SCHELLENBERG, WALTER. *The Schellenberg Memoirs.* London: Andre Deutsch, 1956.

SHIRER, WILLIAM. *Rise and Fall of the Third Reich.* London: Secker & Warburg, 1960.

SWEETS, JOHN F. *Choices in Vichy France: The French under Nazi Occupation.* Oxford: Oxford University Press, 1986.

WHEELER BENNETT, SIR JOHN. *The Nemesis of Power: the German Army in Politics, 1918–1945.* London: Macmillan, 1953.

WIGHTON, CHARLES. *Eichmann: His Career and Crimes.* London: Odhams Press Ltd., 1961.

USEFUL WEBSITES

www.einsatzgruppenarchives.com
For a detailed introduction to the crimes of the mobile killing units who followed in the wake of the Wehrmacht's invasions of Poland and the Soviet Union. Includes official reports, directives and statistics, as well as some eyewitness testimonies and photographs.

www.ghil.co.uk
The German Historical Institute London (GHIL) is an independent academic institution that promotes research on modern German history.

www.lidice-memorial.cz
The official site dedicated to the victims of the Lidice massaccre in Czechoslovakia in 1942.

www.topographie.de
The official site of the Topography of Terror Foundation. This organization provides historical information about National Socialism and its crimes, and organizes exhibitions and special events both at its main address in Berlin (on the site of Prinz-Albrecht-Strasse) as well as in other German cities.

www.wienerlibrary.co.uk
A rich source for modern German history, the Wiener Library specializes in modern Jewish history and the rise and fall of the Third Reich. It also includes extensive collections on antisemitism and post-war Germany. The collection comprises books, periodicals, unpublished memoirs, original documents, eyewitness testimonies, press cuttings, photographs, videos and multi-media resources.

INDEX